CW00486184

HAPPINESS IN JOURNALISM

This book examines how journalism can overcome harmful institutional issues such as work-related trauma and precarity, focusing specifically on questions of what happiness in journalism means, and how one can be successful and happy on the job.

Acknowledging profound variations across people, genres of journalism, countries, types of news organizations, and methodologies, this book brings together an array of international perspectives from academia and practice. It suggests that there is much that can be done to improve journalists' subjective well-being, despite there being no one-size-fits-all solution. It advocates for a shift in mindset as much in theoretical as in methodological approaches, moving away from a focus on platforms and adaptation to pay real attention to the human beings at the center of the industry. That shift in mindset and approach involves exploring what happiness is, how happiness manifests in journalism and media industries, and what future we can imagine that would be better for the profession. Happiness is conceptualized from both psychological and philosophical perspectives. Issues such as trauma, harassment, inequality, digital security, and mental health are considered alongside those such as precarity, recruitment, emotional literacy, intelligence, resilience, and self-efficacy. Authors point to norms, values and ethics in their regions and suggest best practices based on their experience.

Constituting a first-of-its-kind study and guide, *Happiness in Journalism* is recommended reading for journalists, educators, and advanced students interested in topics relating to journalists' mental health and emotion, media management, and workplace well-being.

This book is accompanied by an online platform which supports videos, exercises, reports and links to useful further reading.

Valérie Bélair-Gagnon is an Associate Professor for the Hubbard School of Journalism and Mass Communication, University of Minnesota-Twin Cities, Minneapolis, USA.

Avery E. Holton is Associate Professor and Chair of the Department of Communication, University of Utah, USA.

Mark Deuze is a Professor for the Department of Media Studies, University of Amsterdam, The Netherlands.

Claudia Mellado is a Professor for the School of Journalism, Pontificia Universidad Católica de Valparaíso, Chile.

HAPPINESS IN JOURNALISM

Edited by Valérie Bélair-Gagnon, Avery E. Holton, Mark Deuze, and Claudia Mellado

Routledge
Taylor & Francis Group

LONDON AND NEW YORK

Designed cover image: akinbostanci/E+ via Getty Images

First published 2024
by Routledge
4 Park Square, Milton Park, Abingdon, Oxon OX14 4RN

and by Routledge
605 Third Avenue, New York, NY 10158

Routledge is an imprint of the Taylor & Francis Group, an informa business

© 2024 selection and editorial matter, Valérie Bélair-Gagnon, Avery E. Holton, Mark Deuze, and Claudia Mellado; individual chapters, the contributors

The right of Valérie Bélair-Gagnon, Avery E. Holton, Mark Deuze and Claudia Mellado to be identified as the authors of the editorial material, and of the authors for their individual chapters, has been asserted in accordance with sections 77 and 78 of the Copyright, Designs and Patents Act 1988.

All rights reserved. No part of this book may be reprinted or reproduced or utilised in any form or by any electronic, mechanical, or other means, now known or hereafter invented, including photocopying and recording, or in any information storage or retrieval system, without permission in writing from the publishers.

Trademark notice: Product or corporate names may be trademarks or registered trademarks, and are used only for identification and explanation without intent to infringe.

Access the Instructor and Student Resources: https://www.valeriebelairgagnon.com/happinessinjournalism

British Library Cataloguing-in-Publication Data
A catalogue record for this book is available from the British Library

Library of Congress Cataloging-in-Publication Data
Names: Bélair-Gagnon, Valérie, editor. | Holton, Avery, editor. |
Deuze, Mark, editor. | Mellado, Claudia, editor.
Title: Happiness in journalism / edited by Valérie Bélair-Gagnon, Avery Holton, Mark Deuze and Claudia Mellado.
Description: Abingdon, Oxon ; New York, NY : Routledge, 2024. |
Includes bibliographical references and index.
Identifiers: LCCN 2023022119 (print) | LCCN 2023022120 (ebook) |
ISBN 9781032428550 (hardback) | ISBN 9781032428543 (paperback) |
ISBN 9781003364597 (ebook)
Subjects: LCSH: Journalists--Mental health. | Journalists--Psychology. |
Happiness. | Well-being. | LCGFT: Essays.
Classification: LCC PN4797 .H28 2024 (print) | LCC PN4797 (ebook) |
DDC 070.4023--dc23/eng/20230802
LC record available at https://lccn.loc.gov/2023022119
LC ebook record available at https://lccn.loc.gov/2023022120

ISBN: 978-1-032-42855-0 (hbk)
ISBN: 978-1-032-42854-3 (pbk)
ISBN: 978-1-003-36459-7 (ebk)

DOI: 10.4324/9781003364597

Typeset in Galliard
by Taylor & Francis Books

CONTENTS

CONTRIBUTORS

Achala Abeykoon is Senior Lecturer for Department of Mass Communication, University of Kelaniya, Sri Lanka.

Sajjad Ali, Department of Journalism & Mass Communication, University of Malakand, Pakistan, is a former journalist. He is author of *Community Media of Swat*. He is the Pakistan lead for Global Journalism Trauma Literacy Project (JETREG).

Valérie Bélair-Gagnon is Associate Professor and Cowles Fellow in Media Management, University of Minnesota–Twin Cities, USA.

Santosh Kumar Biswal, Department of Journalism and Mass Communication at Rama Devi Women's University, Bhubaneswar (India).

Diana Bossio is Associate Professor of Media and Communication and program leader at the Social Innovation Research Institute, Swinburne University, Melbourne Australia.

Danielle Deavour is Professor of Media Studies is Assistant Professor of broadcast journalism, Samford University, USA.

Mark Deuze is Professor of Media Studies, University of Amsterdam, Netherlands.

John Crowley is Director of Headlines Network, UK, the organization that exists to create connections and drive conversations towards improving mental health in the media industry.

Jennifer Henrichsen is Assistant Professor, Washington State University, USA.

Avery E. Holton is Associate Professor and Chair of the Department of the Communication, University of Utah, USA.

Shilpa Kalyan is Head of the Department of Liberal Arts, Humanities and Social Sciences, Manipal Academy of Higher Education, Manipal, India.

Archana Kumari, Department of Mass Communication and New Media at Central University of Jammu, India.

Hayes Mabweazara is a Senior Lecturer in Media, Communication & International Journalism, University of Glasgow, UK, where he is affiliated to the Glasgow University Media Group.

Pallavi Majumdar is a communication professional for Royal Thimphu College, Bhutan, with 25 years of media industry and training experience across leading brands in India.

Trust Matsilele is a Senior Lecturer in Journalism, Department of the Cape Peninsula University of Technology, South Africa.

Claudia Mellado is Professor of Journalism, Pontificia Universidad Católica de Valparaíso, Chile.

Kelsey Mesmer is Assistant Professor of Journalism at Saint Louis University, USA.

Logan Molyneux is Associate Professor at the Klein College of Media and Communication, Temple University, USA.

Mou Mukherjee Das, Future Media School, Maulana Abdul Kalam University of Technology (M.A.K.A.U.T), West Bengal, India, is alumnus of Banaras Hindu University.

Jacob L. Nelson is Assistant Professor in the Department of Communication University of Utah, USA.

Elana Newman is McFarlin Professor of Psychology (University of Tulsa) and Research Director at the Dart Center for Journalism and Trauma Research Center, Columbia University, USA.

Lambrini Papadopoulou is an Assistant Professor in Media Political Economy, National and Kapodistrian University of Athens, Greece.

Seth C. Lewis is Professor, Director of Journalism, and the founding holder of the Shirley Papé Chair in Emerging Media in the School of Journalism and Communication, University of Oregon, USA.

Olatunji Ogunyemi is the convener of the Journalism Education and Trauma Research Group and the Media of Diaspora Research Group at the Lincoln School of Film, Media and Journalism, University of Lincoln, UK.

Gregory P. Perrault is Associate Professor of Media Literacy and Analytics, University of South Florida, USA.

Lada Trifonova Price is a Senior Lecturer in Journalism at the Department of Journalism Studies, University of Sheffield, UK.

M. C. Rasmin is a media development specialist and an academician with 15 years of experience in media development, teaching, research and experimentations both locally and internationally.

Mamunor Rashid is Associate Professor in Mass Communication and Journalism in Khulna University, Bangladesh and a Coordinator for Disaster Perception, a voluntary organization.

Jennifer M. Ragsdale is a research psychologist at the National Institute for Occupational Safety and Health (NIOSH), Centers for Disease Control and Prevention (CDC), USA.

Víctor Hugo Reyna García is Professor, Faculty of Communication and Marketing at the Universidad La Salle Bajío, Mexico.

Jana Rick is a Research Associate and doctoral student in the Department of Media and Communication, Ludwig Maximilian University of Munich, Germany. She also is a freelance journalist.

Errol Salamon, Department of Communication and Humanities at the University of Huddersfield, UK.

Mohammad Sahid Ullah, Department of Communication and Journalism, University of Chittagong, Bangladesh.

Muhammad Shahid, journalist for News International and instructor of journalism and mass communication at Abdul Wali Khan University Mardan (AWKUM) as well as University of Peshawar, Pakistan.

Eugenia Siapera is Professor of Information and Communication Studies, School of Information and Communication Studies, University College Dublin, Ireland.

Maja Šimunjak is a Senior Lecturer in Journalism, Middlesex University London, UK and Leadership Fellow of the Arts and Humanities Research Council.

Erin Smith is an Honorary Enterprise Professor, Department of Critical Care at the University of Melbourne, and CEO of the Dart Centre for Journalism and Trauma Asia Pacific.

Richard Stupart is a lecturer at the Department of Communication and Media, University of Liverpool, UK.

Hanne Vandenberghe is a Guest Professor in the Department of Communication Sciences, Ghent University, Belgium.

Sarah Van Leuven, is an Associate Professor at the Department of Communication Studies, Ghent University, Belgium and head of the research group Center for Journalism Studies.

Alexandra Wake, is an Associate Professor in Journalism at RMIT University, Australia, and the elected President of the Journalism Education and Research Association of Australia.

Hermann Wasserman is a Professor of Media Studies and Director of the Centre for Film and Media Studies, University of Cape Town, South Africa.

ACKNOWLEDGEMENTS

This book is a call for action to think about how as a community of practice we, educators and media actors from policymakers and platform companies to news organizations, may improve well-being in journalism, and general state of happiness. We would like to thank the Happiness in Journalism Project participants and those that are part of this group and those who entrusted us in joining this book project. We would also like to thank our respective institutions, the Hubbard School of Journalism at the University of Minnesota-Twin Cities, Department of Communication and the College of Humanities at the University of Utah, the Journalism and Media graduate program of University of Amsterdam and the School of Journalism at the Pontificia Universidad Católica de Valparaíso in Chile. We would also like to thank Alyssa Caitlyn Hill, Audrey Anchirinia, Hannah McKeating, Elizabeth Cox and our family and friends for their support.

1

FOSTERING A CULTURE OF WELL-BEING IN JOURNALISM

Valérie Bélair-Gagnon, Avery E. Holton, Mark Deuze and Claudia Mellado

Globally, journalists face stressors related to their work, including demanding circumstances and a lack of reciprocity on the job. They often give much and receive little in return while public trust, and institutional support, continues to erode. Journalists, especially women, people of color, or practitioners with minority backgrounds experience harassment, bullying, emotional exhaustion, and trauma at work. Outside of the newsroom, journalists are vulnerable to trauma because of the tendency of the news to focus on what goes wrong in society and in people's lives. This has a major impact on the mental health and happiness of reporters and editors, as documented in numerous surveys and research projects. Though not new, problematic aspects of what working in the media is like have been linked to demands for journalists to engage on social media, document and remedy increased political polarization while suffering attempts to vilify the press, the rapid rise of atypical work, and the pressures associated with the pandemic.

The circumstances of work in journalism have implications for individual journalists and for news organizations' bottom lines as they seek to recruit and retain talent and bolster their reporting. Journalists have referred to the impact that all of this has on their professional performance, ranging from self-censorship and burnout from a 24/7 news cycle, addressing toxic workplace cultures, to enduring harassment from news audiences. Researchers, educators, professional associations, and news organizations have come to recognize the occupational hazards involved with journalism and have begun to invest in resources and programs designed to improve journalists' quality of life. Our book documents this global trend while attempting to benchmark an effort for news organizations, researchers, and educators, asking what sustained steps can be taken to help make journalism the profession it is expected to be.

DOI: 10.4324/9781003364597-1

Defining Happiness for Well-Being in Journalism

One of the main findings of researchers outside of the media and journalism studies literature who work on happiness is that we, as individuals, can rewire our brains to experience and understand well-being. Such a rethink is contingent upon who you are, where you are, and what kind of context you work in. Happiness (or subjective well-being) tends to fall into two related categories: enjoying what you do and finding what you do is meaningful. Such an all-too-easy distinction can vary across cultures and contexts. And there is not much evidence to suggest that, once happy, people will be better at their job. What we do know is that the absence or understanding of happiness at work may lead to work-related stress disorders and burnout, among other issues. What is key is that one's experience and state of happiness to a large extent get determined by one's perceptions and belief.

What makes people happy is not always about what they think will happen, especially in capitalistic societies. Rather, individual happiness can be conceived around kindness, mindfulness, belonging, community, savoring, and gratitude, among other things.[1] Such principles tend to manifest in professional and organizational settings primarily as individual-level constructs such as job satisfaction, commitment, and engagement. Issues regarding engaging in work that contributes to the common good, that fosters a sense of belonging, and an overall more holistic appreciation of happiness at work tends to be largely absent from the literature and the management and culture of news organizations.

As in other types of media work and work in creative occupations, journalism is a form of affective labor, blurring the boundaries between personal and professional lines. Practitioners invest in the stories they tell, the people whose lives they cover, the beat they report on, and the communities they engage with. Changes in practices related to digital and social media make the work of journalists almost 24/7, stretching their lives thin across a range of channels and platforms. Journalists report using strategies to disconnect from their work such as blocking comments from social media, which may afford them (the illusion of) greater autonomy and the freedom to just do their work. Reporters covering traumatic events quite often turn to cynicism to handle all the complex negative emotions that they experience. Precariousness and job uncertainty cause significant stress, emotional exhaustion, and turn many promising voices away from the profession. In some parts of the world, journalists have no choice but to be compliant spokespersons or become activists, especially under repressive political regimes or within larger commercial enterprises.

The COVID-19 pandemic of the early 2020s amplified across the news industry and beyond the idea that the mental health, well-being, and happiness of journalists need care and attention if the profession is to continue in a complex world that genuinely needs them. There is now a larger, global platform for journalists, educators, civil society, journalists' allies, and researchers to think about what they can do better. Building on this wealth of practitioners' experiences and research, this book focuses on happiness as a concept, and what it takes to be a happy journalist as an individual and as part of a collective. In this book, we explore multiple approaches to well-being,[2] including an approach to happiness at work, consisting of both hedonic experiences (HWB)—of liking what you do, job satisfaction, being passionate about the work, and so on—as well as eudaimonic aspects (EWB), including personal growth, professional autonomy, and doing work that contributes to the common good.[3] We also consider that happiness or well-being is not only an individual problem but a collective one that should be tackled by the industry, governments, and research. Like climate change, individual approaches can yield limited results. As such, our call is broader and requires a systemic intervention.[4]

For a while, there have been emergency alert signals pointing to journalistic unhappiness in the profession's history. Historians noted that journalists have been expected to embrace gender normative ideals discouraging women to pursue the profession, at times leaving them to write in the society pages. Being a journalist was conceptualized as having a "thick skin" or being aggressive. As the population of journalists (slowly still) started to become more diverse, these analyses compounded the experiences of people of color in the profession, as well as reporters with disability. Intersectionality has long played an important role in understanding the lived experience of journalists. Gendered, sexualized, ableist, and racialized notions of journalism often determine today's workplace cultures in journalism. From a communal perspective, critical issues in journalism cultures around the world include fierce competition, favoritism (and other behaviors indicating a lack of organizational justice), a style of management that discourages speaking out or asking for help, a disconnect with the communities one is supposed to serve, and a worrying lack of public trust underpinning newswork.

Unhappiness in journalism takes multiple shapes and the way the news industry has addressed it over time has evolved. While news media are slowly beginning to take their professionals more seriously, journalists are suffering. There is an urgency to address the challenges facing the news industry in terms of journalists' happiness. With declines in happiness have come deep impacts on the personal lives of journalists, the quality and sustainability of newsrooms and reporting, and the sense of autonomy and agency journalists have long championed. How exactly journalists can bridge the gaps between their professional ideals, news practices, and personal lives—especially within social media spaces—to at once serve the public good as well as the personal, remains an important question.[5]

Civil society and various professional associations like the International Center for Journalists, the Dart Center, Trollbusters, the Media and Entertainment Alliance, and others have been central in helping journalists and providing resources. These have pointed to a major issue that inspires and informs this book: as an industry, and as professionals, organizations, scholars, educators, students, and news audiences, we need to think and act with care regarding journalists' well-being if we want the profession and journalism itself to flourish.

Well-Being in Journalism

Addressing the happiness of journalists is a complex situation without a one-size-fits-all solution. However, there is much that can be done. Change is necessary. There are variations at the individual level and across different working arrangements in journalism, within and between countries and cultures, types of news organizations, and ways of being a journalist. Research has shown that the challenges that journalists experience—how they rate and perceive their autonomy, what precarity means to them—vary substantially across the world.[6] Discussions about better working conditions and happiness may be more prevalent in places where journalists have time to self-reflect on practices and engage in such discussion as opposed to places where journalism needs to be highly focused on keeping populist governments accountable.

The call to take happiness and well-being seriously is urgent. As part of this urgency, the theoretical and methodological approaches used to explore the professional and personal well-being of journalists need to change. These have been mainly focused on how journalists and organizations need to adapt to changing societies, technologies, and the power of platforms, so much so that they have risked the alienation of very real human beings behind the cameras, microphones, keyboards, and touchscreens. This book acknowledges such well-documented challenges to the profession and asks how journalism can be better as both a community of practice, a public service, and a business. How can we be successful and flourish at the same time? What price are we willing to pay for good work and excellent journalism?

That shift in mindset and approach involves exploring what happiness is, how happiness manifests in journalism and the media industry, and what future we imagine that would be better for the profession that we practice, teach, research, and experience. This book is ambitious and hopes to amplify voices that speak to such topics as trauma, harassment, precarity, mental health, and well-being.

Our Approach to Building Resilient Journalism

By understanding the many roadblocks that journalists face, we need to consider carefully what happiness is and how the subjective well-being of professionals may contribute to stronger, more sustainable journalism. We must engage in and amplify conversations about and undertake concrete actions that consider the different challenges of today's journalism across the globe—if only to acknowledge that journalists everywhere are, or can be, struggling.

We thus invited international scholars to discuss happiness in journalism from their unique perspectives and positionalities. The chapters in this book offer a collection of stories, best practices, and advice for journalists, media professionals and organizations, as much as for journalism students, educators, and scholars alike. We hope that this will contribute to the emerging world-wide dialogue on mental health, and subjective well-being at work, providing agency, and spark new and much needed actions to support journalists. The topics addressed include:

- Norms, values, and ethics
- Organizational best practices
- Social media policy best practices
- Approaches in unionized organizations
- Approaches to recruitment and retention
- Approaches to emotional literacy, intelligence, resilience, and self-efficacy
- Approaches to digital security and safety
- Psychological approaches to well-being
- Practical tips for journalism schools and the news industry
- Different concepts of happiness at work
- Challenges related to diversity, equity, and inclusion
- And much more.

This book is for journalists and their audiences, educators, undergraduate and graduate students, and practitioners interested in learning about practices and strategies related to well-being and mental health in the news industry. Chapters are designed to be short and propose concrete solutions on how to bring happiness to journalism. While we do focus on journalism, this book is meant to spark conversations on happiness and well-being across all media professions and inspire and map out a better future for work and labor.

Organization of the Book

All chapters point to concrete solutions for journalists and media professionals, news, and professional organizations for fostering a culture of well-being in journalism. These chapters are meant to empower news and media professionals and the industry leaders to take steps to change culture globally and in unique contexts. While it addresses questions of intersectionality in gender, race, ethnicity, and sexuality, it doesn't address the role that religion has in some cultures. This book is divided into four main parts addressing these challenges.

Part 1 of the book, "Journalists, Joy & the Pursuit of Happiness," focuses on well-being from psychological and, relatedly, individual perspectives. In Chapter 2, "Journalists Considering an Exit," Jana Rick explores job precarity and journalists who seek to leave the profession. In Chapter 3, "The Joy in Journalism," Richard Stupart connects emotional well-being to journalism's moral dimensions by asking, "what moral communities exist within the profession and who we ought to hold responsible for whether or not journalists can live up to the obligations that those communities impose on their members." In Chapter 4, "Finding Joy as Journalists: Motivations for Newswork," Gregory P. Perrault unpacks why journalists stay in the field despite difficult working conditions.

In Chapter 5, "What Psychology Can Offer in Understanding Journalists' Well-Being," Jennifer M. Ragsdale and Elana Newman introduce key ideas and present recommendations for future research to leverage the knowledge of well-being from psychology and occupational health. In Chapter 6's "Building Resilience Through Trauma Literacy in J-Schools," Lada Trifonova Price and Ola Ogunyemi analyze the role of journalism schools and journalism educators in addressing the lack of trauma literacy teaching.

Part 2 of the book, "In Support of Well-Being in Journalism," addresses ways in which organizations can help build more resilience—that is the ability to withstand shocks, survive and adapt when situations arise—in response to contexts and preemptively. Chapter 7, "Recruitment and Retention Practices in a Changing African News Media Ecosystem," by Hayes Mawindi Mabweazara and Trust Matsilele, explores the transformations in African journalism and how those changes have been reshaping recruitment and retention practices, from informal recruitment procedures to the "juniorization" of news organizations affecting journalism's well-being. In Chapter 8, "Developing Psychological Capital to Support Journalists' Well-Being,'" Maja Šimunjak outlines industry-specific interventions that could be useful in the development of personal resources for safeguarding well-being amongst its journalists, including hope, efficacy, resilience, and optimism. In Chapter 9, "How Newsroom Social Media Policies Can Improve Journalists' Well-Being," Logan Molyneux and Jacob L. Nelson provide recommendations on how news organizations can improve their social media policies.

In Chapter 10, "Supporting Digital Job Satisfaction in Online Media Unions' Contracts," Errol Salamon argues that improved language and dialogue around workers' happiness would improve work conditions. Chapter 11, "Establishing Individual, Organizational and Collective Practices for Journalists' Well-Being through Disconnection" by Diana Bossio, suggests that improving journalists' happiness means centering methods of care in the profession, editorial strategy, newsroom resources, and the community of practice. In Chapter 12, "Championing a Security-Sensitive Mindset," Jennifer R. Henrichsen examines journalism safety and security options for journalists and promotes the role of security champions to contribute to a "security culture" in newsrooms. Víctor Hugo Reyna in Chapter 13, "Job Control and Subjective Well-Being in News Work," unpacks the concept of job control as a precondition of journalists' subjective well-being and how it may be contributing to job satisfaction and work–life balance.

Part 3 of the book, "Steps & Practices Towards Happiness," focuses on journalists themselves and what they can do to be resilient in their practices and normative constructs. In Chapter 14, "Cognitive Dissonance in

Journalistic Trauma," Danielle Deavour proposes alternatives for unhealthy coping techniques, such as ignoring the pain and only positive thoughts. In Chapter 15, "Safer Vox Pops and Door Knocking," Kelsey Mesmer shows how vox pop interviews and door knocking may be common reporting techniques used by journalists and at the same time harm them. In Chapter 16, "Teaching Student Journalists to Refill their Happiness Tanks," Alexandra Wake and Erin Smith propose methods for encouraging well-being among journalism students (e.g., the importance of purpose and help seeking).

In Chapter 17, "Self-Employment in the News Industry," Sarah Van Leuven and Hanne Vandenberghe show how the conditions of freelance journalists can be precarious. In Chapter 18, "Workplace Happiness, Journalism and COVID-19 in South Asia," Achala Abeykoon et al. highlight the ways in which South Asian news organizations have positively supported their employees during COVID-19. Chapter 19's "Engaged Journalism and Professional Happiness" by Lambrini Papadopoulou and Eugenia Siapera explores the notion of contentment in journalism engagement. Together, these chapters point to the importance of recognizing one's own boundaries and journalism ethics as a central part of a culture of well-being in journalism.

In Part 4, John Crowley (Chapter 20), Hermann Wasserman (Chapter 21) and Seth C. Lewis (Chapter 22), present essays that reflect on the book chapters, highlight gaps, and propose ways forward for fostering a culture of well-being in journalism practice and education.

This book contends that acknowledging and supporting journalists' happiness and well-being are fundamental first steps towards re-imagining journalism in terms of work and labor, if only because a happy worker in the full and richest sense of the concept is a better worker when it comes to resilience, efficacy, and one's ability to do good work.

Notes

1 Laurie Santos, "The Science of Well-Being." The first editor completed this Coursera course certificate delivered by Dr. Santos in Spring 2022.
2 William Tov, "Well-Being Concepts and Components." In *Handbook of Well-Being* eds. Ed Diener, Shigehiro Oishi and Louis Tay, (Salt Lake City, UT: DEF Publishers, 2008), 30.
3 Cynthia Fisher, "Happiness at Work," *International Journal of Management Reviews* 12, (2010): 384–412.
4 Diana Bossio, Valérie Bélair-Gagnon, Avery E. Holton and Logan Molyneux, *The Paradox of Connection: How Digital Media Is Transforming Journalistic Labor.* (Urbana Champaign: University of Illinois Press, 2024).
5 Claudia Mellado (ed.), *Beyond Journalistic Norms.* (London: Routledge, 2021).
6 Kalyani Chadha and Linda Steiner, *Newswork and Precarity.* (London: Routledge, 2021).

PART I

JOURNALISTS, JOY, AND THE PURSUIT OF HAPPINESS

2

JOURNALISTS CONSIDERING AN EXIT

Jana Rick

Journalism is often described as a "dream job."[1] However, research shows that there has been a decline in satisfaction and increase in intentions to leave the profession.[2] These studies draw attention to journalists who seem to be unhappy in and question their profession. This phenomenon must be taken seriously because a loss of experienced journalists could deplete institutional memory.[3] Researchers should identify early predictors of change to support retention strategies in the media industry.[4] This chapter looks at journalists' intention to exit the profession with the goal to better understand the context in which happiness in journalism is embedded. In doing so, it identifies triggers for changing careers and sheds light on the working conditions of the industry. It provides an overview of studies on the topic and quantitative and qualitative data on German journalists who feel keen to make such a change.

Turnover intention in journalism is a topic of global interest.[5] While there are no reliable statistics on how many journalists leave journalism, studies have provided data on journalists considering such a change. Research demonstrates an increase in intentions to leave the profession are linked to a decline in job satisfaction.[6] The trend is described using percentages in an annual comparison.[7] The literature refers to this as a disturbing development, and warns that the "exodus of journalists is just beginning."[8] For example, 19.3 percent of Estonian journalists expressed intentions of leaving the field.[9] The reasons for journalists thinking about leaving their careers include low salaries, the pace of work and workload, and health issues such as burnout.[10]

A feeling of discontent or frustration is linked to personal and career goals.[11] Regardless of the cause of dissatisfaction in each case, feelings of unhappiness or discontent can accumulate, leading to turnover intention. For some news workers, journalism is no longer seen as a career option.[12]

DOI: 10.4324/9781003364597-3

Research on journalism should explore the phenomenon of exiting the profession and identify possible triggers.

The data presented in this chapter are based on a survey that is part of a larger research project on precarity in German journalism conducted in 2020 that elicited 983 responses from journalists. The project—funded by the German Research Foundation (DFG)—examines the working conditions of journalists. The online survey was distributed via the largest journalism associations and trade unions in Germany (e.g., the German Federation of Journalists, DJV, and the German journalists' union, DJU, part of the Ver.di trade union) and targeted journalists who work in journalism as their main profession. This meant earning more than 50 percent of their income from journalistic activities or spending more than half of their total working hours in journalism.[13] This work was carried out during a time when COVID-19 preventative measures such as lockdowns had a significant impact on (working) life in Germany. German journalism found itself in a situation marked by massive loss of advertising revenue and increasing subscription numbers.[14] Many freelancers suffered huge losses of income.[15]

The average age of journalists in the sample was 48.9, and 37.7 percent of the respondents identified as female. Freelancers were the largest group in the sample, representing 44.4 percent of those surveyed. Compared to similar studies in Germany and the entire workforce in journalism globally, this percentage is relatively high[16] which may be a result of recruiting via the journalism associations. Journalists worked as editors (47.9 percent), and the majority worked for newspapers (37.6 percent) and magazines (17.5 percent).

To capture journalists' willingness to make a change in their professional lives, the survey included a two-part question. First, respondents were asked to answer a yes/no question that addressed possible thoughts about changing profession.[17] Journalists who stated that they were having such thoughts were asked a follow-up question: "Which of the following reasons are causing you to think about a job change/career change?" Twenty possible motives[18] were offered, and respondents were also given the option to give other reasons. Research has shown that career change decisions are often based on multiple reasons, so respondents were allowed to choose more than one answer.[19] The survey also allowed journalists to describe their reasons in greater detail in their own words. Several participants took advantage of that opportunity, and a total of 285 qualitative written answers were collected.

Journalists Feeling Keen to Change

A quarter of the sample (25.7 percent) reported that they were considering changing professions. This group of journalists had an average of 19 years of experience, and their average age was 45.8. Twenty-seven percent of all freelance journalists and 23.8 percent of permanent employees (full-time and part-time) were considering a career change at the time, but this difference is not statistically significant. There was also a small but non-significant difference in terms of gender: while 29 percent of female journalists reported that they were considering a career change, only 23.5 percent of male journalists stated that they were doing so. Age also seems to influence the intention to change ($p = 0.017$, Cramer's $V = 0.15$). Respondents between the ages of 30 and 39 expressed the greatest desire for change, and those over 50 were least likely to do so. Journalists with young children were particularly likely to be considering a switch, with 33.5 percent of them ($\chi2\ (1) = 9.8$, $p < 0.005$, Cramer's $V = 0.1$) stating that they were thinking about a career change. In addition, the desire to change professions depends on income ($\chi2\ (8) = 18.6$, $p = 0.017$, Cramer's $V = 0.15$). Specifically, 37.1 percent of journalists earning between €600–1,200 per month reported that they were thinking about a career change. That number dropped to 15.4 percent for journalists earning €4,800–6,000 per month.

These results help researchers identify vulnerable groups in journalism, such as parenting journalists and low earners, who have a hard time in this profession. The data provide evidence of inequalities in journalists' working conditions. These findings also draw attention to journalists who are particularly dissatisfied with their profession.

The most frequently chosen reasons for considering an exit are "the transformation of journalism" (71.1 percent), "job insecurity" (63.1 percent), and "low income" (61.9 percent). Other frequently mentioned motives were "working conditions" (52.2 percent) and "seeking better social security" (48.4 percent). About a quarter of all female journalists chose "gender inequalities," while this was selected for only 2.1 percent of their male colleagues ($p < 0.01$, Cramer's $V = 0.36$). The pages that follow offer insight into the journalists' comments about the three most frequently selected reasons for thinking about a career change. Recurring themes are discussed, and exemplary comments from individual journalists are quoted.

The transformation of journalism

Answers related to the most frequently selected reason—the transformation of journalism—show that journalists perceive transformation differently and refer to various types of changes. Respondents pointed to a shift in business strategies, digital circumstances, and professional practices. Many addressed *cost-cutting measures* and the resulting *declining budget* in media outlets. One respondent wrote, "Savings are made wherever possible. Ideally, an article including photos does not cost anything." This led to frustration, as seen in a comment from a female freelancer who complained, "I am sick of hearing the word budget!" Journalists believe that limited resources in newsrooms can have *negative consequences for the quality* of journalism. As a 30-year-old freelancer explained, "It's incredibly annoying that savings are being made in all areas, but the quality is supposed to remain the same. That's not possible. It simply makes journalism worse." Journalists referred to a decline in the quality of journalistic content by claiming that *quantity seems to win over quality*. They wrote about the number of articles that must be produced in one day and the importance of *clicks* in times of digital journalism. This phenomenon also impacts research practices, and "important stories for society" are becoming increasingly rare in the eyes of one respondent. Journalists also linked these changes to a perceived increase *in competition from bloggers and influencers* on the internet.

Job insecurity

The comments about "job insecurity" reflect the increasingly uncertain and precarious situation of the journalistic working world. As a 37-year-old employed journalist wrote, "Even though I work at a big newspaper, my job is not secure. I'm thinking of quitting before I get laid off." He is not the only one playing with the idea of anticipating a layoff. This is indicative of the constant fear of losing a job in journalism. "It can be over from one day to the next," wrote a 50-year-old female freelancer who works for a magazine. This anxiety reflects workers' dependency on the gig economy and the "casualization of journalistic labor,"[20] a phenomenon that is currently on the rise in journalism.

A glimpse into the future seems to trigger anxiety among many journalists regardless of whether it is caused by the pandemic, a temporary contract, or the thought of getting older. A 64-year-old journalist shared her fears, explaining that job insecurity can get "dangerous" at her age. Overall, the respondents seem to struggle with the uncertain future of their media outlets. The pandemic, which was ongoing at the time of the survey, influenced feelings of uncertainty in times of short-time work and income losses for journalists. Freelance journalists were especially likely to list "job insecurity" as the reason they are considering a change ($\chi2$ (3) = 17.4, p = 0.001, Cramer's V = 0.26). The reasons seem to depend heavily on the journalists' employment status, as 75.2 percent of all freelancers and only 47.2 percent of the full-time permanently employed journalists identified it as an important reason for considering a change.

Low income

Journalists who participated in this survey and stated that they are thinking about changing professions have an average monthly income of €2,137.28 per month (after taxes). This means they earn over €200 less than journalists in the sample who deny having thoughts of changing their profession (The average income of the latter group is €2,410.01). For those considering a change, "low income" was an especially popular response among freelancers ($\chi2$ (8) = 59.6, p = 0.001, Cramer's V = 0.51). The average monthly income for this group was reported as €1,829.91 in our survey. Given that journalists were asked to report their income before the COVID-19 crisis, we can only imagine how challenging the pandemic was or still is for them. Indeed, 79.4 percent of all surveyed freelancers stated that they have lost income due to the pandemic.[21]

The issue of low income led to the highest number of comments from respondents. Some of them highlighted their decision to select this reason by mentioning their exact income. For example, a 58-year-old photojournalist working for a newspaper stated, "My hourly salary is equivalent to approx. €3.50." When describing their income as "low," some respondents compared their salaries to those provided in other fields. For example, one said, "Earning less than the babysitter gives you food for thought" (44-year-old female freelancer earning €900 per month). Another noted, "I earn less than I did ten years ago with my student job" (36-year-old female permanent journalist earning €1,280 per month).

Others discussed their income in the context of their experience and training. "I studied abroad for six years in three countries, attended a journalism school, and won journalism awards. Yet I earn less than the average for my age" (27-year-old employed journalist earning €2,200 per month). Journalism salaries are also perceived as low in relation to the workload and responsibilities associated with the profession.

In many cases, participants view low income as an acute problem. Compensation is a key issue in the here and now, as journalists do not make enough money to support themselves or achieve certain standards of living. A 32-year-old female photojournalist who reported that she earned €2,100 per month wrote, "Too low for living in the city, too low for having a family, and there is no hope for a higher income." Others were concerned about the future. A 57-year-old female journalist stated, "I am approaching retirement with increasingly difficult conditions and falling payments." Experiencing poverty later in life was an issue for several of the journalists who participated in the survey.

Keeping Journalists in Journalism: Practical Suggestions

This chapter is focused on journalists who are considering a career change. The fact that about a quarter of the journalists surveyed in this study are doing so points to a dynamic labor market in the field of journalism. The percentage could also imply that the journalism profession makes a lot of its practitioners unhappy. The respondents' comments do not suggest that the surveyed journalists were dissatisfied with journalistic work itself. One could conclude that it is not journalism as a profession that makes people unhappy, but the conditions under which it takes place. This incongruence contributes to feelings of unhappiness when, on the one hand, journalists have no power over their own working conditions, but at the same time they love their profession and do not want to give it up.

The findings identify catalysts for turnover in journalism and triggers for those leaving. Those who leave do not do so for one single reason, but due to many factors. While the quantitative data made visible groups that are more likely to consider an exit than others, the open answers made possible reasons for leaving more concrete. Journalists' comments about why they intended to leave the profession show that some felt forced to do so because they were anticipating a job loss or looking to prevent becoming impoverished later in life. Many of the long-form responses were characterized by frustration and hopelessness.

Some respondents already had a plan B in mind and were close to leaving. Given that every journalist who leaves can be seen as a loss for the industry, the reasons for this should be taken seriously. Each reason for career change cited can be seen as an important parameter that must be addressed so that journalists can practice their profession instead of leaving it. These findings are consistent with previous research, in that they suggest that low salaries are one of many problems in journalism.[22] There may be several different reasons for journalists' dissatisfaction, as the determinants of their decisions to leave the profession are diverse. The transformation of journalism, the resulting job insecurity, and low-income levels are the leading triggers identified in this study.

In this study, it is still not clear whether the journalists surveyed will be happy once they leave the profession. Previous studies have shown that journalists seem to live happier after having left journalism.[23]

It is up to media companies to implement retention strategies. Reinardy concludes that "keeping employees satisfied" is essential to preventing turnover, and policies are needed to keep journalists in their jobs and keep them happy.[24] This would also improve journalism itself by providing favorable conditions for producing quality journalism. Retention strategies inevitably involve *listening to journalists* and *increasing awareness of factors that cause unhappiness* in newsrooms. Academia, media management, trade unions, journalism associations, and society should *listen to journalists when they discuss the problems they face and their dissatisfaction. Regular employee appraisal interviews* and *anonymous internal surveys* can be the first steps towards identifying sources of dissatisfaction. Discussions between journalists and decision-makers should also consider *the problems and challenges faced by freelancers and parenting journalists.*

Journalists should be involved in processes that lead to changes, as *transparency* can reduce feelings of insecurity. Preventing an outflow of news professionals could be achieved by *letting them participate in processes of change* and respecting their opinions. Regarding levels of compensation, journalists want media outlets to respect *collective bargaining agreements.* These can prevent pay inequities and ensure a minimum level of income for all journalists. One way to improve journalists' labor conditions is collective bargaining.[25] This would allow unions to address income precarity of self-employed journalists but also legal precarity.

Given that respondents' comments point to frustration and feelings of hopelessness, it is important to consider the possibility of providing *professional psychological help* to journalists. In the ongoing discussion on journalists' mental health,[26] experts have pointed to therapy sessions as opportunities to help journalists identify the sources of their dissatisfaction by reflecting on their work. *Talking openly* about existential worries, feelings of insecurity, and fears about the future should be seen as a critical step towards happiness. Journalists should *express possible worries and dissatisfaction* at an early stage and discuss their problems with the management. Journalists might also find it helpful to *connect with colleagues*, for example in an online forum or groups on social media. The Facebook group "What's Your Plan B?" can be seen as an example for this, it allows journalists to share ideas and worries. Another idea would be to *prepare junior journalists* for the uncertainties of the industry.

Questions remain as to how many of the 252 "doubtful" journalists have already left the profession or will do so in the future. We can only assume that thoughts about changing careers point to possibilities in some cases and are already a reality in others. This study shows that targeting potential career changers can help researchers understand the urgent problems facing journalism professionals. The findings highlight the challenging labor conditions in this field and support the stream of research that describes journalism as a profession of precarity.[27] That 25 percent of respondents are considering a career change but are still working in journalism may speak to the great passion that is associated with the profession. Research should continue putting the focus on those journalists to make inequalities in the media industry visible and to give them a voice.

Notes

1 Roman Hummel, Susanne Kirchhoff, and Dimitri Prandner, "'We used to be Queens and Now We Are Slaves'," *Journalism Practice* 6, no. 5–6 (2012): 722–731.
2 Signe Ivask, "Stressed out Print, Digital and Converged Newsroom Journalists Consider Leaving the Field," *Media and Communication* no. 8 (2017): 83–99; Scott Reinardy, "Female Journalists More Likely to Leave Newspapers," *Newspaper Research Journal* 30, no. 3 (2009a): 42–57.
3 Haeyeop Song and Jaemin Jung, "Factors Affecting Turnover and Turnaway Intention of Journalists in South Korea," *Journalism & Mass Communication Quarterly* 99, no. 4 (2021): 1072–1098.
4 Scott Reinardy, "Beyond Satisfaction," *Atlantic Journal of Communication* 17, no. 3 (2009b): 126–139.
5 Víctor Hugo Reyna, "'This Is My Exit Sign'," *Journalism Practice* 15, no. 8 (2021): 1129–1145; Heui-Ling Liu and Ven-Hwei Lo, "An Integrated Model of Workload, Autonomy, Burnout, Job Satisfaction, and Turnover Intention among Taiwanese Reporters," *Asian Journal of Communication* 28, no. 2 (2018): 153–169.
6 Weaver and Wilhoit, *The American Journalist* (1986, Indiana University Press).
7 Reinardy, "Beyond Satisfaction," 126–139.
8 Reinardy, "Beyond Satisfaction," 126–139.
9 Ivask, "Stressed out Print," 83–99.
10 Ivask, "Stressed out Print," 83–99.

11 Indah Setiawati, "To Quit or not To Quit," MA thesis, (Missouri-Columbia: University of Missouri-Columbia, 2020).

12 Marjoribanks, Timothy, Lawrie Zion, Penny O'Donnell, and Merryn Sherwood (eds.), *Journalists and Job Loss*. (London: Routledge, 2022), 93–105.

13 Siegfried Weischenberg, Maja Malik and Armin Scholl, *Die Souffleure der Mediengesellschaft. Report über die Journalisten in Deutschland.* (Konstanz: UVK Verl.-Ges, 2006).

14 Dieter Keller and Christian Eggert, Zur wirtschaftlichen Lage der deutschen Zeitungen, (Branchenbeitrag. Berlin: Bundesverband Digitalpublisher und Zeitungsverleger (BDZV), 2021).

15 Barbara Witte and Gerhard Syben, "Erosion von Öffentlichkeit. Freie Journalist*innen in der Corona-Pandemie," *OBS-Arbeitsheft* 109, (Otto-Brenner-Stiftung). https://www.otto-brenner-stiftung.de/erosion-von-oeffentlichkeit

16 Beate Josephi et al., "Profiles of Journalists." In *Worlds of Journalism* eds. Thomas Hanitzsch, Folker Hanusch, Jyotika Ramaprasad and Arrie de Beer, (New York, Chichester, West Sussex: Columbia University Press, 2019), 67–102.

17 Survey question: Are you thinking about a job change or even a career change? (yes/no)

18 The list of reasons was based on journalistic research on already established reasons for leaving the profession.

19 Natalie Helka, *Redaktionsschluss – warum Journalisten aussteigen.* (Wiesbaden: Springer VS, 2014).

20 Mirjam Gollmitzer, *Employment Conditions in Journalism.* (Oxford: Oxford University Press, 2019).

21 Thomas Hanitzsch and Jana Rick, Prekarisierung im Journalismus. Erster Ergebnisbericht März 2021. https://survey.ifkw.lmu.de/Journalismus_und_Prekarisierung/Prekarisierung_im_Journalismus_erster_Ergebnisbericht.pdf.

22 Gollmitzer, *Employment Conditions in Journalism.*

23 Merryn Sherwood, "Newly Branded." In *Journalists and Job Loss* eds. Timothy Marjoribanks, Lawrie Zion, Penny O'Donnell, and Merryn Sherwood, (London: Routledge, 2022), 42–54; Zion, "Australian Journalists," 17–30.

24 Reinardy, "Female Journalists More Likely to Leave," 42–57.

25 Gollmitzer, *Employment Conditions in Journalism.*

26 International Federation of Journalists, Journalists' Mental Health During the Pandemic. https://www.ifj.org/media-centre/news/detail/category/press-releases/article/journalists-mental-health-during-the-pandemic-we-need-to-talk.html.

27 Henrik Örnebring and Raul Ferrer Conill, "Outsourcing Newswork." In *The SAGE Handbook of Digital Journalism*, eds. Tamara Witschge, C. W. Anderson, David Domingo, and Alfred Hermida, (London: Sage, 2016), 207–221.

3

THE JOY IN JOURNALISM

Richard Stupart

That journalism can be hard, often thankless and poorly paid has become a background to industry conversations and university classes where journalism is taught. The harassment of female journalists in particular[1] raises concerns that journalism has become increasingly vulnerable to attacks from the communities it serves. In difficult subfields such as investigative and conflict reporting, the challenges and risks of the job are even more starkly reflected in the running counts of the dead published by the Committee to Protect Journalists.[2]

There is less said about how such work might produce *good* feelings for those who do it, in spite of—and perhaps in part *because* of—the risk and sacrifices that are involved in being a journalist. In this chapter, I argue that we should take seriously the possibility that for at least particularly morally-entangled forms of journalism—such as conflict and investigative reporting—it might be the case that these can be deeply emotionally fulfilling. This happiness is of a particularly eudaimonic kind, a fulfillment or sense of flourishing that derives from acting in accordance with strongly held/valued moral ideas. In line with the broader views developed in this book, this chapter suggests that there is a moral happiness to journalism, but that it is inextricably tied up with how the profession is socially constructed—both in the sense of its identity as a (moral) form of work and in terms of the institutional, political, and other contexts in which it takes place.

To make the case for eudaimonia in this chapter, I begin at the opposite end of the emotional spectrum with the current consensus on the existence of moral injury as a distinct form of emotional harm. I argue that we can view this moral injury as a specific case of "moral feeling" in the sense described in moral philosophical work that connects emotion and normative ethics. The idea that "bad" feelings about oneself might come about in response to violations of personal ethics in turn suggests the possibility of its opposite: "good" feeling in recognition of moral work well done: a kind of eudaimonia.

DOI: 10.4324/9781003364597-4

Connecting emotional well-being in journalism to its moral dimensions has some potentially significant (and perhaps inconvenient) implications for journalists, their employers, and the wider communities they are a part of. It links journalistic ethics (in an expansive, practical sense) to what it feels like to do the work itself. This prompts us to ask what moral communities exist within the profession and who we ought to hold responsible for whether journalists can live up to the obligations that those communities impose on their members. In other words, what does "good journalism" look like in different specializations, countries, or newsrooms, for example, and who is responsible for the feelings in those spaces when journalists succeed (or fail) to do morally good work well? Finally, thinking "eudaimonically" about journalistic work gives us an approach to understanding how the apparently paradoxical satisfactions of risky, often poorly paid work come about.

Moral Work and the Case for Positive Feeling

McDonald theorizes that certain forms of journalistic work can result in trauma, echoing a prevailing distinction between forms of harm anchored in experiences of fear such as post-traumatic stress disorder (PTSD) and those deriving from the feelings of shame (moral injury) that come from violating one's moral norms.[3] Scholars make the point that moral injury is an emotional harm that comes about after transgressing strongly held moral beliefs, whether through action, inaction, or witnessing egregious acts or betrayal by those who have authority over an agent (as in the case of being placed in an impossible moral position by a superior).[4]

The term "moral injury" has its origins in studies of the experiences of soldiers and trying to understand the causes of emotional distress in those who have had little or no obvious exposure to enemy fire or danger. The prevalence of PTSD-like symptoms in U.S. drone pilots clearly illustrates the long-term psychological and emotional harm that unethical work (from the point of view of an agent) can have.[5] The kinds of egregious contraventions of moral norms that might give rise to moral injury are by no means limited to the military. Journalists with a professional interest in injustice and suffering often find themselves in a position that risks moral injury, positioned as they are between those who are wronged and the audiences that they work to inform.[6] The literature on witnessing, for example, captures the moral awkwardness of the journalist's precarious position between voyeur and witness. Scholars have argued that the latter involves being unavoidably caught up in the causal (and moral) calculus of the suffering one encounters.[7] Journalists are close enough to the developments that they cover to have privileged knowledge of others' wrongs, and this is part of what animates a need to bear witness for them to emerge from such encounters as morally praiseworthy.[8]

Moreover, journalists may also be among the first or more privileged responders to situations of suffering and injustice, which can lead to a double interpellation as someone who can provide direct assistance (as general moral norms might require) or who ought to remain at a distance and tell others (a colder professional norm).[9] Such conflicts around how much to help personally and how much to report animate encounters between such journalists and their subjects frequently enough that they are a significant source of replayed regret or anxiety.[10]

Reactive Attitudes

The link between norms and feelings has been much discussed by moral philosophers as well. Arpaly has argued against seeing emotions as unreasoned or irrational feelings, suggesting that in many cases they are directing our attention to important subjective facts about the situations we find ourselves in.[11] She gives an example of a hypothetical "Sam the student" who decides that in order to pass his exams, he will give up all time with his friends and concentrate on work alone for the next month. Sam soon discovers that he finds this situation deeply emotionally unsatisfying not because he is feeling irrational, but because his feelings are pointing him to something he in fact deeply values—the sociality of friendship—that was not part of his explicit reasoning beforehand.

One case in which emotions follow from contexts is what Strawson calls "reactive attitudes": feelings that follow moral judgements and can exert a disciplinary force on us or affirm appraisals of the situations we find ourselves in.[12] Anger, shame and embarrassment are feelings of this kind, consequences of our judgements of others' (or our own) transgressions. Anger has been understood as a legitimate response to injustice for some time.[13] The same is true of positive feelings such as pride or a satisfied righteousness in our (or others) success in behaving in a morally exemplary way.

Also, one might feel moral emotions are in no way enough to advocate for one specific moral system over another. Manne has described how actions can feel entirely righteous within a moral system that might horrify those not included in it (such as the case of misogynistic violence).[14] The point, here, is the more general one that moral communities—that is, shared worlds of moral belief—can conjure positive emotions in members as a result of performing "good" acts, as judged by the normative lights of the community in question.

A Matter of Degrees

The hopefully uncontroversial observation that moral emotions might arise from the evaluation of our behavior in the context of rules established based on strongly held moral norms includes (at least) two observations that are worth spelling out. The first is the suggestion that our moral evaluations of our acts can be *positive*, and that it would not be surprising to see positive feelings (such as pride or righteousness) associated with such evaluations. Just as "bad feelings" may arise when we break important moral rules, such as in cases of moral injury, "good feelings" may arise when we adhere to or exceed our moral norms.

Second, we seem to experience *degrees* of feeling that correspond to the significance of the moral norms that are violated and the degree to which they are violated. All else being equal, a minor violation of a major rule—while perhaps not insignificant—would inspire less shame or regret than a major one. A violation of a minor rule would—all things considered—be less of a source of shame or regret than the violation of a major one. The case of positive feeling appears to be analogous. Contributing significantly to achieving something that is valued as a profound moral good (such as saving a life or righting an egregious wrong) could be expected to provide a greater sense of good feeling than achieving a minor good. The same gains would also apply in terms of our self-assessed contribution to achieving that good, or the extent to which it was realized.

Examples of Satisfying Moral Norms

I have argued in favor of the in-principal possibility of a deep emotional satisfaction where work satisfies strongly held (moral) principles. Yet this is more than simply a theoretical maybe. Reflections offered by actual news professionals working in (at least) conflict, investigative and activist journalism, offer evidence of such positive feeling as a valued component of the work.

One example of important moral norms guiding a sense of fulfillment in the work of journalists comes from studies focused on witnessing and journalism. Journalists of conflict have often adopted a language of witnessing and the duty to "bear witness" as an obligation that distinguishes journalism from voyeurism.[15] Succeeding in their work can be emotionally rewarding for journalists within a moral universe that affirms the value of witnessing. In investigative or activist journalism, bringing attention or remedy to situations of injustice produces feelings like those that result from engaging in doing virtuous work.

Implications of Moral Feeling in Journalism

The argument that (certain forms of) journalism carries moral commitments and that making good on those commitments might be a source of good feeling has several implications. First, it suggests that journalists' emotional well-being is intimately tied to the normative moral evaluations involved in their work. Such moral evaluations can take the form of (at least) professional, "journalistic" ethical evaluations, and more general societal moral norms. In other words, good moral feelings may depend on the extent to which one is being both a *good journalist* and a *good person* (however that might be understood).

A second implication is that the ability to "make good" on strongly felt moral principles is not the responsibility of the journalist alone. The literature on moral injury makes it clear that moral feelings can arise in situations in which agents feel betrayed by others who place them in impossible ethical positions. For example, Newman describes the case of a journalist whose agreements with victims about how they would be portrayed were betrayed by the editorial decisions of the news organization.[16] The implication in this case is that editorial (and other) staff in a news organization may play a role in whether journalists feel their work to be eudemonic or morally injurious in nature.

The approach to seeing feeling and ethics as bound up with one another developed here suggests that the same process that can help to minimize moral injury—aligning actions with values—can create feelings of eudaimonia in the profession. A more relativist view of moral norms, however, also implies the possibility of eudemonic feeling arising in work that may have very different (and even conflicting) moral norms to "orthodox" journalism. There is nothing in this account that ties the possibility of eudemonic feeling to any set of normative values. It requires only that they are held to be important in a particularly fundamental way by journalists themselves.

The project of understanding eudemonic feeling in journalism would therefore involve understanding which virtues are fundamental to moral communities within journalism, rather than assuming that eudemonic feeling is tied to any broad "journalistic value" of the kind taught in an undergraduate journalism class. Understood in this light, many of the challenges posed by contemporary journalism, such as increased precarity and risk, may offer paradoxical routes to eudemonic feeling even as they make the work ever harder to perform. If doing "good" journalism is satisfying in general, succeeding in doing it in the face of resistance from a hostile state, mafia or other bad actor would be more satisfying.

While it might be true that the difficulty of doing this type of journalistic work might contribute to the moral satisfaction of getting the job done, this should not be read as an endorsement of news organizations getting away with placing journalists in precarious positions, states targeting conflict reporters or other acts of malfeasance. Impairing journalists' ability to do their work successfully and to a standard that would fulfill their strongly held moral commitments is (all things considered) likely to prevent them from succeeding. It may contribute to journalists experiencing degrees of moral injury rather than eudaimonia due to self-perceptions of having failed those they work with/on behalf of. Seeing risk and precarity, normative ideals and emotional satisfaction as connected might, however, help explain what continues to motivate talented journalists to do work that is often poorly paid, undersupported and even dangerous. From the point of view of newsrooms, this insight should prompt conversations about the support offered by news organizations. Do institutional contexts enable the pursuit of (morally) good journalism? Or are journalists set up for failure through underfunding, shifting the responsibility for safety onto individual journalists and undermining the expectations that journalists and those they report on have for one another?

Much more could be said about the implications of this approach to thinking about journalism as eudemonic. I have hopefully demonstrated, however, that the same basic mechanism by which moral injury is understood to function can be used as a basis for theorizing the existence of its opposite—eudaimonia. Taking such an approach seriously in turn opens interesting connections between the norms of journalistic (sub)fields, the moral communities we belong to more generally, and the very real satisfactions that come from doing "good" journalism.

Notes

1 Trond Idås, Kristin Skare Orgeret, and Klas Backholm, "# MeToo, Sexual Harassment and Coping Strategies in Norwegian Newsrooms," *Media and Communication* 8, no. 1 (2020): 57–67.
2 "Explore CPJ's Database of Attacks on the Press," Committee to Protect Journalists, accessed 27 February, 2023, https://cpj.org/data/killed2.
3 Joseph McDonald, "What is Moral Injury?" In *Moral Injury*, (2020), 7–16.
4 McDonald, 7–16; Sonya Norman and Shira Maguen, "Moral Injury," *US Department of Veteran's Affairs*, Accessed April 4, 2022, https://www.ptsd.va.gov/professional/treat/cooccurring/moral_injury.asp
5 Christian Enemark, "Drones, Risk, and Moral Injury," *Critical Military Studies* 5, no. 2 (2019): 150–167.
6 Elana Newman, "The Bridge between Sorrow and Knowledge." In *Sharing the Front Line and the Back Hills*, (2018), 316–322.
7 Andrew Linklater, "Distant Suffering and Cosmopolitan Obligations," *International Politics* 44 (2007): 19–36.
8 John Durham Peters, "Witnessing," *Media, Culture, and Society* 23, no. 6 (2001): 707–723.
9 Richard Stupart, "Forgotten Conflicts." In *Routledge Handbook of Humanitarian Communication*, (Routledge, 2021), 220–234.
10 Richard Stupart, "Feeling Responsible," *Media, War & Conflict* 14, no. 3 (2021): 268–281.
11 Nomy Arpaly, "On Acting Rationally Against One's Best Judgment," *Ethics* 110, no. 3 (2000): 488–513; Nomy Arpaly, *Unprincipled Virtue*, (Oxford University Press, 2002).
12 Peter Frederick Strawson, *Freedom and Resentment and Other Essays*, (Routledge, 2008).
13 Audre Lorde, "The Uses of Anger," *Women and Language* 11, no. 1 (1987): 4.
14 Kate Manne, *Down Girl*, (Oxford University Press, 2017).
15 Richard Stupart, "Forgotten Conflicts," In *Routledge Handbook of Humanitarian Communication*, (Routledge, 2021), 220–234.
16 Newman, "The Bridge between Sorrow and Knowledge," 316–322.

4

FINDING JOY AS JOURNALISTS

Motivations for Newswork

Gregory P. Perreault

Deborah D. Douglas is the visionary leader of *The Emancipator*, a collaborative journalism project between *The Boston Globe* and Boston University's Center for Antiracist Research. *The Emancipator* is named for the first abolitionist newspaper in the United States and tackles topics of racial justice, structural inequality, and white supremacy. Douglas readily acknowledges that the seriousness of these topics can give journalists pause in engaging with the above issues. Journalists, Douglas argues, often feel a tension between who they are and what they must report. According to Douglas, the key to the success for *The Emancipator* is in erasing that tension. "We built into our mission that joy underlines our ethos," says Douglas ... "Journalists should not have to create from tension [who they are and what they must report on] ... Journalism is not where I work. Journalism is who I am."[1]

Journalism scholars often find themselves at the crossroads of two very different experiences: (1) those of the journalists we often study who describe working conditions that are stressful, hostile, and wearying; and (2) those of the journalists they often educate as they enter the field, who see the field in the broad brushstrokes of what it *can be*. These are not always mutually exclusive experiences, yet they necessitate a robust consideration on the motivations for entering the field to reflect on what happiness may mean for journalism.

Research reflects that aside from the normative claims of the field, the work experience of journalists bears much in common with medical professionals: stressful, yet with a vision that the work they do will make a difference. Journalism studies literature indicates numerous issues facing news work: hostility in reporting,[2] the hidden labor of many journalists in their work,[3] the exodus of journalists leaving the field,[4] and difficulties in navigating the divide between who they are and what they do.[5] The latter often is referenced

DOI: 10.4324/9781003364597-5

broadly in critique of the *objectivity* norm, a norm aimed at "remaining completely unbiased in covering the news" and promoting "'he-said-she-said' reporting."[6] As Wahl-Jorgensen puts it: "The governing assumption of the profession has been that journalists are objective, impartial, and distanced observers of events, and that emotion is anathema to responsible journalistic storytelling."[7] Taken together, these challenges reflect a number of exhausting, frustrating stressors placed on journalists.

While it is important to consider why journalists may leave the profession, it is also important to explore why journalists *stay*. Where do journalists find happiness? As such, this chapter plumbs a simple yet pernicious question within the field: given the well-known challenges, why do journalism? This chapter considers the experience of joy, an ingredient in personal happiness, among journalists. This chapter applies the lens of joy as a news value,[8] a conceptual framework aimed at "reorienting the minds of journalists and audiences toward affective characteristics of people and events that evoke well-being, delight, and courage," and based on interviews with U.S.-based journalists from several specialties including politics, gaming, and sport, this chapter explores the joys of journalism that motivate their work in the field as a way to understand and explore solutions for how journalists may find happiness in their profession. Journalists in the U.S. face challenging labor conditions given the commercial system—high market profit expectations with low pay and benefits[9]—as well as a rising degree of press criticism.[10] The American media system receives little support from the state which has exacerbated problems in the profession.[11] While the U.S. presents an exceptional case, it is nevertheless an important one, given that the trends of harsh work conditions and criticism are well represented across the globe.[12]

Joy as a News Value

This study builds on Parks's call to establish joy as a news value motivational to the work of journalism.[13] Joy reflects an essential aspect of happiness. Kövecses elaborates: happiness is not defined by the absence of unpleasant experiences but rather navigating those experiences with joy.[14] To consider journalism in this way "would help reorient the minds of journalists and readers toward the affective characteristics of people and events that produce a sense of well-being, delight and even courage."[15] The news value reflects the constructed values that journalists use to motivate their reporting—Galtung and Ruge laid the foundation of this concept with the values of frequency, threshold, unambiguity, meaningfulness, consonance, continuity, composition and unexpectedness.[16] Later scholars emphasized that a heavier weight in these values was on "bad news" or conflict-oriented stories, distilled in the newsroom refrain *if it bleeds, it leads.* [17] Intuitively, this focus leaves a gaping hole in the rationale: given that journalists are as human as their readers, wouldn't they be motivated in similar ways? And bad news, while unavoidable in human experience, is simultaneously not the *whole* of human experience. "Joy can be cognitively apprehended only in and amongst being felt. Its recognition demands a life-altering reorientation to what we perceive as the meaning and essence of news."[18]

Parks offers several dimensions of how joy presents in news content— built off the dimensions developed by spiritual leaders the Dalai Lama, and Anglican Archbishop Desmond Tutu: the dimensions include perspective, humility, humor, acceptance, forgiveness, gratitude, and compassion.[19] Joy may serve a strong normative function within journalism in that a joyful mind is "better prepared to confront injustice than a mind that is contracted and confused."[20] Yet it is worth considering that this joy—like other news values—does not just present in the news content but also the news production. In this study, I apply this framework to conceptualizing the motivations of journalists in their specialty to uncover the happiness in journalism.

Interviews with Journalists

This study is based on 126 interviews with U.S. journalists. From 2015 to 2019, three different interview-based studies were conducted with journalists from the specialties of politics (63), sports (46) and gaming (17). In each of these questionnaires, journalists were asked about their central motivations for working in journalism with questions such as "how did you decide to get into XX journalism" (here XX was replaced by the specialty in which journalists worked), "how did you choose XX journalism?" and "What motivates you to do this form of journalism?" Each of the questionnaires dealt with a range of other topics such as role conception,[21] labor challenges,[22] and boundary work.[23]

All interviews were semi-structured. Interviews with sports and political journalists were conducted and transcribed by trained research students at Appalachian State University, while interviews with gaming journalists were conducted solely by the primary investigator. All interview protocols were conducted following approval from the Institutional Review Board. For this study, journalists were deidentified, and quotes are attributed to journalists only regarding their specialty and with context deemed relevant.

Gratitude as Motivating the Work of Journalists

The first joy journalists articulated motivating happiness in their work was one of gratitude. Gratitude is the recognition of "all that has made it possible to have the life that we have and the moment that we are experiencing."[24] Journalists here articulated their work to recapture something magical from their past and pay tribute to the people who granted it to them. In other words, journalism provided them a way to express gratitude for their experiences.

Journalists tied this gratitude to their family and their childhood. As one political journalist (J9) put it, "It's sort of a family business. My father was a journalist for the Associated Press and his stepfather was a journalist and my mother is also a writer, so I just kind of grew up in a family of writers and journalists." Similarly, a gaming journalist grew up with game systems in his house and recounted his original ColecoVision—a 1980s video game system best known for an at-home version of *Donkey Kong*—which he played with his family. During the interview, he noted that he still had the steering wheel controller for the system in the other room. His kindergarten class started later in the day—12:30 p.m.—"I remember waking up, showering, getting ready for the day and then I would be playing *Zelda 2* until the last second before my mom made us leave the house and go to school" (J113). As a new father, this journalist noted that "I am certainly looking forward to sharing a hobby" with his son when he is old enough. His own experience made him feel strongly "video games have gone from being just a product or even a toy to being something that has a real cultural impact."

Similarly, other journalists mentioned formative experiences in their schooling that they were grateful for with one political journalist noting that it was her middle school classes that made her realize that she could have the opportunity to be in the "middle of talking to people who make very important decisions" (J74). Another described falling in love with journalism through covering high school sports for the *High Point Enterprise* (J104) and another noted that during schooling he found "sports as a passion, but I wasn't good enough to play any of them very well so I figured I could write about them—it has been a good decision" (J70). Hence sports reporting "made it possible to have the life" that he had. All of this reflects the degree to which journalists were motivated in their reporting by gratitude for early experiences that introduced them to either the specialty or to writing more broadly.[25]

The Opportunity to Provide Perspective

Journalists were also motivated by their personal identity and life experiences they felt that, if shared, could allow others more expansive responses. As Parks put it, "actively taking perspective frees us from narrow or habituated responses."[26] This was a particularly prominent dimension of joy shared by political journalists. As a political journalist said, "I remember being young and watching the news on tv and not really seeing anyone who looked like me. I'm a young black woman, and you don't often see young black women on news and TV talking about politics. I knew that I wanted to do it then, and I had always loved writing since I was a kid" (J10). What is at stake in having access to different perspectives? Almost everything if you're in political journalism. Hence, journalists articulated a passion for helping readers gain alternative ways of viewing the world. "It's sort of a public service and overall, it would mean that people are more informed because people don't really have the time to vet every single candidate. It's a way to learn from people who have spent the time," voiced a journalist (J13), and others "enjoyed it immensely, especially getting to know politicians of different parties and long-time practitioners who could offer insightful perspectives," said another (J8).

While the importance of sharing multiple perspectives–including your own—was dominant in political journalism, this theme was nevertheless reflected in other specialties as well in that good sports journalists can give "readers an insight ... they wouldn't have had without your work" (J106). Similarly, a gaming journalist drew joy from linking a game experience to larger worldwide issues.

> I think that adds a bit of insight to context you don't usually see, and it is usually something that tackles an interesting or important issue. So, those stories have included things like what it's like to be a developer in the Middle East, how GameStop's policies of fingerprinting can be a major invasion of privacy.
>
> *(J116)*

Journalists found joy in learning about a range of perspectives on a topic—and at times elaborating on their own as a part of that. As a dimension of joy, this also reflects that those normative expectations of journalism (e.g., representing the full picture in a story) would seem to still be addressed by centering joy as a news value.

Compassion for the Audience

Journalists articulated compassion for their audience. Compassion, according to the Dalai Lama, Tutu and Abrams, reflects the desire to reduce suffering in the world in that in "alleviating other people's suffering, our own suffering is reduced."[27] Political journalists were motivated to provide "context for readers why these decisions matter and how it impacts their lives," (J11) and for their readers who at times "may not have big voices or [are] getting screwed over by the government in some way" (J24). The journalist added that he was motivated "to get political information to people who need it." As another said:

> Having lived in West Virginia my whole life, I have a personal connection to doing this work because it absolutely affects the people I know and love the most, and I have a lot of good, practical knowledge about the history of the state that really lets me dig deep into issues in a way that connects politics and law making with the actual lived experience of our readers.
>
> *(J21)*

But this compassion for the readers wasn't just about providing information but also sharing joy with them. Journalists "want the readers to be happy" (J110) even as it's "not important in the sense of like if someone is going to live or die over this topic but it's still journalism...just satisfy a different itch," said another (J116). In gaming journalism, many respondents enacted this by finishing video games they were not personally interested in and in doing so they felt that they were able to connect with their readers (J119). Sports journalists described reporting on games and teams wanting their readers to "feel like they're a part of it" (J109). There is joy in sharing, as a sports journalist (J24) described, the stories that readers do not yet know. This reflects the degree to which journalists articulated being embedded in their passions and that they were a part of their audience.[28]

For the Joy of Journalism

Wright Thompson is a sports writing legend. While known for genre-defining pieces on Tiger Woods and the Ole Miss football team's 1962 perfect season, Thompson commonly finds memories of his late-father working their way into his stories. While his father's love of sports inspired Thompson's reporting, it was the way he viewed his work that informed so much of how Thompson approached his own. In an article about the birth of his daughter, Thompson notes,

> His old shoe-shine kit is framed and hangs above the door to my office, and near my desk is a print he once had in his own office: WHEN YOUR WORK SPEAKS FOR ITSELF, DON'T INTERRUPT ... He wrote me a lot of letters, which I still have in a box. Years later, I'm still trying to make peace with his absence ... [My daughter] doesn't know what I know now: There's no place she can ever go where I won't be with her, part of her, which is something my father surely felt about me but I never understood.[29]

Wright Thompson found connection with his late father through his reporting, and in writing about the birth of his own daughter, realized there were totems he had carried unnecessarily for years—unnecessarily, because there was no need to recapture the experience of his father, because it had never been lost.[30]

While much scholarship has focused on professional roles and professional motivations, there are also personal roles and motivations that are at least as important.[31] Through the lens of joy as a news value, we see that journalists were motivated by three key dimensions of joy:

- Gratitude—for their childhood and early experiences.
- Perspective—the opportunity to provide a different way of looking at things.
- Compassion for their readers—reflected in a desire to, conversant with professional role conception literature—provide them information they needed but also to bring them stories that shared joy.

Noteworthy are the dimensions of joy *not* mentioned by journalists, notably forgiveness and acceptance. This is perhaps given the nature of the sample of journalists interviewed who may not have encountered these forms of story as often. Politics can be, of course, famously unforgiving, and sport and gaming provide few avenues for these forms of stories. Politics can be exceptionally interpersonal in its reporting, but political journalism has placed an emphasis on interpersonal conflict.[32] Centering joy as a news value would encourage a very different approach to political journalism that would, in contrast, emphasize interpersonal cooperation.

Much attention within U.S. journalism studies has been placed on the binary notion of the objectivity norm—the need to provide balance for stories but also encourage verification and independence.[33] We see this norm in Douglas's statement from the introduction that "journalists should not have to create from tension." This tension of course calls journalists, to some degree, to divorce *who they are* from *what they do*. It is worth considering that tension, while perhaps more acute in the U.S., may not be a solely U.S. phenomenon. Globally and across fields, the digital information scape has facilitated a collapsing of roles that would seem to expect the professional in all settings. This has required journalists, particularly in the wake of the pandemic, to reconstitute digital boundaries that allow them to find joy.[34]

As research explores the serious concerns related to why journalists leave the industry,[35] this chapter prescribes that more studies are needed to understand the things that encourage journalists to stay. While mitigating the issues that journalists face on the job is unquestionable—indeed the labor expectations and experiences of harassment would be untenable in nearly any profession[36]—it may be that journalism's salvation relies on giving journalists the opportunity to report on the topics and in the ways that bring them joy. If gratitude is indeed "an antidote to negativity bias" in the news,[37] then it is worth considering the degree to which the cure to what ails journalism may be found in the aspects that spark joy.

Notes

1 Michele Weldon, "Equity, Humanity, Power and Joy." *Take the Lead*, (2021). https://www.taketheleadwomen.com/blog/equity-humanity-power-and-joy-black-journalist-leaders-on-addressing-history-with-solutions
2 Avery E. Holton, Valérie Bélair-Gagnon, Diana Bossio, and Logan Molyneux, "'Not their fault, but their problem,'" *Journalism Practice* (2021): 1–16.
3 Karin Wahl-Jorgensen, "An emotional turn in journalism studies?" *Digital Journalism* 8, no. 2 (2020): 175–194.
4 Nick Mathews, Valérie Bélair-Gagnon, and Matt Carlson, "Why I quit journalism?" *Journalism* (2021).
5 Karin Wahl-Jorgensen, "Questioning the ideal of the public sphere," *Social Media + Society* 5, no. 3: (2019): 674.
6 Jane Singer, "The journalist in the network," *Blanquerna School of Communication and International Relations* (2008): 72.

7 Wahl-Jorgensen, "Questioning the ideal of the public sphere," 674.
8 Perry Parks, "Joy is a news value," *Journalism Studies* 22, no. 6 (2021): 820–838.
9 Carey L. Higgins-Dobney, "Not on air, but online," *Electronic News* 15, no. 3–4 (2021): 95–108.
10 Matt Carlson, Sue Robinson, and Seth C. Lewis, *News after Trump*, (Oxford University Press, 2021).
11 Paul Clemens Murschetz, "State aid for independent news journalism in the public interest?" *Digital Journalism* 8, no. 6 (2020): 720–739.
12 Silvio Waisbord, "The vulnerabilities of journalism," *Journalism* 20, no. 1 (2019): 210–213.
13 Parks, "Joy is a news value."
14 Zoltán Kövecses, "Happiness: A definitional effort," *Metaphor and Symbol* 6, no. 1 (1991): 29–47.
15 Parks, "Joy is a news value," 821.
16 Johan Galtung, and Mari Holmboe Ruge, "The structure of foreign news," *Journal of Peace Research* 2, no. 1 (1965), 64–90.
17 Deirdre O'Neill, and Tony Harcup, "News values and selectivity," In *The handbook of journalism studies*, (Routledge, 2009), 181–194.
18 Parks, "Joy is a news value," 833.
19 Dalai Lama, Desmond Tutu, and Douglas Carlton Abrams, *The Book of Joy*, ([New York]: Penguin, 2016).
20 Parks, "Joy is a news value," 833.
21 Gregory P. Perreault, and Travis R. Bell, "Towards a 'digital' sports journalism," *Communication & Sport* 10, no. 3 (2022): 398–416.
22 Gregory P. Perreault, Volha Kananovich, and Ella Hackett, "Guarding the firewall," *Journalism & Mass Communication Quarterly* (2022).
23 Gregory P. Perreault, and Tim P. Vos, "The GamerGate controversy and journalistic paradigm maintenance," *Journalism* 19, no. 4 (2018): 553–569.
24 Lama, Tutu, and Abrams, *The Book of Joy*, 242.
25 See also Lama, Tutu, and Abrams, *The Book of Joy*, 242.
26 Parks, "Joy is a News Value," 829.
27 Lama, Tutu, and Abrams, *The Book of Joy*, 254.
28 Greg Perreault and Valérie Bélair-Gagnon, "The lifestyle of lifestyle journalism," *Journalism Practice* (2022): 10.
29 Wright Thompson, "Like father, like son, like daughter," *Garden & Gun* (2018), https://gardenandgun.com/articles/wright-thompson-essay-father-son-daughter/
30 Thompson, "Like Father, Like Son, Like Daughter."
31 Wahl-Jorgensen, "Questioning the ideal of the public sphere," 674.
32 Guus Bartholomé, Sophie Lecheler, and Claes de Vreese, "Manufacturing conflict?" *The International Journal of Press/Politics* 20, no. 4 (2015): 438–457.
33 Michael Schudson, "The objectivity norm in American journalism," *Journalism* 2, no. 2 (2001): 149–170.
34 Bélair-Gagnon, Valérie, Diana Bossio, Avery E. Holton, and Logan Molyneux. "Disconnection," *Social Media + Society* 8, no. 1 (2022).
35 Nick Mathews, Valérie Bélair-Gagnon, and Matt Carlson, "Why I quit journalism," *Journalism* 24, no. 1 (2023): 62–77.
36 Kaitlin Miller and Seth C. Lewis, "Journalists, Harassment, and Emotional Labor," *Journalism* 23, no. 1 (2022): 79–97.
37 Parks, "Joy is a news value," 832.

5

WHAT PSYCHOLOGY CAN OFFER IN UNDERSTANDING JOURNALISTS' WELL-BEING

Jennifer M. Ragsdale and Elana Newman

Estimates suggest that people spend an average of 90,000 hours working in their lifetimes.[1] Journalists may work even more hours,[2] hours which vary considerably due to breaking news and particular assignments.[3] Journalists, like others, desire to spend that work time doing work that is fulfilling or meaningful to them—something that contributes to their well-being, including happiness.[4] In this chapter, we introduce the psychological science of well-being as applied to the work of journalists. First, we define well-being, which includes happiness, and we distinguish it from related psychological concepts of resilience and recovery. Using the National Institute for Occupational Safety and Health (NIOSH)s Total Worker Health®[5] as an organizing framework, we discuss opportunities for improving research and interventions aimed at improving journalists' well-being. This review will introduce key ideas and outline recommendations for future research as a step toward leveraging the vast knowledge of well-being from psychology and occupational health to amplify knowledge and promote evidence-based actions to enhance journalists' well-being and occupational success.

Introducing Well-Being

Well-being is a fuzzy concept that represents living in a subjective state that is somehow good.[6] Researchers have suggested that well-being is more an area of study than it is a "thing."[7] That is, well-being may be better thought of as an umbrella term under which concepts are organized that represent positive emotional states, attitudes about many aspects of one's life, and experiencing fulfillment. There are two prevailing approaches to describing well-being: *hedonic* and *eudaimonic* well-being. Aside from communication studies on hedonic and eudaimonic entertainment preferences,[8] journalist-focused

DOI: 10.4324/9781003364597-6

research has not used this specific terminology when studying different indicators of journalists' well-being.

Hedonic well-being

Hedonic well-being, also referred to as subjective well-being,[9] is characterized by experiencing more frequent positive emotions, less frequent negative emotions, and evaluations or judgements that life is good.[10] Emotional states differ in their valence—positivity/pleasure or negativity/displeasure—and their arousal—how physiologically activated a person feels (affective circumplex).[11] Feeling happy and excited are positive emotional states with higher activation, whereas feeling content and calm are positive emotional states with lower activation. Similarly, feeling anxious and angry are negative emotional states with higher activation, and feeling sad or tired are negative emotional states with lower activation. These emotional states represent the affective well-being dimension of hedonic well-being, which is typically assessed using a list of emotional states, and people are asked to indicate to what degree they have experienced that emotion (e.g., POMS-SF and PANAS-X). The traditional stereotype that journalists are tenacious, miserable pessimists may run counter to the notion of hedonic well-being, although many journalists experience positive moods from their work. Thus far, journalism research has examined general positive and negative affect as outcomes of working conditions and worker characteristics.[12]

Subjective judgements about how well one's life is going relative to some standard or ideal state represents cognitive well-being, i.e., life satisfaction.[13] Cognitive well-being is measured by asking people to rate the extent to which they agree with statements like "As a whole, I am satisfied with my life"[14] and "In most ways, my life is close to ideal."[15] Journalism research has largely examined job satisfaction[16] over other cognitive well-being outcomes. Cognitive and affective well-being have different antecedents. Affective states are reactions to specific events, like giving a presentation at work, and are more easily recalled when asked to respond in the moment or reflect on an entire day, whereas cognitive well-being is less impacted by individual events (e.g., an argument with a spouse) and more so by factors that stabilize or destabilize general life conditions, like a well-resourced work environment driving higher job satisfaction.[17]

Eudaimonic well-being

Eudaimonic well-being is characterized by fulfilling one's potential[18] and is rooted in pursuit of goals that are consistent with a person's values and identity.[19] Eudaimonic well-being is less well-studied compared to hedonic well-being so there is no unified definition or set of concepts that represents an optimally functioning person.[20] However, common indicators of eudaimonic well-being include a sense of meaning or purpose, self-acceptance, autonomy, and growth. Given the nature of journalists' work, eudaimonic well-being is important to examine. Many journalists view their job as a calling, dedicated to truth telling, the democratic ideals, and public service.[21] Further, the opportunity and privilege to tell interesting stories and witness historical events unfold are identified as key aspects of the professional role,[22] and the joy of daily challenges and working against deadlines are part of journalists' professional identity.[23]

Although eudaimonic well-being is related to hedonic well-being, they are distinct concepts.[24] For example, experiencing and overcoming challenges are associated with higher eudaimonic well-being and lower hedonic well-being.[25] Rather than considering hedonic and eudaimonic well-being separately, some researchers take an integrated view. Flourishing is defined broadly as feeling good and functioning well.[26] It is conceptualized as a combination of eudaimonic and hedonic well-being characterized by experiencing more positive emotions, engagement, positive relationships, meaning, and achievement.[27] Work engagement is a positive affective and motivational state of well-being. It is experienced as the effort/intensity of doing work, attention/absorption to work tasks, and enthusiasm/energy during work. Similarly, thriving at work is a combination of vitality (energy, positive affect) and growth.[28] Flow, which is total immersion in an activity,[29] is another well-being indicator that is not clearly organized in one category or another. However, flow may reflect eudaimonic more than hedonic well-being,[30] because it involves higher levels of engagement that are not always accompanied by positive emotions. Flow has been examined in journalism research. Among 211 Norwegian journalists, those with higher levels of flow reported more work enjoyment, positivity, and efficacy; however, flow was unrelated to negative feelings.[31] Specifically, flow levels were unrelated to negative affect, emotional exhaustion, cynicism, and absenteeism. Hence, the positive experiences associated with being in a flow state do not negate the experience of negative emotions like frustration.

Context of Well-Being

Researchers have studied well-being as "context-free," representing well-being that is not tied to a specific setting (e.g., happiness, life satisfaction, meaningful life) and "domain specific," such that factors within a specific domain or environment (e.g., job or family satisfaction, occupational calling) more strongly contribute to well-being within that same domain, environment,[32] or possibly culture. For instance, work-related well-being represents indicators of well-being that are connected to the work setting, occupation, or job requirements. For research on work-related well-being, the hedonic perspective is more dominant (e.g., job satisfaction, burnout), however increasing attention has been directed toward the eudaimonic view (e.g., meaningfulness at work).[33] Research on journalists seems to focus primarily on work-related hedonic well-being (e.g., job satisfaction, burnout); however, one study on work–family conflict in Indian journalists incorporated both work (job satisfaction) and nonwork (family and life satisfaction) indicators of well-being[34] showing that as work interfered with family, journalists had lower family satisfaction, and as family interfered with work, journalists had lower work satisfaction. The research on the intersection between work and home and the impact on well-being is complex,[35] but is important for understanding how journalists' work follows them home and how home situations impact work.

Positive well-being, negative well-being, and ambivalence

For the longest time, psychology followed a "disease model" focused on fixing what was wrong with people[36] by identifying factors that predicted negative well-being or unwell-being, such as burnout, depression, or fatigue.[37] The advent of positive psychology promoted a focus on positive outcomes, including work engagement, work-related flow, and meaningful work.[38] This shift in emphasis does not signify that one view is more important than the other or that these perspectives are opposite sides of the same coin. Further, the concept of well-being does not reflect the absence of negative emotions or a lack of suffering.[39]

Indicators of positive well-being can co-occur with negative outcomes, especially in work-related challenges.[40] For example, a study of 69 U.K.-based print and broadcast journalists found that personal life-threatening risk was positively correlated with both post-traumatic growth (positive outcome) and post-traumatic stress symptoms (negative outcome).[41] Feeling both good and bad is characteristic of ambivalence, a psychological state that is hardly measured but is needed within the context of well-being.[42] Most studies on trauma-related mental health difficulties in journalists focus on solely negative outcomes,[43] except for the few studies on post-traumatic growth.[44] Especially when studying trauma exposure among journalists, a sole focus on positive well-being has the risk of invalidating journalists' experiences.

Summary and recommendations

Well-being is a multi-faceted area of study, and so consistent use of terminology is important for future research on journalists' well-being. For example, affective well-being is a specific category of well-being that reflects various emotional states. Using terminology like "emotional well-being" to connote mental health problems about journalists,[45] creates conceptual confusion. Although mental health is a component of well-being,[46] psychopathology is distinct. Individuals with mental disorders or maladaptive behaviors may experience positive emotional states. Journalists who respond to everyday work stressors (e.g., deadlines) with negative emotional responses are not experiencing psychopathology. Using appropriate terminology is critical for advancing understanding of journalists' well-being so that information about journalists can be contextualized and compared to other professions and contextualized in the field of occupational health psychology.

Similarly, the various well-being concepts described above are not interchangeable and each concept has unique correlates. Inferences about one aspect of well-being do not necessarily generalize to others. For example, inferences that journalists are "doing well" based on measures of job satisfaction alone ignore when journalists are dissatisfied in other domains. Caution is warranted when including multiple well-being concepts in a single study. It is important that the measures selected reflect the intended concept, and measures should be avoided that have considerable overlap. For example, items from some measures of fatigue, burnout, and depression have strong conceptual overlap.[47] Recently, NIOSH developed the Worker Well-Being Questionnaire (WellBQ), which is a theoretically driven, comprehensive assessment of worker well-being across multiple spheres, including quality of working life, circumstances outside work, and physical and mental health status.[48] This WellBQ is freely available for public use and is intended to help researchers, employers, workers, practitioners, and policymakers understand the well-being of workers and develop interventions to improve their well-being. Future research examining journalists' well-being should consider using the WellBQ.

Distinguishing Well-Being from Related Concepts of Recovery and Resilience

Other phenomena that are sometimes discussed interchangeably with well-being are recovery and resilience. These are processes that promote well-being in response to stress. Recovery may be considered a pathway to daily well-being (at and outside of work) that disrupts the development of unwell-being and ill health in the long term. Resilience, on the other hand, may be considered a pathway to well-being following exposure to a unique type of stressor or adversity. Below, we explain these different processes and how they affect well-being.

Recovery

Recovery is the psychophysiological process of unwinding or undoing the stress response whereby psychophysiological states and resources return to a pre-stressor state.[49] It is a process of recharging one's "batteries" to prevent build-up of negative reactions to stressors and conditions like burnout, depression, and increased risk for ill health, like cardiovascular disease.[50] The success of the recovery process is often indicated by changes in hedonic well-being, such as positive and negative affect[51] and fatigue and energy/vitality.[52] Although studies have examined eudaimonic well-being as an outcome of recovery[53] (e.g., flow), a great deal of research has identified work engagement, a combination of hedonic (energy, dedication) and eudaimonic (absorption/flow) well-being, as improved by pursuing recovery opportunities.[54]

Recovery as an area of study has focused on what people do (recovery activities) and how people perceive their experience (recovery experiences) during their time off work (i.e., work breaks, evenings, weekends, vacations).[55] Overall, social and physical activities are more consistently linked to higher vigor and lower exhaustion or fatigue,[56] whereas continuing to do work or engage in work-like tasks (e.g., paying bills) reduces happiness and vigor[57] and increases exhaustion.[58] Recovery experiences of psychological detachment and relaxation have the strongest and most consistent associations with improved well-being (e. g., increased energy, reduced fatigue).[59] Mastery experiences, however, are only sometimes related to improved well-being (e.g., work engagement and burnout avoidance),[60] which may be a function of personality differences.[61]

The technology-connectedness characteristic of modern work creates a situation where people always have work with them, whether they are actively continuing to do work during "off-work" time or passively receiving work-related notifications. On the one hand, this keeps people engaged with work, while also keeping stress responses activated and leaving people overtaxed and depleted when they return to work.[62] For journalists, the 24-hour news cycle creates a need to be aware of up-to-the-minute changes in a story, which interferes with having sustained time off work to recover. Yet, journalists can practice intentionally monitoring the news related to their work, rather than monitoring all news. Furthermore, journalists can take advantage of 1–2-minute microbreak opportunities (e.g., breathing exercises) and news organizations should encourage microbreaks. Journalists and news organizations might actively plan longer periods of recovery time when they are not tethered to technology and the news. Novel scholarship on connection and disconnection in digital media[63] which addresses these issues will benefit from leveraging existing recovery research, especially those related to technology.

Resilience

Resilience is "the process by which individuals are able to positively adapt to substantial difficulties, adversity, or hardship."[64] It is largely evidenced by a unique response, a "bounce back" or positive adaptation, that occurs after experiencing adversity.[65] Adverse experiences are not well-defined, but represent acute or chronic experiences of difficulty or hardship that can cause disruption or disequilibrium in a person's functioning.[66] Some forms of adversity constitute traumatic stressors which are events that potentially threaten a person's physical integrity such as serious injury and sexual violence.[67] The characteristic resilient response is indicated by adversity first triggering a reduction in functioning. Over time, however, people "bounce back" and return to pre-adversity levels of functioning.[68]

Thus far in understanding journalists' occupational health, scholars have used the term "resilience" in a variety of ways. For example, resilience has been operationalized generally as coping with trauma, or as a process "to minimize trauma" or "address the problems of journalists' adversity,"[69] without clarifying if the bouncing back is essential. Similarly in journalism education, resiliency training is sometimes equated with a more general trauma informed approach[70] or general well-being or self-care as opposed to returning to equilibrium. Clarity of the term is necessary as important scholarship may be disregarded or combined in ways that obfuscate important information about journalists' experiences of bouncing back and experiencing happiness after adversity from general wellness.

Summary and recommendations

Recovery and resilience are processes that are distinct from one another but contribute to journalists' well-being. When developing a study, clarity is needed on what type of process (recovery or resilience) best fits the research question and considers the journalists' work context (chronic stressors or adversity), as few studies on journalists' work-related stress distinguish between daily work experiences and the distress of reporting on major adverse events[71] or they have focused solely on trauma exposure.[72]

Addressing these conceptual issues will inform selection of the research design, variables, and associated measures.[73] Of particular importance to the issue of resilience and recovery is the characteristic that these processes change over time. This means repeated measures are an important feature of any resilience or recovery study, whereas studies on well-being can be examined as a single snapshot in time. Journalists are busy and may be difficult to keep engaged, so researchers need to balance the research design with the burden on the participants.[74]

Improving Journalists' Well-Being

Improving journalists' well-being requires a holistic picture of the person, work context, personal or family context, and socio-political context. Together, NIOSH's Total Worker Health® (TWH) holistic framework and Hierarchy of Controls can guide researchers identifying and prioritizing research questions, developing workplace interventions, and measuring the effectiveness of interventions that prioritize journalists' well-being.[75] TWH approaches recognize that employee health and well-being are impacted by more than just the traditional occupational safety and health concerns such as chemical, biological, and physical workplace hazards.[76] All aspects of work, including psychosocial factors (e.g., organizational culture, workload, co-worker and supervisor interactions, pay and benefits) contribute to the well-being of employees, their families, and their communities.[77]

Journalism as an occupation offers a unique combination of exposures to physical hazards and psychosocial hazards emanating from economic, cultural, organizational, and job-related challenges, all of which present intervention opportunities for improving the well-being of journalists. In line with the Hierarchy of Controls, approaches that eliminate or replace job-related hazards are argued to be most effective.[78] However, many journalists are required to do hazardous work, such as reporting in high-risk locations, and it is often impossible to remove or replace the hazard. Existing solutions focus on risk reduction by enhancing physical and digital safety protections, individualized safety planning, restricting how often journalists are assigned to cover dangerous or emotionally difficult stories by rotating staff and enforcing breaks, but their effectiveness has not been evaluated.

The next most effective strategy is to redesign the work environment by adding or enhancing aspects of the work environment that reduce barriers and improve employees' ability to do their work, including introducing or increasing job control, social support, feedback on how their job contributes to the organization's mission.[79] Bolstering resources like these also provides an environment that fosters resilience.[80] Management support addressing staff distress appears to be a critical variable in promoting job satisfaction and reducing turnover for journalists.[81] Typically, middle managers (editors, producers, bureau chiefs) see themselves as the sole support for trauma exposed staff yet have no training and are often peers in age or experience to those they supervise. Relatedly, inconsistent leadership styles, supervisory conflicts, and changes in organizational policies predicted trauma-related symptoms,[82] and so these appear to be fruitful areas for potential redesign for well-being. Newsrooms have experimented with extra days off on a rotating basis, hazard pay, formally trained mentors, peer support programs,[83] game nights for staffers, check-ins with staff, enhancing mental health benefits, and management training; however, none of these interventions have been formally evaluated.

Less effective are education strategies and encouraging personal change.[84] These interventions shift the burden onto the employee. They are more commonly implemented as they are perceived as easier and more cost effective.[85] These individually focused interventions typically focus on stress management, recovery from work stress, and self-care.[86]

Many trainings have been proposed or developed to promote recovery and resilience among journalists especially those exposed to traumatic events,[87] but few have been formally evaluated.[88] Typically, these programs include trauma-education and coping strategies including mindfulness training. With respect to organizational strategies in newsrooms that focus on individual-level support, peer support programs,[89] informational briefings on physical and psychological safety and management training have been implemented. Some newsrooms, especially during difficult prolonged new reporting cycles have brought in massage therapists, emotional support animals, and therapists although none of these interventions have been tested.

Summary and recommendations

We have noted several interventions directed at improving journalists' workplaces, access to resources, and developing skills and routines for recovery and self-care, but little evaluation research exists to form conclusions about their effectiveness. Given the financial pressures and rapid changes in journalism, intervention or program evaluations are often seen as costly time investments. However, it may be more costly in terms of productivity, health insurance, and even mortality if news organizations continue to implement strategies that are ineffective or even harmful. Existing tools, such as NIOSH's TWH program, including the WellBQ, can be used as a baseline needs assessment to inform the design of an intervention, and can be used in multiple follow up assessments to track the success of the program over time. The assessment of journalists at multiple time points during and after the intervention is recommended for determining the extent to which any intervention was effective.[90]

However, typical outcomes that might be included in a program evaluation such as employee turnover are difficult to interpret given that many journalists are changing jobs within the industry, there is a reduction in number of journalist positions, and an increase in the use of freelancers. As the industry relies more on freelancers, many current organizational approaches will not address the needs of these groups. Instead of newsrooms, alternative organizations, such as unions for freelance journalists (e.g., Freelance Journalists Union, National Union of Journalists) may provide opportunities for supporting freelance journalists' well-being.

Conclusion

This review links the general psychological literature on health and well-being with the emerging literature about journalists' well-being to enhance our understanding of journalists' experiences. Hedonic well-being, typically measured as positive affect and job satisfaction among journalists, is one distinct aspect of well-being. Eudaimonic well-being, typically measured as an aspect of professional identity and mission among journalists, is less studied. In other fields, facing challenges is sometimes associated with higher eudaimonic well-being but lower hedonic well-being;[91] focusing on journalistic mission as an intervention may be more effective to increase one's sense of purpose and professional identity but less effective for improving journalists' fatigue. Addressing the work environment by improving resources in the face of challenging work demands can improve both types of well-being in the form of work engagement and flow.[92] Understanding ambivalence as it applies to well-being among journalists is also an area for exploration.

In addition, the Total Worker Health® framework provides a broader basis for identifying economic, cultural, organizational, and job-related challenges for journalists and presents opportunities for improving the well-being of journalists by combining risk reduction strategies and work redesign. Currently, many of the well-being strategies used for journalists focus on the individual, which while helpful, certainly are not as effective as preventive strategies at the organizational level.

Finally, this review suggests many avenues for future scholarship. There is a need to continue to study well-being and the effectiveness of well-being promotion campaigns. Careful attention to methodology, such as clearly defining constructs, using appropriate measurement tools, and using rigorous repeated measures can further enhance knowledge about the well-being of journalists. Importantly, greater efforts need to be made to evaluate the effectiveness of existing and emerging interventions aimed at improving journalists' well-being.

Notes

1 Jessica Pryce-Jones, *Happiness at Work: Maximizing Your Psychological Capital for Success.* (Hoboken: Wiley, 2010), https://doi.org/10.1002/9781118313978.ch17
2 Angela Fu, "Journalists Report Working Hundreds of Hours of Unpaid Overtime at Gannett Papers," *Poynter*, September 30, 2021, https://www.poynter.org/business-work/2021/journalists-report-working-hundreds-of-hours-of-unpaid-overtime-at-ga nnett-papers/
3 Bureau of Labor Statistics, "Occupational Outlook Handbook," *Bureau of Labor Statistics*, last modified September 8, 2022, https://www.bls.gov/ooh/
4 Anita L. Schill, "Advancing Well-Being through Total Worker Health®," *Workplace Health Safety* 65, no. 4 (2019): 158–163.
5 National Institute for Occupational Safety and Health, "What Is Total Worker Health®?," last modified June 29, 2020, https://www.cdc.gov/niosh/twh/tota lhealth.html#:~:text=Total%20Worker%20Health%20is%20defined,to%20advance%20worker%20well%2Dbeing.
6 Peter Warr, "Work, Well-Being, and Mental Health." In *Well-Being* eds. D. Kahneman, E. Diener, and N. Schwarz, (New York: Russell Sage Foundation, 1999), 547–573.
7 Despoina Xanthopoulou, Arnold B Bakker, and Remus Ilies, "Everyday Working Life," *Human Relations* 65, no. 9 (2012): 1051–1069, https://doi.org/10.1177/0018726712451283.
8 Mina Tsay-Vogel and K. Maja Krakowiak, "Effects of Hedonic and Eudaimonic Motivations on Film Enjoyment through Moral Disengagement," *Communication Research Reports* 33, no. 1 (2016): 54–60, DOI: 10.1080/08824096.2015.1117443.
9 Ed Diener et al., "Subjective Well-Being," *Psychological Bulletin* 95, no. 3 (1984): 276–302.
10 See Sabine Sonnentag, "Dynamics of Well-Being," *Annual Review of Organizational Psychology and Organizational Behavior* 2 (2015): 261–293, https://doi.org/10.1146/annurev-orgpsych-032414-111347.
11 James A. Russell, "A Circumplex Model of Affect," *Development and Psychopathology* 17, no. 3 (2005): 1161–1178.
12 E.g., Ronald J. Burke, "Flow, Work Satisfaction and Psychological Well-Being at the Workplace," *Archives of Nursing Practice and Care* 2, (2016): 237–48, DOI: 10.17352/2581-4265.000007.
13 William Tov, "Well-Being Concepts and Components." In Ed Diener, Shigehiro Oishi, & Louis Tay eds. *Handbook of Well-Being*, (Salt Lake City, UT: DEF Publishers, 2018), 1–15.

14 Gwenith G. Fisher, Russell A. Matthews, and Alyssa Mitchell Gibbons, "Single-Item Measures in Organizational Research," *Journal of Occupational Health Psychology* 21, no. 1 (2015): 3–23, DOI: 10.1037/a0039139.

15 Ed Diener et al., "The Satisfaction with Life Scale," *Journal of Personality Assessment* 49, no. 1 (1985): 71–75, https://doi.org/10.1177/008124630903900402

16 Randal A. Beam and Meg Spratt, "Managing Vulnerability," *Journalism Practice* 3, no. 4 (2009): 421–438.

17 Tov, "Well-Being Concepts and Components," 1–15.

18 Richard M. Ryan and Edward L. Deci, "On Happiness and Human Potentials: A Review of Research on Hedonic and Eudaimonic Well-Being," *Annual Review of Psychology* 52 (2001): 141–166, https://doi.org/10.1146/annurev.psych.52.1.141.

19 Tov, "Well-Being Concepts and Components," 1–15.

20 See Samantha J Heintzelman, "Eudaimonia in the Contemporary Science of Subjective Well-Being." In *Handbook of Well-Being* eds. Ed Diener, Shigehiro Oishi, and Louis Tay, (Salt Lake City, UT: DEF Publishers, 2018).

21 Bill Kovach and Tom Rosenstiel, *The Elements of Journalism: What Newspeople Should Know and the Public Should Expect*. (New York: Three Rivers Press, 2001).

22 Rosemary J. Novak and Sarah Davidson, "Journalists Reporting on Hazardous Events," *Traumatology* 19, no. 4 (2013): 313–322, https://doi.org/10.1177/1534765613481854.

23 Patric Raemy, "A Theory of Professional Identity in Journalism," *Community Theory* 31, no. 4 (2020): 841–861, https://doi.org/10.1093/ct/qtaa019.

24 Tov, "Well-Being Concepts and Components," 1–15.

25 Giovanni B. Moneta and Mihaly Csikszentmihalyi, "The Effect of Perceived Challenges and Skills on the Quality of Subjective Experience," *Journal of Personality* 64, no. 2 (1996): 275–310, DOI: 10.1111/j.1467–6494.1996.tb00512.x.

26 Henry C. Ho and Ying Chuen Chan, "Flourishing in the Workplace," *International Journal of Environmental Research and Public Health* 19, no. 2 (2022): 922, DOI: 10.3390/ijerph19020922.

27 William Tov, "Well-Being concepts and components," 1–15.

28 Sonnentag, "Dynamics of Well-Being," 261–293.

29 Mihaly Csikszentmihalyi, *Flow: The Psychology of Optimal Experience*. (New York: HarperCollins, 2008).

30 Tov, "Well-Being Concepts and Components," 1–15.

31 Burke, "Flow, Work Satisfaction and Psychological Well-Being at the Workplace," 37–48.

32 See review by Warr, "Work, Well-Being, and Mental Health," 547–573.

33 Sonnentag, "Dynamics of Well-Being," 261–293.

34 Abha Bhalla and Lakhwinder Singh Kang, "Domain-Specific and Nonspecific Outcomes of Work-Family Interface," *Evidence-based HRM* 7, no. 2 (2019): 127–142, https://doi.org/10.1108/EBHRM-10-2017-0053.

35 Gloria M. González-Morales, Lois E. Tetrick, Ryan Ginter, "Measurement Issues in Work–Family Research." In *Research Methods in Occupational Health Psychology* eds. Robert R. Sinclair, Mo Wang and Lois E. Tetrick, (New York: Routledge, 2012), 55–72.

36 Wilmar B. Schaufeli, "The Future of Occupational Health Psychology," An *International Review* 53, no. 4 (2004): 502–517, https://doi.org/10.1111/j.1464-0597.2004.00184.x.

37 Warr, "How to Think About and Measure Psychological Well-Being," 76–90.

38 Arnold B. Bakker and Kevin Daniels, *A Day in the Life of a Happy Worker*. (London: Psychology Press, 2013).

39 Lois E. Tetrick and James C. Quick, "Overview of Occupational Health Psychology: Public Health in Occupational Settings." In *Handbook of Occupational Health Psychology* eds. Lois E. Tetrick and James C. Quick, (Washington: American Psychological Association, 2011), 3–20.

40 See meta-analyses by Joseph J. Mazzola and Ryan Disselhorst, "Should We Be 'Challenging' Employees?" *Journal of Organizational Behavior* 40, no. 8 (2019): 949–961, https://doi.org/10.1002/job.2412.

41 Sian Williams and Tina Cartwright, "Post-Traumatic Stress, Personal Risk and Post-Traumatic Growth among UK Journalists," *European Journal of Psychotraumatology* 12, no. 1 (2021): DOI: 10.1080/20008198.2021.1881727.

42 Warr, "How to Think About and Measure Psychological Well-Being," 76–90.

43 See review by River J. Smith, Elana Newman, Susan Drevo, Autumn Slaughter, "Covering Trauma: Impact on Journalists," Dart Center for Journalism and Trauma, July 1, 2015, https://dartcenter.org/content/covering-trauma-impact-on-journalists.

44 E.g., Trond Idås, K. Backholm, and J. Korhonen, "Trauma in the Newsroom," *European Journal of Psychotraumatology* 7, no. 10: (2019): DOI: 10.1080/20008198.2019.1620085.

45 E.g., Jonas Osmann et al., "The Emotional Well-Being of Journalists Exposed to Traumatic Events," *Media, War & Conflict* 14, no. 4: 476–502, https://doi.org/10.1177/1750635219895998.

46 American Psychological Association, *APA Dictionary of Psychology,* n.d. https://dictionary.apa.org

47 Renzo Bianchi, Irvin Sam Schonfeld and Eric Laurent, "Burnout-Depression Overlap," *Clinical Psychology Review* 36, (2015): 36–45, doi: 10.1016/j.cpr.2015.01.004.

48 Ramya Chari et al., "Development of the National Institute for Occupational Safety and Health Worker Well-Being Questionnaire," *Journal of Occupational and Environmental Medicine* 64, no. 8 (2022): 707–717, DOI:10.1097/JOM.0000000000002585.

49 Sabine Sonnentag, Laura Venz and Anne Casper, "Advances in Recovery Research," *Journal of Occupational Health Psychology* 22, no. 3: 365–380, DOI: 10.1037/ocp0000079.

50 Sabine AE Geurts and Sabine Sonnentag, "Recovery as an Explanatory Mechanism in the Relation between Acute Stress Reactions and Chronic Health Impairment," *Scandinavian Journal of Work, Environment & Health* 32, no. 6 (2006): 482–492, DOI: 10.5271/sjweh.1053.

51 Charlotte Fritz, Sabine Sonnentag, Paul E. Spector and Jennifer A. McInroe, "The Weekend Matters," *Psychology Faculty Publications* 31, no. 8 (2010): 1137–1162, https://doi.org/10.1002/job.672.

52 Andrew A. Bennett, Arnold B. Bakker and James G. Field, "Recovery from Work-Related Effort," *Journal of Organizational Behavior* 39, no. 3 (2017), 262–275, https://doi.org/10.1002/job.2217.

53 Maike E. Debus, Sabine Sonnentag, Werner Deutsch and Fridtjof Nussbeck, "Making Flow Happen," *Journal of Applied Psychology* 99, no. 4 (2014): 713–722, DOI:10.1037/a0035881.

54 See reviews by Sabine Sonnentag, Laura Venz and Anne Casper, "Advances in Recovery Research," 365–380; Sabine Sonnentag, Bonnie Hayden Cheng and Stacey L. Parker, "Recovery from Work," *Annual Review of Organizational Psychology and Organizational Behavior* 9, no. 33 (2022): 33–60, https://doi.org/10.1146/annurev-orgpsych-012420-091355.

55 Sonnentag, Cheng and Parker, "Recovery from Work," 33–60.

56 Hoover, Ragsdale and Ayres, "An Experimental Test of Resource Recovery from Physical and Relaxation Work Break Activities," 477–489.

57 E.g., Arnold B. Bakker et al., "Workaholism and Daily Recovery," *Journal of Organizational Behaviour* 34, no.1 (2012): 87–107, https://doi.org/10.1002/job.1796.

58 E.g, Lieke L. ten Brummelhuis and John P. Trougakos, "The Recovery Potential of Intrinsically versus Extrinsically Motivated off-Job Activities," *Journal of Occupational*

   and Organizational Psychology 87, no. 1 (2013): 177–199, DOI:10.1111/
   joop.12050.
59 Bennett, Bakker and Field, "Recovery from Work-Related Effort," 262–75.
60 Marjo Siltaloppi, Ulla Kinnunen and Taru Feldt, "Recovery Experiences as Moderators between Psychosocial Work Characteristics and Occupational Well-Being,"
   Work and Stress 23, no. 4 (2013): 330–348, DOI:10.1080/02678370903415572.
61 Jennifer M. Ragsdale, Coty S. Hoover, and Kaylen Wood, "Investigating Affective
   Dispositions as Moderators of Relationships between Weekend Activities and
   Recovery Experiences," *Journal of Occupational and Organizational Psychology* 89,
   no. 4 (2016): 734–750, https://doi.org/10.1111/joop.12150.
62 Jennifer M. Ragsdale and Coty S. Hoover, "Cell Phones During Nonwork Time:
   A Source of Job Demands and Resources," *Computers in Human Behavior* 57,
   (2016): 54–60, https://doi.org/10.1016/j.chb.2015.12.017.
63 Valérie Bélair-Gagnon, Diana Bossio, Avery E. Holton and Logan Molyneux,
   "Disconnection," *Society Media + Society* 8, no. 1 (2022): https://doi.org/10.
   1177/20563051221077217.
64 David M. Fisher, Jennifer M. Ragsdale and Emily C.S. Fisher, "The Importance of
   Definitional and Temporal Issues in the Study of Resilience," *Applied Psychology*
   68, no. 4 (2018): 583–620, https://doi.org/10.1111/apps.12162.
65 Thomas W. Britt et al., "How Much Do We Really Know about Employee Resilience?" *Industrial and Organizational Psychology* 9, no. 2: 378–404,
   DOI:10.1017/iop.2015.107.
66 Margaret O'Dougherty Wright and Ann S. Masten, "Resilience Processes in
   Development." In *Handbook of Resilience in Children* eds. Sam Goldstein and
   Robert B. Brooks, (Manhattan: Springer, 2007), 15–37.
67 American Psychiatric Association. *Desk Reference to the Diagnostic Criteria from
   DSM-5 (R)*. (American Psychiatric Association Publishing, 2013).
68 David M. Fisher, Jennifer M. Ragsdale and Emily C.S. Fisher, "The Importance of
   Definitional and Temporal Issues in the Study of Resilience," 583–620.
69 E.g., Ola Ogunyemi and Joseph Akanuwe, "Should Journalism Curriculum
   Include Trauma Resilience Training?" *Journalism Education and Trauma Research
   Group* 10 (2021): 34–43; 3.
70 Ola Ogunyemi and Joseph Akanuwe, "Should Journalism Curriculum Include
   Trauma Resilience Training?" 34–43.
71 Susana Monteiro, Alexandra Marques Pinto and Magda Sofia Roberto, "Job
   Demands, Coping, and Impacts of Occupational Stress among Journalists," *European Journal of Work and Organizational Psychology* 25, no. 5 (2016): 751–772,
   DOI: 10.1080/1359432X.2015.1114470.
72 Jasmine B. MacDonald, Gene Hodgins and Anthony J. Saliba, "Trauma Exposure
   and Reactions in Journalists," *Fusion Journal* (2015).
73 David M. Fisher and Rebekah D. Law, "Organizing Framework for Resilience
   Measurement," *Advances in the Psychology of Workplace Coaching* special issue 70,
   no. 2 (2021): 643–673.
74 David M. Fisher, Jennifer M. Ragsdale, and Emily C.S. Fisher, "The Importance of
   Definitional and Temporal Issues in the Study of Resilience," 583–620.
75 Michelle P. Lee et al., "Fundamentals of Total Worker Health Approaches,"
   (Washingon D.C.: National Institute for Occupational Safety and Health, 2016);
   National Institute for Occupational Safety and Health, "What Is Total Worker
   Health®?"
76 Paul A. Schulte, "Considerations for Incorporating 'Well-Being' in Public Policy
   for Workers and Workplaces," *American Journal of Public Health* 105, no. 8
   (2015): 31–44, DOI: 10.2105/AJPH.2015.302616.
77 National Institute for Occupational Safety and Health, "What Is Total Worker
   Health®?"

78 National Institute for Occupational Safety and Health, "Hierarchy of Controls Applied to NIOSH Total Worker Health®," last modified December 28, 2020, https://www.cdc.gov/niosh/twh/guidelines.html
79 James C. Quick et al., *Preventive Stress Management in Organizations*; Norbert N. Semmer, "Job Stress Interventions and Organization of Work," *Scandinavian Journal of Work, Environment & Health* 32, no. 6 (2006): 299–318, DOI: 10.5271/sjweh.1056.
80 David M. Fisher, Jennifer M. Ragsdale, and Emily C.S. Fisher, "The Importance of Definitional and Temporal Issues in the Study of Resilience," 583–620.
81 Randal A. Beam and Meg Spratt, "Managing Vulnerability," *Journalism Practice* 3, no. 4 (2009): 421–438.
82 River J. Smith, Susan Drevo and Elana Newman, "Covering Traumatic News Stories," *Stress & Health* 34, no. 2 (2017): 1218–1226, https://doi.org/10.1002/smi.2775.
83 Amanda Svachula, "The Newsroom Trauma Equation," *Medium*, May 22, 2019, https://medium.com/news-to-table/the-newsroom-trauma-equation-60d28fa94127.
84 National Institute for Occupational Safety and Health, "Hierarchy of Controls Applied to NIOSH Total Worker Health®."
85 Terry A. Beehr, "Interventions in Occupational Health Psychology," *Journal of Occupational Health Psychology* 24, no. 1 (2019):1–3, https://doi.org/10.1037/ocp0000140.
86 Cait McMahon, "Building Resilience in the War Zone against Hidden Injury," *Pacific Journalism Review* 16, no. 1 (2010): 39–48, DOI:10.24135/pjr.v16i1.1006.
87 E.g., Mark Pearson et al., "Building Journalists' Resilience through Mindfulness Strategies," *Journalism* 22, no. 7 (2019): 1647–1664.
88 Colm Murphy et al., "A New Pedagogy to Enhance the Safety and Resilience of Journalists in Dangerous Environments Globally," Education Sciences 10, no. 11 (2020): https://doi.org/10.3390/educsci10110310.
89 Mark H. Massé, *Trauma Journalism: On Deadline in Harm's Way*. (London: Continuum, 2011).
90 See for review Joyce A. Adkins et al., "Program Evaluation." In *Handbook of Occupational Health Psychology* eds. James Campbell Quick & Lois E. Tetrick (Washington D.C.: American Psychological Association, 2003): 399–416, https://doi.org/10.1037/10474-019.
91 Giovanni B. Moneta and Mihaly Csikszentmihalyi, "The Effect of Perceived Challenges and Skills on the Quality of Subjective Experience," *Journal of Personality* 64, no. 2 (1996): 275–310, https://doi.org/10.1111/j.1467-6494.1996.tb00512.x
92 Arnold B. Bakker and Kevin Daniels, *A Day in the Life of a Happy Worker*.

6

BUILDING RESILIENCE THROUGH TRAUMA LITERACY IN J-SCHOOLS

Lada Trifonova Price and Ola Ogunyemi

This chapter is concerned with the hazards of practicing journalism that can impact the psychological safety of media workers, and more specifically the institutional issue of work-related trauma that journalists in all parts of the world are exposed to, sometimes daily. Our focus is on the current response to this problem by journalism education that often fails to adequately prepare and foster trauma literate reporters that can cope with the challenges of covering traumatic events and human suffering, and to take care of their sources and themselves. Many journalists like the British Broadcasting Corporation's (BBC) veteran international correspondent Lyse Doucet point to the dark side of practicing journalism and feeling the pressure to stay safe and survive in increasingly dangerous and hostile environments globally. Thousands of journalists have been killed in the course of daily work in the past three decades, while many others have been kidnapped, imprisoned, threatened, physically attacked, and abused online (see CPJ.org[1] and UNESCO.org).[2]

As journalism has become more dangerous to practice, the mental health and well-being of journalists is increasingly at risk.[3] Female journalists and journalists of color are subjected to a tide of intimidation and harassment online in the form of hatred, rape and death threats, and misogynist attacks. This leads to adjustment in behaviors online where journalists may limit their engagement with readers, adjust their reporting, and consider leaving journalism altogether.[4] These avoidance strategies are in response to stress caused by attacks towards them but harms also include trauma and psychological distress.[5] Female journalists are at greater risk than their male colleagues of symptoms of post-traumatic stress disorder (PTSD).[6] Because of online abuse, which involves trolling and harassment, it has become an "ethical necessity" for journalism educators to teach students about online abuse and how to spot and manage it throughout their careers.[7]

DOI: 10.4324/9781003364597-7

In some countries, like Iran, where journalists are faced with extreme degrees of danger, journalists report facing high emotional distress and are inclined to self-medicate with sedatives of sleep-inducing pills barbiturates in order to alleviate their symptoms.[8] War correspondents often suffer the effects of repeated exposure to trauma, which is a predictor for PTSD in journalists.[9] For instance, BBC former war correspondent Fergal Keane has talked openly about his PTSD and the impact his trauma experiences have had on his mental health and well-being. Throughout his three-decade long career of reporting from the frontline, he has suffered depression, hospitalization, and anguish in his personal life, all of which have placed his health in "grave danger."[10] In a candid account, Keane describes symptoms such as guilt, insomnia, anxiety, stress and "a powerful compulsion to prove that I can survive,"[11] symptoms that are common for journalists who report on war and conflict.[12]

Another significant issue is the risk of "moral injury," which can happen when journalists must step outside their roles as observers of events and, for example, are faced with a choice to help someone in need without appropriate training. Moral injury relates to the powerful emotions of guilt and shame that "can be debilitating, disorienting and lead journalists to become disillusioned or drop out of the industry altogether."[13] For example, in a milestone case, a crime reporter (YZ) who worked for a decade in one of Australia's well-known daily newspapers was awarded A$180,000 in damages for suffering psychological injury. The case is the first in its kind in Australia to acknowledge the risk of such injury on journalists and the duty of care newsrooms have to their employees.[14]

Research shows that courses which teach future journalists how to be resilient to psychological trauma and how to interact with victims and survivors of trauma are few and far between. In the U.S. only one such specific course was identified out of 41 accredited institutions in the study's analysis despite the fact that educators and j-schools recognize the importance of trauma literacy.[15] Other studies point to a confusion about what and how to teach trauma awareness in journalism education;[16] inconsistency around fostering resilience among students and teaching the risks of vicarious trauma;[17] a gap between classroom approaches and newsroom realities when it comes to trauma education and a lack of recent research exploring educators' understanding of trauma and its effects on journalists.[18]

This chapter builds on previous work to show that journalism education in institutions across the world continues to neglect the subjects of mental health, emotional safety and trauma, and there is still a reactive or "accidental" approach to trauma-informed teaching and learning. To examine how the subject is approached in journalism education, we spoke to 20 journalism educators from higher education institutions in 13 countries who teach a range of theoretical and practical journalism courses and modules to undergraduate and postgraduate students. They shared their experiences and observations of teaching trauma to student journalists. Given the scope of this chapter, we focus on three main themes: (1) educators' risk awareness of exposure of journalists to vicarious trauma; (2) teaching experience, content and trauma-informed practices in the classroom; and (3) challenges and barriers as well as competence to teach trauma. We conclude this chapter with some recommendations for trauma-informed teaching in journalism education and training.

Risk Awareness of J-Educators

It was encouraging to find that participants demonstrated a very high recognition of the risks that witnessing and experiencing trauma, and human distress, can potentially have on all journalists, not just those covering war, conflict, and disaster. This awareness stemmed from the fact that all but one participant had worked as a journalist for several years before they moved to academia and teaching. These interviewees recalled personally experiencing trauma in the course of their work and suffering the impact of this trauma in cases that have stayed with them for decades. All knew a former colleague or a journalist that they had seen struggle to cope with the effects of vicarious trauma and the effect it had on their personal and professional life, such as drinking, isolating themselves from colleagues, friends and family and failed marriages and relationships. The following quotes illustrate this well.

> The only way I could sleep was that I went out to a local martial arts supply store and bought a weapon that I was trained to use and stuck it under the mattress so that I could get to it without even getting out of bed, and unless I had that stuff you know, like within hand's reach, I could not go to sleep. (P5)
>
> I used to be a night news reporter at the regional newspaper in Cape Town, and if you work at night, particularly in South Africa there is lots of murder and mayhem at night, […] there were a lot of gang shootings. I remember one very traumatic incident; I went for trauma counselling which we got through work […] they created opportunities for us to seek counselling so that was the first time I really realized how traumatic it can be. (P15)
>
> You just hold it within yourself, you don't want to share it with anybody and most journalists in Africa or in the UK don't want to talk about things they saw when they were out in the field, because they bring those nasty memories, which they are trying to forget. And that's why most of the time they resort to drinking to forget temporarily when they are sober. Those thoughts come back to them again. (P6)

Despite witnessing colleagues' or having their own struggles, our participants point to a culture in newsrooms that attached stigma to the topic of mental health, being traumatized and having psychological problems as one interviewee said:

a lot of journalists have that same gung-ho macho mentality. They were also a category of people who would deny post-traumatic stress disorder when it was evident to other people ... Some of them say there's no such thing as post-traumatic stress disorder, some of them even go so much further to say, well so and so is a wimp if they can't do the job, they should leave it. (P8)

The awareness of potential risks of exposure to vicarious trauma, death and people suffering was at the root of the attitude among all educators who expressed a strong belief that it is important to teach journalism students how to take care of themselves but also how to take care of their sources. Educators stress that emotional literacy skills on how to minimize the harm to victims and survivors, how reporters behave towards them, and how they talk to them and how to cope after, should be taught hand in hand as reporting skills.

Teaching Experience, Content and Trauma-Informed Practice

We wanted to find out whether journalism educators teach trauma literacy and how. It is important to study the pedagogical responses of journalism educators to a persistent work-related problem that many have themselves encountered. Our interviewees' experience as journalists with links to the industry, regardless of country or context, often guides their teaching practices. For example, the most common and widely used method to introduce the topic of trauma in journalism is to invite a guest speaker who is willing to share their personal real-life experience, coping strategies and offer some advice to aspiring reporters. This is usually a journalist, a victim/survivor or both, which raises the question of re-traumatizing the speaker in the short or long term, although some inter-viewees point out that they use the same speakers regularly. While our inter-viewees[19] noted that their institutions have no dedicated courses or specific modules on trauma literacy, trauma-informed content is mostly embedded in teaching on media and journalism ethics, conflict journalism, media law, crime and suicide reporting, photography, and investigative journalism.

It's never overtly used so it's not like I maybe have a session on trauma ... I mean it's something that might come in conversation, but more orga-nically, I would say. (P14)

A great deal of the material I use involves traumatic content even in media law we are dealing with particularly nasty things. So, we deal for instance with things like defamation ... I also teach human rights law. And I also teach conflict journalism so when you're teaching conflict journalism, you're having to deal with particularly nasty events. (P8)

We don't have it, we have just elements, but we don't have a structured curriculum from the beginning to the end, where we can teach students to become aware of trauma and collective trauma, and what is the responsibility to report about that. (P1)

The teaching strategies educators use tend to generally fall within the main principles of trauma-informed approach to training, teaching, and learning, which give educators a framework to develop their own discipline specific methods. These include: physical, emotional, social and academic safety; trust and transparency; support and connection; collaboration and community; empowerment; voice and choice; social justice, and resilience, growth and change.[20] There is emphasis on safety in professional journalism practice, creating safe spaces for students to discuss emotionally challenging topics and be mindful of their mental health and well-being, but also a high level of sensitivity among participants that any method, discussion and approach could trigger students' hidden traumas. There is evidence that by the time young people enter higher education, a significant number have trauma history and as many as 50 percent of students are exposed to an event that could potentially traumatize them in their first year of study.[21]

Educators also resort to role play (students and tutors acting) and attending simulations (e.g. fire brigade training; Emergency Room (ER), use of first aid courses, cardiopulmonary resuscitation (CPR), even writing "fake obituaries") as these examples of practice show:

> In the classroom what I've already been doing is like a simulation. Invite one of the students out: Okay, you act as a victim let's talk about it, then you give them some rules, this is what you've got to do, assuming, you are a sex worker and this has happened to you, and so what would you do, then we'll have to have a counsellor and also have a reporter then we will ask the reporter how will you report that particular story, based on what you have heard now. (P11)
>
> I choose how to work on that being very careful not to create negative reaction, and tend to say these are the videos, these are the academic articles, this is the research, and I would like you to look into any of them and then we can discuss, we can talk about these instead of showing classroom a video full of difficult situation and have a kind of bad reaction from them. (P3)

Educators state that emphasis should be on teaching to redress the impact of trauma both on the journalists but also on their sources. They stress the need for additional training, resources, methods and structure that help them to teach students how to recognize and respond to signs or symptoms of trauma in their own behavior and that of others.

Barriers to Teaching and Learning Trauma

Participants shared that there are several challenges that they face as educators on an individual and institutional level. The biggest issue is their lack of any resilience or trauma literacy training that they have completed as educators or previously as journalists. Only one of our respondents had taken a train-the-trainer workshop on trauma, and this training was not recent. The rest of our interviewees expressed low confidence in their ability to teach trauma literacy due to perceived "insufficient knowledge," "not being a psychologist," "no time and resources," and "limited interdisciplinary approach," and "no staff to teach this." Our findings reinforce findings[22] from previous[23] studies,[24] which shows a worrying lack of progress in this area given the current challenges that journalists are facing in the field. The attitude of journalism educators towards trauma literacy is in contrast with the perceived attitude of their own institutions, described as not taking the topic seriously, not willing to include additional courses or modules in a crowded or inflexible curriculum, and the passive attitude of journalism accreditation bodies that do not yet insist on making trauma and emotional resilience training an essential element of journalism education and training.

There is also a cultural aspect of these barriers such as societal attitudes that may not recognise the need for an open conversation on trauma in journalism and psychological harm that reporters suffer. Educators are very much conscious of the stigma attached to mental health in newsrooms and how this bleeds to academia, which tends to hire former journalists. In more conservative environments, the issue is brushed under the carpet by older generations of tutors in j-schools whose views amount to "keep it to yourself and just get on with the job," according to interviewees. Participants agree that Higher Education institutions in their countries are slow to respond to the trauma needs of educators, students and ultimately the industry due to bureaucracy, cumbersome quality administrative process, and accreditation issues. The large gap in accessible teaching and learning resources in their own countries, tips and examples of best discipline-specific practice is making an impossible task even more difficult. These quotes illustrate the pattern of the main identified challenges:

> I think it's generally still not considered that important [...] it's still a taboo and it's very hard to talk about it from a personal perspective and personal experience [...] sometimes face even administrative challenges, you know it takes time to decide something as a team and then try and implement it and it might take a quality process and couple of years before we actually see it implemented in our courses. (P2)
>
> Resources are always a problem, time is always a problem, and you know so, for instance, it would be great I think if we could require every student to take a trauma journalism class. [...] But the bigger problem is that there are already so many required elements of the curriculum for AEJMC accreditation that it's hard to fit anything else in. (P5)
>
> Sometimes I feel like when you try to bring something to the institution, I don't know it's a university. Generally, they are very conservative in a sense. (P13)

Towards More Resiliency in Journalism Education

Scholars note in relation to the severe occupational hazards that journalists currently face: "It is difficult to envision effective responses to the formidable challenges in the short term without professional and personal resilience embedded in the field of journalism."[25] Journalism education needs urgent change in teaching trauma and emotional literacy to address growing mental health and well-being crises for journalists. The educators we interviewed from different parts of the world said that they were very attuned to their student journalists' needs, highly aware of the importance of a trauma-informed approach in journalism practice and education; humble on the limitations of their own teaching and courses, but resourceful, with examples of trauma-informed approaches to teaching and learning.

Becoming trauma-informed is an ongoing process and an ongoing lesson for students as well as educators. What should also be stressed is the responsibility and role of newsrooms who, according to the interviewees, must invest in resources and training after graduation and in the field. "With good support systems in place, journalists will successfully absorb the impact of traumatic events and be able, willing even, to continue their work."[26] Journalists should also play a role in this by taking part in the conversation and helping to break the taboo and stigma attached to trauma and other mental health disorders.

New journalists are the ones who are often sent to knock on doors and interview bereaved family members, yet they rarely feel prepared to cope with the emotional impact witnessing human suffering has on their own psyche and that of victims and survivors.[27] Based on our interviews with educators and our own "accidental" experience of teaching trauma, we recommend for journalism education to start actively building or enhancing resilience rather than rely on reactive approaches in supporting students and future journalists once problems have already appeared. Flexible, innovative, interdisciplinary approaches and radical thinking are needed so we can better prepare newcomers to journalism for the challenges that they will inevitably face in the course of their work and in response to the growing mental health crisis among young people.[28] Implementing emotion instruction in journalism courses and textbooks is a good starting place.[29] As researchers we can continue to work on understanding the "science of suffering,"[30] which ties together the alleviation and prevention of suffering from traumatic stress. There is a strong pattern that we identified when it comes to barriers educators encounter in their efforts to embed trauma literacy in the curriculum.

These can be overcome by an increasingly aware, networked, active and determined groups of journalism educators, scholars and trainers who are willing to embrace change and "implement classroom training that incorporates theory and practice; provide essential literature, contacts, networks, and resources to students; and promote normalization of reactions to trauma in journalism work."[31] We also propose that journalism schools carry out annual well-being surveys among their staff and students, and student population surveys such as the National Student Satisfaction survey in the U.K. should include a score for well-being, resilience and a culture of trauma-informed learning and teaching, which would encourage higher education institutions to take notice of trauma informed approaches to learning and teaching not just in journalism but in other disciplines.

Notes

1 Committee for Protection of Journalists, "Special Reports & Publications," Accessed February 23, 2023 https://cpj.org/reports/
2 UNESCO, Director-General's Report on the Safety of Journalists and the Danger of Impunity, (Paris: UNESCO, 2022), https://en.unesco.org/themes/safety-journalists/dgreport.
3 Lisa Clifford, "Under Threat," International News Safety Institute, 2016, https://newssafety.org/underthreat/.
4 Lea Stahel and Constantin Schoen, "Female Journalists Under Attack?" *New Media & Society* 22, no.10 (2020): 1849–1867.
5 Emma A. Jane, "Gendered Cyberhate as Workplace Harassment and Economic Vandalism," *Feminist Media Studies* 18, no. 4 (2018): 575–591.
6 Anthony Feinstein, Jonas Osmann, and Bennis Pavisian, "Symptoms of Posttraumatic Stress Disorder in Journalists Covering War and Conflict," *Traumatology: An International Journal* 26, no. 26 (2020): 35–39.
7 Jay Daniel Thompson, "Can Trolling be Taught?" *Ethical Space: The International Journal of Communication Ethics* 17, no. 2 (2020): 30.
8 Anthony Feinstein, Saul Feinstein, Maziar Behari, and Bennis Pavisian Bennis, "The Psychological Well-Being of Iranian Journalists," *JRSM Open* 4, no.12 (2016), http://doi: 10.1177/2054270416675560.
9 Gabriella Tyson and Jennifer Wild, "Post-Traumatic Stress Disorder Symptoms among Journalists Repeatedly Covering COVID-19 News," *International Journal of Environmental Research and Public Health* 18, no. 16 (2021): 8536.
10 Fergal Keane, "How I Found a Way to Live with PTSD," May 8, 2022, https://www.bbc.co.uk/news/world-61350174
11 Keane, "How I Found a Way to Live with PTSD."
12 Anthony Feinstein, John Owen, and Nancy Blair, "A Hazardous Profession: War, Journalists, and Psychopathology," *American Journal of Psychiatry* 159 (2002): 1570–1575.
13 Clothilde Redfern, "There's a Bigger Risk to Journalists' Mental Health than PTSD," July 14, 2022, https://www.newstatesman.com/politics/media/2022/07/journalists-moral-injury-bigger-hazard-than-ptsd.
14 Alexandra Wake and Matthew Ricketson, "Trauma in the Newsroom," *Ethical Space: The International Journal of Communication Ethics* 19, no. 1 (2022): 39–49.
15 Gretchen Dworznik and Adrienne Garvey, "Are We Teaching Trauma?" *Journalism Practice* 13, no.3 (2019): 367–382, http://doi.org/10.1080/17512786.2018.1423630.
16 Lyn Barnes, "Trauma Training in Australia and New Zealand," *Australian Journalism Review* 37, no.1 (2015): 121–131.
17 Doug Spechts and Julia Tsilman, "Teaching Vicarious Trauma in the Journalism Classroom," *Journal of Applied Journalism and Media Studies* 7, no. 2 (2018): 407–427, http://doi.org/10.1386/ajms.7.2.407_1
18 Elyse Amend, Linda Kay, and Rosemary C. Reilly, "Journalism on the Spot," *Journal of Mass Media Ethics* 27, no. 4 (2012): 235–247, http://doi.org/10.1080/08900523.2012.746113.

19 The results of a global survey with more than 120 educators that we conducted in 2021 demonstrated that dedicated trauma literacy courses/modules are not widespread.

20 Janice Carello, "Trauma-informed teaching & learning principles," 2020, https://tra umainformedteachingblog.files.wordpress.com/2020/04/titl-general-principles-3.20. pdf.

21 Janice Carello and Phyllis Thompson, *Lessons from the Pandemic.* (Cham, Switzerland: Palgrave Macmillan, 2021).

22 Stephanie Anderson and Brian Bourke, "Teaching Collegiate Journalists How to Cover Traumatic Events Using Moral Development Theory," *Journalism and Mass Communication Educator* 75, no.2 (2020): 233–246, https://doi.org/10.1177/ 1077695819891020

23 Natalee Seely, "Fostering Trauma Literacy," Journalism & Mass Communication Educator 75, no. 1 (2020): 116–130, http://doi.org/10.1177/1077695819859966.

24 Doug Spechts and Julia Tsilman, "Teaching Vicarious Trauma," 407–427.

25 Jeannine Relly and Silvio Waisbord, "Why Collective Resilience in Journalism Matters," *Journal of Applied Journalism & Media Studies* 11, no. 2 (2022): 164, https://doi.org/10.1386/ajms_00089_1.

26 Alexandra Wake and Matthew Ricketson, "Trauma in the Newsroom," 39–49.

27 Gretchen Dworznik, and Adrienne Garvey, "Are We Teaching Trauma?" 367–382.

28 Suleman et al., *Unequal Pandemic, Fairer Recovery. The COVID-19 Impact Inquiry Report* ([location: The Health Report, 2021, https://www.health.org. uk/publications/reports/unequal-pandemic-fairer-recovery?gclid= Cj0KCQjwz96WBhC8ARIsAATR25OUUNcjCHaBg2mdXTljmf_vCUz-2Dh5Ja vDUC7ML-0nDQ9JFoMuk9kaAquVEALw_wcB.

29 Megan K. Hopper and John Huxford, "Emotion Instruction in Journalism Cour-ses," *Communication Education* 66, no. 1 (2017): 90–108, https://doi.org/10. 1080/03634523.2016.1210815.

30 Sandra. L. Bloom, "Human Rights and the Science of Suffering." In Lisa Butler, Filo-mena Critelli, and Janice Carello eds. *Trauma and Human Rights,* (Cham, Switzerland: Palgrave Macmillan, 2019), https://doi.org/10.1007/978-3-030-16395-2_13.

31 Desiree Hill, Catherine A. Luther, and Phyllis Slocum, "Preparing future journal-ists for trauma on the job," *Journalism and Mass Communication Educator* 75, no. 1 (2020): 67–68, https://doi.org/10.1177/1077695819900735

PART II
IN SUPPORT OF JOURNALISM WELL-BEING

7

RECRUITMENT AND RETENTION PRACTICES IN A CHANGING AFRICAN NEWS MEDIA ECOSYSTEM

Hayes Mawindi Mabweazara and Trust Matsilele

This chapter explores how transformations in African journalism are (re)shaping recruitment and retention practices and, by extension, journalists' happiness and well-being in the workplace. Understanding these practices demands an exploration that stretches beyond examining traditional media to include practices associated with new players that have claimed legitimacy and gained notable traction within the African news media ecosystem.

Developments in digital technologies have resulted in an increasingly complex African journalism ecosystem in which the stability and professional hegemony that characterized the legacy media for decades is now history.[1] The organization of newswork and the rise of multiple forms of producing news that do not conform to traditional journalism have direct implications for the recruitment and retention of journalists as diverse news organizations compete to recruit and retain talent to bolster their reporting.

This chapter draws its data from semi-structured interviews with senior editors, proprietors, and founders of the news organizations selected from a mix of well-established traditional legacy news organizations and emerging news media start-ups purposely selected from three Southern African countries: Lesotho, South Africa, and Zimbabwe. These countries have similarities which relate to their complex news media environments, in which, as elsewhere, the hegemony of traditional media institutions as sole arbiters of news is under unprecedented threat from equally complex peripheral news players.[2] Across the three countries, flourishing media start-ups coexist with traditional news media that are beset by both professional and economic instability.

There are radical differences in the countries' news media systems, which stretch from well-developed and technologically advanced newsrooms in South Africa to fledgling and struggling media operations in Lesotho and Zimbabwe. For these reasons, most of the mainstream news organizations

DOI: 10.4324/9781003364597-9

selected for this study were largely drawn from South Africa (*Eyewitness News*, established in 2008; *News24*, established in 1998; *Cape Times*, established in 1876 and *Cape Argus*, established in 1857). One mainstream news organization was selected from Lesotho (*The Post*, established in 2014). Start-ups (*Centre for Innovation & Technology (CITE)*, established 2016; *Review & Mail*, established in 2020 and *TellZim*, established in 2012) were selected from Zimbabwe, which has been teeming with alternative media activity as a response to the political pressures that have impacted the plurality and vibrancy of traditional news media in the country.[3]

To set the context for the study, we first position the notion of happiness in African journalism studies.

Positioning Happiness in African Journalism

The notion of *happiness* in Africa can be connected to "entrenched cultural practices and concepts that often filter into the practice of journalism," such as the traditional communitarian notion of *ubuntu*, which encapsulates what it means to be human to frame our overarching conception of happiness. Despite Africa's cultural diversity, "threads of underlying affinity run through the beliefs, customs, value systems, and socio-political institutions and practices of the various African societies." By invoking the culturally mediating communitarian notion of ubuntu, we are in essence acknowledging that "actions and decisions (individually or collectively) are inherently linked to the complex web of social connections—the whole *cultural milieu* that shapes and constrains actions from within and from outside." This cultural notion can explain "some of the most distinct professional practices and cultures," including recruitment and retention practices. Approaches to the latter, as with other aspects of journalism practice, are "manifest in the way that news outlets and their reporters think and act, as well as imitate one another, quite often unconsciously, by sharing "a recognizable style and other identifiable characteristics." These factors are "adaptive to various structural influences and conditions, especially the *structures of ownership and control*" as well as the digital and economic pressures that are shaping (and redefining) journalism.[4]

The centrality of the cultural context is that it connects news institutions to the dynamics of everyday life, which have been shown to significantly encroach into and affect the work environment but are often not considered when assessing the professional activities of journalists. African journalism scholars have tended to overlook the connections between news institutions and the broader routines of everyday life, a relationship sharply emphasized by scholars such as Grint,[5] who maintains that "the spheres of work, employment and home are all necessarily intertwined, and to separate them as if they could exist independently is to misconceive the complex reality of work and misunderstand the significance of the relationships which it embodies." Journalistic work, like any other paid work, can thus be interpreted as an important stabilizing factor that connects journalists to their everyday lives.

When employment security is threatened, the extent to which journalists invest their energies towards positive organizational outcomes diminishes.[6] Thus, having an employer who enables journalists to provide for themselves and their families as well as providing stability is, in essence, among the key reasons why journalists go to work. There is a formal contract (labour for money) and an informal contract between journalists and their employers. As Matthews and Onyemaobi say, "[j]ob stability is recognized as important to the professional standing and the activities of journalists." They further note that African journalists, as members of a professional community and as paid workers, are "acutely aware of the role that [working conditions and] the level of remuneration plays in their wider social position and speak often of the advances that similarly educated peers achieve as a source of comparison." Similarly, "stability around financial matters underpins [journalists'] sense of self and their professional performance."[7]

If the news organization does not work on retaining its key journalists, they are more likely to seek better opportunities elsewhere. Thus, employment security benefits news organizations because it helps them retain their most experienced staff and maintain the critical institutional memory, professional standards, and skills central to the achievement of organizational goals.[8]

In the next sections, we present the key findings of the study, beginning with the broad dynamics of issues around recruitment and retention.

The Dynamics of Recruitment and Retention

While traditional journalistic norms, in their various forms, remain significant in influencing recruitment and retention practices, important differences in approaches point to divergences in organizational cultures, everyday practices, economic sustainability pressures, and the news organization's period in operation. These factors implicate notions of staff happiness within news organizations. We discuss the recruitment practices in detail in the sections below.

Influences of Traditional Journalistic Norms, Skills, and Practices

The recruitment strategies deployed by news organizations are broadly influenced by traditional journalism practices that apply globally but also stretch beyond the established norms of what constitutes journalism in ways that reflect radical changes in the boundaries and social practice of journalism. For mainstream news organizations, traditional professional qualities such as curiosity, adaptability, and connectedness were highly valued. As one senior editor at *Cape Argus* put it, "We need someone who is curious. […], who is connected and […] who wants to learn." Echoing similar sentiments, an editor at *Eyewitness News* pointed to "hard work, good attitude to work, openness to learning" and an understanding that "no day as a reporter is the same."

The dynamics of these generic considerations differed along the lines of the level of seniority for the job at hand as the Managing Editor of *News24.com* explained. "At entry level, I look for someone energetic and curious, someone who tries to soak up all the opportunities that come up in the newsroom." When recruiting at the senior level, some mainstream news organizations look for journalists who have established themselves as brands with potential to add value to the organization through individual professional reputation and recognition they have gained over the years. *News24.com*'s managing editor explained: "When someone has established themselves in a particular niche, *that journalist adds respect to our newsroom.*" This strategic hiring of senior journalists points to the pressures that African news organizations contend with to maintain their legitimacy in a competitive media environment.[9]

The search for flexibility and open-mindedness was also ranked highly across news organizations, as explained by a senior editor at *Cape Argus*: "If you have a comfort zone seeker [who is] rather rigid and wants to only do one thing, that person we don't recruit because they might become a cog in the system." This quest for flexibility among recruits highlights how recruitment strategies are also a response to the instability and ongoing transformations in the news media industry, a point noted by the *Eyewitness News* assistant editor: "Employers in the mainstream media are under pressure to deliver fresh, breaking news. Staff [...] who are able to adapt in a high-pressure industry [are] strongly considered over someone who is not." It further reinforces an additional expectation for reporters to do more outside working hours. This was implicit in the expectation for cub reporters at *News24.com* to do more in their spare time as the managing editor put it, "let's take, for example, a metro reporter, I want to know that during their spare time they are reading the municipal and local papers about water burst issues."

The pursuit of staffers who can adapt and work under pressure in unfamiliar areas was particularly defined in the recruitment strategies of start-ups. They went a step further to emphasise multitasking as a top attribute of their everyday operations, as explained by the editor of *TellZim*:

> We identify specific talent, largely, the ability to adapt to an environment where you are not confined to one skill [...] you may be a journalist who is a good writer, but *we expect someone who has ability to generate revenue such as bringing sponsored advertorial.*

This expectation for start-up journalists to contribute to income generation activities beyond their primary role as journalists points to a radical shift in the social practice of journalism as well as to heightened work intensification in start-ups.

Between Digital Savviness and Traditional Attributes

For established news organizations, digital savviness, prominence, or success on social media were not something they took seriously. As one senior editor at *News24.com* explained, "we prioritize company brand accounts, so we don't look at personal social media savviness or following." An assistant editor at *Cape Times* similarly averred, "We are not currently considering someone's adeptness with social media, [...]. We only ask if they can use these media platforms and technologies due to the importance of the news sharing economy." The editor of *The Post* was equally upfront in highlighting how social media was not at the heart of his newsroom's agenda: "We do *not* focus on social media as our type of journalism does not rely on engagement."

In contrast, start-ups took a radically different stance on digital skills. The expectations for flexibility among their staffers discussed above were inextricably linked to effectively deploying the latest digital tools, keeping abreast with the latest developments, and pushing professional boundaries, as explained by the editor of CITE:

> We [operate] mainly online relying on videos and use social media. So, ideally, we go for youngish people aged between 25 and 30 years. We find this age group flexible. [...] We need journalists who can write, take videos and pictures and are adept at using social media.

These sentiments were echoed by the founder and head of content at *Review & Mail*: "we would want to have writers and creatives with a good social media base and aptitude as [...] social media offers side doors for the consumption of our content."

The centrality of digital skills for some start-ups was further exhibited in their assessment of potential candidates' personal social media accounts: "We look at potential [candidates]' social media accounts and assess their ability to upload videos across platforms. A person with these abilities has a higher chance of being hired and retained at *TellZim*." Reinforcing similar sentiments, a senior editor at CITE stated, "when we recruit, we ask people to submit their social media profiles so we can see the kind of content they post and determine how active and versatile they are on social media." These invasive approaches to recruitment highlight an uncomfortable blurring of lines between journalists' personal spaces, employability, and by extension, journalistic labour itself.

Informal Recruitment Procedures

Within start-ups and a new generation of mainstream news organizations such as *The Post*, there is a pervasive culture of informal recruitment practices that revolve around referrals and internships. This culture is also linked to Deuze and Witschge's[10] observation that start-ups position themselves as pioneering and experimental and as being at the forefront of media-related transformation. As the founder of CITE explained, start-ups "can afford to experiment and innovate in their recruitment and retention practices as they don't feel bound by established notions of 'good practice'." Thus, rather than leveraging traditional methods of hiring staff such as classified ads, they tend to ask employees, friends, or relatives to recommend new hires as articulated by the *TellZim* editor: "When hiring we no longer advertise, instead, we identify potential among those who come for internship, or we recruit through referrals." These informal approaches lead to the appointment of friends and associates without due regard for appropriate qualifications, a practice that relates to pervasive cultures of patronage and cronyism in African news organizations.[11]

Beyond start-ups, emerging mainstream news organizations also deploy informal recruitment practices, particularly in their reliance on interns. As the editor-in-chief of *The Post* explained, "ninety percent of our newsroom was recruited as students who came for attachment. [...]. It's only our deputy news editor who came from another newsroom, everyone else came directly from school." Giving further rationale for this approach, he stated: "We use the system of [internships] because we want to make our timber. Most journalists are trained in a conventional way, but we have our style, which is largely explanatory in nature, as we rely more on profile and feature reporting."

The next sections focus on the dynamics around staff retention across the news organizations studied.

Retention Dilemmas and Dynamics

Precarity, conditions of service, pay and benefits packages

While mainstream media organizations offer relatively secure and longer-term contracts, start-ups predominantly offer fixed-term contracts that are occasionally attached to foundation grants. This is in addition to relying extensively on freelancers who are paid per news item. What is evident from that scenario is that economic imperatives and funding pressures are central to shaping and influencing retention strategies particularly within start-ups. As the founder of *Review & Mail* explained, "we offer fixed term, largely short-term positions as we assess and monitor our capacity. We are [...] mindful of our economic standing and challenges of sustainability as a venture." This approach was also confirmed by the founding editor of *TellZim*: "We have fixed term contracts, and *they are tied to performance and fundraising capabilities*." The latter approach highlights how journalists in start-ups have the added pressure to contribute to their own job security through direct involvement in revenue generation activities.

The study also shows that retaining key staffers was hampered by attractive salaries offered elsewhere, particularly in the Public Relations industry and international non-governmental organizations (NGOs). The editor-in-chief of *The Post* lamented this situation:

> Retention is very tough as we don't compete with our peers, but international NGOs. Some of these organizations will be trying to recruit our people as public relations managers or stakeholder relations managers and it's tough competing with such [...] When our journalists decide to leave, we do an exit interview, and the common reason is always money.

The economic pressures facing established news organizations such as *Cape Times* similarly render it difficult for them to outcompete organizations that have the capacity to pay more, as one senior editor said:

> [...] retention is hard due to shoestring budgets, especially if someone wants to leave because of monetary reasons. If someone comes and tells me, they have been given a better offer, I encourage them to take the big offer and develop themselves.

Staff turnover due to salaries was also linked to other factors, including conditions of service and general access to everyday tools of the trade. Start-ups fared very well on all these aspects primarily because of their donor dependence and multiple revenue streams. As the founder of CITE explained, "Over the last four years [...], we never lost a journalist because we are paying some of the best salaries and we do that in U.S. dollars. Our journalists also have a good working space, [including] reliable internet." Thus, while start-ups predominantly offer fixed term contracts, their pay, benefits and working conditions are unrivalled by most mainstream news organizations.

Economic value, contribution to institutional agenda and staff cohesion

Throughout our sample, the retention of journalists was largely based on the economic and professional value they contribute to the organization. In the words of one assistant editor at *Eyewitness News*, retention is prioritized: "If the employee has shown that they are of great value. They have a very good work ethic, are highly dependable and perform well [...] For instance, they produce unique [...] news stories and have a wide contact base." This was corroborated by a senior editor at *Cape Times*: "We try and retain journalists who are *performing exceptionally well*, this is also how we evaluate those whom we transition from being interns to full-time journalists."

Start-ups were more likely to retain journalists based on their perceived economic value. As the editor of *TellZim* explained, "retention is informed by the *value the person brings to the organization in terms of revenue generation*.

We also need someone who is good with marketing." Reinforcing the overall point on journalists' value to the news organization, the founder of *Review & Mail* pointed to several interconnected issues, including their contribution to team cohesion: "We retain journalists *because of their capabilities and outputs,* multimedia skills, work culture and *team cohesion.*" Team cohesion was also noted at mainstream organizations such as *Cape Argus:* "We consider people's skills and the *ability to blend with other staff members, this is crucial for anyone we hire or retain on a permanent basis.*"

The pervasive "juniorization" of news organizations

The predisposition and inclination towards recruiting and retaining younger journalists alluded to by the CITE editor earlier is pervasive across news organizations in the region. While for established mainstream news organizations such as *Cape Argus,* "juniorization" is an inadvertent culmination of ongoing retrenchments and the increasingly precarious conditions that push senior journalists out,[12] for start-ups such as CITE, juniorization is a deliberate policy based on the assumption that younger journalists are professionally agile, flexible, and digitally savvy.

This "juniorization" of newsrooms is not without problems, particularly regarding the mentorship of cub reporters. As Tzoneva[13] observed in South Africa, young journalists are missing out on the opportunity to learn from experienced journalists, thus leading to notable depreciation of journalistic standards. Reinforcing this observation, Ndlovu[14] writes: "[t]he era of an older generation of journalists who were trained on the job has disappeared" in South African mainstream newsrooms.

Emerging and Extant Retention Strategies

Despite the clear retention challenges, news organizations are striving to retain their most productive and talented journalists through strategies aimed at engendering job satisfaction and a positive work environment. The retention strategies include succession planning and career development plans targeting young journalists, as explained by a senior editor at *News24.com*:

> Retention is important for me, especially *when working with Generation-Z employees because they are self-centric, and their loyalty is short-lived.* So, what we have started doing is working around succession plans. We *identify people who can do more than one thing* [and] try to expose them to different skill sets and roles.

Career development and training through exposing talented journalists to different areas of specialization and skills was complemented by switching beats or roles periodically to keep journalists happy and motivated.

In efforts to ward off competition from organizations that pay higher salaries, some news organizations invested in cultivating a positive work environment and culture. This is partly connected to the cultural values of *ubuntu*. In the words of *The Post*'s editor-in-chief, "We try to impress upon our journalists the importance of our culture as it is not hierarchical and most of our journalists find it an attractive reason to stay." Favourable working conditions and a positive organizational culture have occasionally resulted in journalists sacrificing higher salaries and returning to their old jobs, as *The Post* editor further explained, "We had about three journalists returning over the past two years even though they had moved for more money. What this tells us is that more than money, culture plays a role when it comes to retention."

This effort to create an inspiring and favourable work environment was complemented by conducting exit interviews with departing staff. Beyond helping senior editors and newsroom managers to understand what needs improvement to retain top talent, exit interviews also equipped news organizations with information for providing new staffers with "a realistic picture of the job" and as Thige[15] notes elsewhere, matching their *"personality* and *values* with *the organization's values and culture."*

In efforts to develop an attractive organizational culture, start-ups cultivate feelings of belonging and institutional attachment by involving all staff members in strategic decision-making processes and workshops, a privilege that most journalists in established news organizations are rarely afforded. While this highlights how start-ups are defying orthodoxy and pushing boundaries,[16] it also points to the very nature of their organizational culture, which shies away from the traditional top-down newsroom hierarchies, as the founder of CITE explained: "We take [our staff] for strategic meetings, and they are part of every decision we make. We try to make journalists feel they are part of the owners."

The scenario above highlights "a picture of unique structural conditions,"[17] which shape retention strategies across the news organizations studied.

Conclusion

This chapter has attempted to map out the contours of *recruitment* and *retention* practices in an increasingly complex African news media ecosystem. The study shows that recruitment and retention practices in start-ups and traditional mainstream news organizations are shaped by the immediate contexts in which the news organizations operate, and are heavily influenced by pressures that are transforming everyday newswork. These factors directly implicate aspects of staff happiness and well-being within news organizations.

The study offers insights that challenge taken-for-granted assumptions about recruitment and retention practices in African news organizations and how the conditions shaping practices directly affect journalists' well-being. It also highlights a range of solutions that news organizations are implementing in their effort to retain experienced staffers. However, further studies could deepen and expand the research by including data from practicing journalists drawn from a wider range of African countries and news organizations.

Notes

1 Mabweazara, Hayes M. "Normative Dilemmas and Issues for Zimbabwean Print Journalism in the Information Society," *Digital Journalism*, 1 no. 1 (2013): 135–151.
2 Cheruiyot, David et al. "Making News Outside Legacy Media," *African Journalism Studies*, 42 no. 4 (2021): 1–14.
3 Mabweazara, Hayes Mawindi. "When your 'Take-Home' can Hardly Take you Home," in *Newsmaking Cultures in Africa*, eds, Mabweazara, Hayes Mawindi. (London: Palgrave Macmillan, 2018a): 99–117.
4 Mabweazara, Hayes Mawindi. "Reinvigorating 'Age-Old Questions'," in *Newsmaking Cultures in Africa*, ed., Mabweazara, Hayes Mawindi. (London: Palgrave Macmillan, 2018b): 1–27.
5 Grint, Keith, *The Sociology of Work*. (Cambridge: Polity, 2005).
6 Ndlovu, Musawenkosi W. "What is the State of South African Journalism?" *African Journalism Studies* 36, no. 3 (2015): 114–138.
7 Matthews, Julian and Kelechi Onyemaobi. "Precarious Professionalism," *Journalism Studies* 21, no. 13 (2020): 1836–1851.
8 Thige, Susan W. "Perceived Factors Influencing Retention of Journalists at Kenya Broadcasting Corporation." MBA diss. (University of Nairobi, 2016).
9 Matthews, Julian and Kelechi Onyemaobi. "Precarious Professionalism," 1836–1851.
10 Deuze, Mark and Tamara Witschge, "Beyond Journalism." (London: Polity, 2020).
11 Mabweazara, Hayes M. "Reinvigorating 'Age-Old Questions'," 1–27.
12 Ndlovu, Musawenkosi W. "What is the State of South African Journalism?" *African Journalism Studies* 36, no. 3 (2015): 114–138.
13 Tzoneva, Desei. "Junior Newsrooms Lack Professionalism of the Past," https://www.mediaupdate.co.za/media/22170/junior-newsrooms-lack-professionalism-of-the-past [accessed 20 November 2022].
14 Ndlovu, Musawenkosi W. "What is the State of South African Journalism?" *African Journalism Studies* 36, no. 3 (2015): 114–138.
15 Thige, Susan W. "Perceived Factors Influencing Retention of Journalists at Kenya Broadcasting Corporation." MBA diss. (University of Nairobi, 2016).
16 Deuze, Mark and Tamara Witschge, "Beyond Journalism." (London: Polity, 2020).
17 Matthews, Julian and Kelechi Onyemaobi. "Precarious Professionalism," 1836–1851.

8

DEVELOPING PSYCHOLOGICAL CAPITAL TO SUPPORT JOURNALISTS' WELL-BEING

Maja Šimunjak

The issue this chapter deals with stems from journalism being a high emotional labor job with multiple stressors faced in everyday work. These include, but are not limited to, work conditions such as long and irregular work hours, constant digital connectedness, pressures of meeting deadlines, dealing with abusive audiences, covering trauma and conflict, and so on. Facing these everyday stressors has been found to lead to burnout, decreased job satisfaction and performance, and concerning levels of journalists considering a change of profession.[1] In light of this, this chapter focuses on happiness as subjective well-being, exploring ways in which journalists' well-being can be supported with development of personal resources in the form of psychological capital (PsyCap), including resilience, efficacy, optimism, and hope.

There is a conceptual overlap and evidence of high positive correlations between happiness and subjective well-being, meaning that the two concepts are often used interchangeably.[2] According to Diener and Ryan, subjective well-being is an "umbrella term used to describe the level of wellbeing people experience according to their subjective evaluations of their lives."[3] Importantly, research in the field suggests that high well-being is positively correlated with both better health and job satisfaction and performance, although the causal relationship remains unclear.[4] Hence, supporting journalists' well-being has the potential to benefit them personally, as well as their employers and industry at large.

Research in the field shows that there are multiple and complex interventions that can contribute to an improved sense of well-being. Literature on organizational and social support theory suggests a worker's well-being can and should be supported through several key pillars of support—from the structures of organizational support, over social support from managers and peers to employment of individual-level resources.[5] While organizational and

DOI: 10.4324/9781003364597-10

social support systems are discussed elsewhere in this volume, this chapter focuses on personal resources in the form of psychological capital. It does so by drawing on the research informing development of psychological capital and mapping against it the recommendations for supporting journalists' well-being made by key stakeholders in a 2022 working group held in the United Kingdom. By doing this, the chapter outlines industry-specific interventions that could be useful in the development of personal resources for safeguarding well-being amongst its journalists.

Psychological Capital

Psychological capital is considered a positive psychological state based on a worker's hope, efficacy (confidence), resilience and optimism (also known as H-E-R-O resources).[6] These characteristics are viewed as state-like and hence able to be changed and developed, as well as measured.[7] In their seminal work on development of psychological capital, Luthans, Youssef and Avolio define the factors and outline strategies for their development in the following way.[8] *Hope* refers to a state of positive motivation which is focused on goal achievement—it can be developed by practice in goal setting, mental rehearsals for achieving them, and contingency planning for managing obstacles. *Efficacy*, i.e., confidence or sense of accomplishment, is a worker's belief in their own abilities to accomplish goals and manage challenges. It can be developed by experiencing and recognizing success, peer support and encouragement (particularly if it entails developmental feedback), as well as participating in mentoring schemes involving observation and imitation of role models.

Resilience is understood as the ability to cope with a difficulty and bounce back from it, and as such, is the only primarily reactive resource in psychological capital. There are three established strategies for developing resilience in the workplace: through asset-focused strategies, such as gaining skills and experience for dealing with issues in the workplace; risk-focused strategies, such as proactive self-care through healthy eating and regular exercise to minimize risk from stress and/or burnout; and process-focused strategies, including developing emotional intelligence to be able to recognize, understand and manage one's own and others' emotions which could have potentially negative outcomes.

Finally, *optimism* refers to a positive outlook on past, present, and future events and developments. It can be enhanced with training in emotional intelligence, which allows workers to actively rethink and reframe thoughts that are driving negative evaluations of past experiences; using positive affirmations to internalize positive outlook on the present; and with encouragement to seek and interpret future developments as opportunities to be welcomed and excited about.

In short, a worker with high psychological capital has "the confidence to succeed, maintaining a hopeful and optimistic mindset, persevering in the face of obstacles, redirecting and adapting efforts and resources when necessary, and bouncing back resiliently from problems and adversity."[9] The evidence suggests that higher levels of psychological capital are linked to improved well-being, lower stress, increased job satisfaction, and organizational commitment,[10] as well as improved job performance.[11]

A range of interventions to enhance each characteristic has been developed and tested. For example, it has been found that organizational and social support contribute to efficacy.[12] There is also evidence that psychological capital can be increased with "micro-interventions," such as 1–2-hour-long workshops, including online training sessions, which introduce workers to the H-E-R-O resources combined with practical exercises designed to develop each of them.[13] Importantly, as mentioned earlier, there is evidence that high and/or increased psychological capital is correlated, directly or as a mediating factor, with workers' well-being and performance. And scholars warn that the majority of studies in the field rely on self-reported data, which raises the question of the influence of common method bias and the social desirability response bias on studies' findings.[14] Also, research on psychological capital indicates that the extent of the relative contribution of each component, that is, efficacy, resilience, hope and optimism, on established outcomes of psychological capital remains inconclusive.[15] And while psychological capital and its relationships with a range of work-related variables have been examined across the world, Da et al. warn that there is still much to learn about the role of cultural differences when it comes to the effects of interventions on workers' psychological capital.[16]

Developing Psychological Capital in Journalism

There is little empirical insight into the development or impact of psychological capital in journalism. This is not surprising as the general discussion of journalists' well-being has been neglected until recently.[17] That said, several studies appear to have engaged with individual components of psychological capital. For example, there are studies examining journalists' *resilience*, particularly in relation to those reporting on trauma and conflict.[18] Swart offers an interesting analysis of resilience from the perspective of neuroscience.[19] Her analysis revealed that one of the key issues affecting resilience among journalists was poor quality of sleep, brought about partly with caffeine and alcohol consumption, which contributed to higher stress levels. *Efficacy* has also been occasionally studied.[20] Studies in the U.S. have examined newspaper journalists' efficacy, often considering it as a counterbalance to burnout. Building on earlier research, Reinardy's survey study of American newspaper journalists reports increasing levels of exhaustion and decreasing rates of efficacy, indicating that efficacy's ability to mitigate risks from burnout among American journalists is diminishing.[21] Hope and optimism in the journalist population are scarcely mentioned. For example, a rare discussion of *hope* can be inferred from Chen and Javid-Yazdi's conceptual work in which they call for better career counseling in the industry to alleviate job stress and prevent burnout by drawing on narrative career theory and social learning theory.[22] Another conceptual work by Pearson et al. suggests that mindfulness training in the industry could be seen as a strategy to develop *optimism*.[23] They argue that engaging in mindfulness-based meditation would enable journalists to develop emotional intelligence, which is one of the key pathways to increasing optimism, as outlined in the psychological capital literature.

There are also several notable industry initiatives, often set to increase journalists' *resilience*, such as training and resources offered by the Rory Peck Trust, Self-Investigation, and Headlines Network. British Women in Journalism's mentorship program can be seen as geared towards developing early career journalists' *efficacy*, but also *hope* (via discussions involving goal setting and contingency planning) and *optimism* (via prompts to reflect and reframe negative thoughts, appreciate the present, and identify career paths). And while the potential benefits of such initiatives are evident, there is rarely clear and public data on their outcomes and achieved impact.

More could and should be done to support journalists' development of personal resources to manage stressors in their everyday work. Similar initiatives, from which journalism can learn from, have already been taken in related industries. For example, The Film and TV charity has in early 2022 launched the "Mentally healthy productions" toolkit that contains advice on how to protect staff well-being in all stages of the production process. While at a level of anecdotal data, a representative from Offspring Films said in a testimonial that implementing this resource has: "given visibility to mental health issues within production, raised awareness, helped us feel more equipped to provide support within the company, and importantly helped people know where they can find outside support if they need it."[24] The charity also offers a set of well-being resources for freelancers, as well as counseling and therapy sessions.[25]

To establish best practice and ways forward in journalism, the working group on journalists' well-being met in the Spring of 2022 featuring a dozen key stakeholders—including representatives of the British Broadcasting Corporation (BBC), British National Union of Journalists (NUJ), Centre for Media Monitoring, European Federation of Journalists (EFJ), Headlines Network, Reach, Rory Peck Trust, Society of Freelance Journalists and UNESCO, as well as UK and Netherlands researchers. These stakeholders exchanged knowledge and best practice in the field and discussed the ways in which journalists' well-being could be supported to benefit their mental health and job satisfaction, as well as the quality of journalism. The working group was organized as part of the project titled "Journalists' Emotional Labor in the Social Media Era," funded by the Arts and Humanities Research Council and led by Middlesex University London.

Through discussion, the working group has agreed to a set of recommendations for supporting journalists' development of personal resources to manage their well-being at work. While journalists should seek opportunities to increase their psychological capital, the development of such resources should be supported by wider structures and practices in a systematic manner. Recent qualitative studies show that journalists often must rely on their personal resources to deal with stressors in the job, with often limited training or support in development of these resources.[26] The key recommendations of the working group,[27] outlined below, demonstrate that the responsibility to equip journalists with psychological capital needed for effective dealing with job stressors should be on a range of stakeholders, and not solely on journalists themselves, including media organizations, editors and supervisors, journalist organizations, training and education institutions, and so on.

Training for development of psychological capital

- Journalism educators, news organizations, professional associations and unions should offer training, including micro-interventions in the form of short workshops, for development of personal resources to deal with occupational stressors in the job. This training can focus on emotional intelligence, resilience, mindfulness, active listening, mental health literacy, and so on.
- Managers/supervisors in news organizations would benefit from training and developing their psychological capital, which could enable them to recognize signs, understand and adequately support their staff when faced with stressors more effectively.
- Good examples include self-investigation's free courses in digital well-being for journalists and their managers; Headlines Network's resources on how to manage your own mental health and support others; and Rory Peck Trust's resilience programme for freelancers.

Regular briefings and debriefings

- Journalists should have access to regular briefings and debriefings, in forms of individual and collective critical reflective practice. These can help prepare journalists for challenging aspects of work, assist them in recognizing and understanding their own triggers of stress, anxiety, and burnout, offer support in their efficient management, and contribute to a collegiate and supportive culture of sharing and caring in journalism.
- Developmental feedback should be regularly provided to journalists by supervisors/editors. This would allow them to identify work processes that are efficient and those that need further development; plan for contingencies in future work; develop confidence in their work; and more effectively process past actions and identify future opportunities.

- Good practice has been observed in a young digital newsroom in Germany in which the editor has instituted a regular weekly collective debriefing in which journalists talk through the issues they have faced in their work and receive emotional release and support from peers.[28] Also, an informal British peer support network NewsBreak holds informal online chats where journalists can engage in a critical reflective practice.

Structures and systems of organizational support

- A system of regular and meaningful reviews/appraisals that go beyond performance evaluations should be implemented in media organizations. These should contain developmental feedback, creation of personally valuable, challenging, yet realistic goals with clear timelines and identification of activities that will lead to successful outcomes, as well as planning contingencies for overcoming obstacles in the process.
- Proactive check-in systems should be instituted in newsrooms to enable prevention and/or early detection and support with issues that might affect journalists' well-being. These interventions could involve contingency planning, briefings on assets and processes that are in place to support them, and coaching in practice of "positive self- talk."
- News organizations should adopt the principle of equity wellness, meaning that everyone has a fair and efficient access to transparent and easy to use systems supporting their psychological capital, including, for example, counseling, mentoring schemes, training offers, regular debriefings and career planning.
- There are several good examples of media organizations, but primarily larger companies, following the principle of equity wellness. For example, the BBC and *The Guardian*, among others, offer their staff free and confidential counseling and therapy sessions, as well as a range of training opportunities aimed at supporting journalists' mental health and well-being.

Practical and emotional social support from peers

- Peer support networks should be instigated, encouraged, supported, and promoted by all stakeholders for social support systems, particularly peer-to-peer, to become a resource in developing journalists' psychological capital.
- Peers can offer practical advice and support by, for example, sharing their own risk and stress management strategies, signposting useful assets, and providing feedback. They can also offer emotional support in the form of active listening that allows their colleagues to gain emotional release, including acknowledgment and legitimization of their actions and emotions, which promotes efficacy and a sense of belonging.
- A good example of organizationally led development of social support is Reach plc's "Online safety rep network" which has been running since

2022. Journalists at Reach can volunteer to be trained in supporting their colleagues in connection to online harms, and hence offer peer support, practical and emotional, when needed.

Hope, Efficacy, Resilience, and Optimism

Each of these recommendations has the potential to develop several if not all elements of psychological capital: hope, efficacy, resilience, and optimism. This matters as it is argued that psychological capital factors interact and, while they can be developed and measured on their own, an individual's psychological capital is not merely the sum of its parts. Rather, the interaction of components creates a synergistic effect, meaning that they are a stronger resource when combined than each on their own.[29]

In line with the psychological capital literature, there are suggestions here for brief and focused micro-interventions, as well as longer-term structures and processes that can help journalists to practice and maintain their psychological capital.[30] They represent a clear call for a range of stakeholders, and in particular media organizations, to take more responsibility, and invest more, in supporting journalists to develop their personal resources to deal with job stressors. Normative declarations of care for journalists' well-being would not suffice. In the first place, implementation of these recommendations requires dedication of resources which could include paying for the services of qualified trainers and employing staff who can organize and support certain structures (e.g., set up and run peer support networks, offer career counseling). On the other hand, it is necessary to recognize the engagement with recommended practices and tools in journalists' workloads.

Second, setting up structures and processes might not be sufficient on its own in an industry that has historically been based on "thick skin" narratives and successful workers being seen as those who are able to "handle it."[31] As discussed in the working group, there is a need for the industry, and in particular media bosses and newsroom supervisors, to not only acknowledge that journalists face a range of occupational hazards in their line of work which often have a negative impact on their well-being, but also to play a pivotal role in normalizing the discussions about mental health and well-being in the workplace.

While personal resources such as those discussed in this chapter are deemed instrumental in managing stress, anxiety and burnout, which seem rampant in the industry, the care for journalists' well-being should not rely solely on development of journalists' psychological capital. Rather, their personal resources should be one pillar of support, alongside wider elements of the organizational and social support systems. Several of these institution-level solutions to supporting journalists' well-being are discussed in Part 4 of this volume. These diverse yet complementary support systems should work in synergy to safeguard journalists' well-being, and consequently also, the quality of journalism.

Notes

1 Sallie Hughes, et al., "Coping with Occupational Stress in Journalism," *Journalism Studies* 22, no. 8 (2021); Samuel Pantoja Lima et al., *Perfil do Jornalista Brasileiro 2021*. (Florianópolis: Brasil, 2022); Matthew Pearson, and Dave Seglins, "Taking Care," published 2022, https://static1.squarespace.com/static/60a28b563f87204622eb0cd6/t/6285561b128d0447d7c373b2/1652905501967/TakingCare_EN.pdf.

2 Oleg N. Medvedev and Erik Landhuis, "Exploring Constructs of Well-Being, Happiness and Quality of Life," *PeerJ* 6 (2018).

3 Ed Diener and Katherine Ryan, "Subjective Well-Being," *South African Journal of Psychology* 39, no. 4 (2009): 391.

4 Diener and Ryan, "Subjective Well-Being."

5 Hamid Roodbari et al., "Organisational Interventions to Improve Employees' Health and Wellbeing." *Applied Psychology* 71, no. 3 (2022).

6 Alexander Newman et al., "Psychological Capital," *Journal of Organizational Behavior* 35, no. S1 (2014).

7 Carolyn M. Youssef-Morgan and Jeff P. Dahms, "Developing Psychological Capital to Boost Work Performance and Well-Being." In *Research Handbook on Work and Well-Being* eds. Ronald J. Burke and Kathryn M. Page, (Cheltenham: Edward Elgar, 2017).

8 Fred Luthans, Carolyn M. Youssef, and Bruce J. Avolio, *Psychological Capital*. (Oxford: Oxford University Press, 2007).

9 Youssef-Morgan and Dahms, "Developing Psychological Capital to Boost Work Performance and Well-Being," 332.

10 James B. Avey, et al., "Psychological Capital: A Positive Resource for Combating Employee Stress and Turnover," *Human Resource Management* 48, no. 5 (2009); James B. Avey et al., "Meta-Analysis of the Impact of Positive Psychological Capital on Employee Attitudes, Behaviors, and Performance," *Human Resource Development Quarterly* 22, no. 2 (2011).

11 Fred Luthans et al., "The Development and Resulting Performance Impact of Positive Psychological Capital," *Human Resource Development Quarterly* 21, no. 1 (2010).

12 Paul Chou, "The Effects of Workplace Social Support on Employee's Subjective Well-Being," *European Journal of Business and Management* 7, no. 6 (2015).

13 Luthans, Youssef, and Avolio, *Psychological Capital*; Fred Luthans et al., "Experimental Analysis of a Web-Based Training Intervention to Develop Positive Psychological Capital," *Academy of Management Learning & Education* 7, no. 2 (2008); Youssef-Morgan and Dahms, "Developing Psychological Capital to Boost Work Performance and Well-Being."

14 Newman et al., "Psychological Capital."

15 Niklas Nolzen, "The Concept of Psychological Capital," *Management Review Quarterly* 68, no. 3 (2018).

16 Shu Da, et al., "Effectiveness of Psychological Capital Intervention and Its Influence on Work-Related Attitudes," *International Journal of Environmental Research and Public Health* 17, no. 23 (2020).

17 Maja Šimunjak and Manuel Menke, "Workplace Well-Being and Support Systems in Journalism," *Journalism* (2022), https://doi.org/10.1177/14648849221115205.

18 Colm Murphy et al., "A New Pedagogy to Enhance the Safety and Resilience of Journalists in Dangerous Environments Globally," *Education Sciences* 10, no. 310 (2020).

19 Tara Swart, "Study into the Mental Resilience of Journalists," published 2017, https://www.taraswart.com/mental-resilience-of-journalists/.

20 See, for example, Ronald J. Burke, and Stig Berge Matthiesen, "Correlates of Flow at Work Among Norwegian Journalists," *Journal of Transnational Management* 10, no. 2 (2005); Justin D. Martin, "Professional Efficacy among Arab American Journalists," *Journal of Middle East Media* 7, no. 1 (2011).

21 Scott Reinardy, "Newspaper Journalism in Crisis," *Journalism* 12, no. 1 (2011).

22 Charles P. Chen, and Madia Javid-Yazdi, "Career Counselling Strategies to Enhance the Vocational Wellness of Journalists," *Australian Journal of Career Development* 28, no. 1 (2019).

23 Mark Pearson et al., "Building Journalists' Resilience through Mindfulness Strategies," *Journalism* 22, no. 7 (2021).

24 "The whole picture toolkit" (also known as the "Menally healthy productions" toolkit.

25 "Your mental well-being," The Film and TV Charity, published 2019, https://filmtvcharity.org.uk/your-support/mental-wellbeing/.

26 Avery E. Holton et al., "'Not Their Fault, but Their Problem': Organizational Responses to the Online Harassment of Journalists," *Journalism Practice* (2021), https://doi.org/10.1080/17512786.2021.1946417; John Huxford and Megan Hopper, "Reporting with Emotion," *Journal of Applied Journalism & Media Studies* 9, no. 1 (2020); Šimunjak and Menke, "Workplace Well-Being and Support Systems in Journalism."

27 For more recommendations: https://europeanjournalists.org/wp-content/uploads/2022/06/Recommendations-wellbeing-in-journalism.pdf.

28 Šimunjak and Menke, "Workplace Well-Being and Support Systems in Journalism."

29 Luthans, Youssef, and Avolio, *Psychological Capital*.

30 Newman et al., "Psychological Capital."

31 Šimunjak and Menke, "Workplace Well-Being and Support Systems in Journalism."

9

HOW NEWSROOM SOCIAL MEDIA POLICIES CAN IMPROVE JOURNALISTS' WELL-BEING

Logan Molyneux and Jacob L. Nelson

Journalists' use of social media has become a source of contention as journalists, their managers, their audiences, and their critics advance varying and sometimes contradictory values. Such contention is often a source of unhappiness and affects perceptions of well-being. Journalists feel pressure to publicize their own work and the work of their colleagues; managers worry their journalists' posts will drive away an already fickle audience; and despite a desire for the visibility and job security a broad social media following may afford, journalists experience harassment from audiences and fear reprimands from their bosses. Such contention and uncertainty are direct contributors to stress and anxiety, but more to the point of this volume, the persistence of negative experiences around social media leaves many journalists unhappy.

A growing body of literature has illustrated journalists' challenges with social media and their frustration with newsroom managers they feel do little to protect them from the dark side of this form of audience engagement.[1] It's naturally difficult to provide and sustain solutions to these ongoing issues as the social media landscape continues its rapid development. To address this need, this chapter provides strategies to reconcile the desires of journalists and their managers in policies that support and protect both these groups' interests. We draw on a discourse analysis of newsroom social media policies, and in-depth interviews with U.S. journalists focused on their reactions to the newsroom social media policies they have worked under, and their recommendations for how those policies could be improved.

We find that social media policies focus primarily on maintaining the institution's image and reputation, implying that newsroom leaders are more concerned with social media's effects on perceptions of their news organizations than they are with anything else about the platforms. As a result, journalists feel abandoned by their managers, as well as anxious

DOI: 10.4324/9781003364597-11

about navigating online abuse alone rather than with the help, support, and guidance of their organization. We conclude with recommendations offered by the journalists interviewed, which center around creating safeguards and building in opportunities for reporters to meaningfully contribute to newsroom policy-making. A key recommendation for newsroom managers is to carefully consider their organization's overarching values and use these to inform policy and process guiding journalists' social media use.

Journalism and Social Media

Journalists have adopted social media as a reporting tool[2] as well as for professional connections[3] and distribution.[4] Journalists frequently describe social media platforms as an invaluable tool they have come to depend on in order to find sources, build their own journalistic "brands," and cultivate deeper relationships with the public.[5] Yet the advent of social media as a journalistic tool has been accompanied by unanticipated risks and challenges for journalists and their managers. The two primary examples of these challenges include the harassment that journalists endure at the hands of online trolls, as well as the fact that journalists' use of social media to present themselves as three-dimensional human beings often is in tension with newsroom managers' desire to project an image of objective and neutral reporting.[6]

This tension is exacerbated by the fact that journalists are constantly doing their work with the anxiety-inducing awareness of the precarity of their profession generally and their own jobs specifically.[7] Journalists who feel less secure in their employment feel even more compelled to use social media to build a professional network and professional identity.[8] Yet this sort of brand-building that relies on the sharing of personal life details further puts these journalists at risk of even more aggressively personal attacks and harassment and further increases their likelihood of being penalized by their managers for acting in ways that go against their organization's "neutrality."[9] In short, increased visibility is an asset in an industry where revenues depend on attention, but increased visibility also brings increased exposure and vulnerability. Nobody is fired or attacked over an insensitive post that remains obscure; it's a different story if the post goes viral.

As journalists increasingly find themselves facing vicious harassment and attacks via social media—what Quandt refers to as "dark participation"—there is a growing awareness throughout the industry that newsrooms have little to offer little in the way of protection and resources for combating them.[10] Instead of support from newsroom managers when it comes to navigating the pitfalls of social media, journalists tend to encounter social media policies that restrict journalists' ability to take advantage of social media's network and identity building functions.[11] In many cases, the policy is simply "don't be stupid."[12] These circumstances have led to frustration on the part of journalists, who feel pressured to use social media to help bring readers and revenue to their organization, yet also feel a constant looming threat of punitive measures from those same organizations for posting something that online audiences may perceive as harming the organization's reputation. Women journalists and journalists of color are especially harmed by this situation, as they "face the highest risks when it comes to social media, while maintaining the lowest levels of control when it comes to the resources and protection their organizations make available for them."[13] Freelancers and other content creators, who rely on online followings even more than institutionalized journalists, face even greater pressure and risks.[14]

This situation creates a valuable lens through which to understand an unfolding tension between journalists and newsroom managers, with implications not only for journalistic practice but for journalists' mental health as well. News organizations use social media policies to impose order and boundaries on their journalists' social media use, hoping to secure the benefits of greater digital reach while minimizing the risk that the organization will be exposed to reputational damage because of employees' indiscretion online. This focus leaves journalists feeling doubly frustrated, as they feel abandoned by their managers when they encounter hostility via social media, as well as unfairly punished by those same managers when their actions on social media are perceived as out of step with the organization's overarching values. In light of this frustration, we ask what newsrooms should do to improve the well-being of journalists who routinely encounter "dark participation" via social media.

Method

This chapter examines how newsroom managers attempt to oversee journalists' use of social media, and how journalists respond to these attempts at guidance. It does so by drawing on a dataset that comprises a literature review and discourse analysis of newsroom social media policy; and in-depth interviews with 37 U.S. journalists—primarily women journalists and journalists of color—focused specifically on their reactions to the social media policies within the newsrooms in which they have worked.

Literature and discourse analysis

The literature reviewed covers roughly 2012–2022, with studies of newsroom social media policies having picked up once social media use became widespread and even required in newsrooms across the globe. This literature comprises studies of newsroom social media policies and interviews of supervisors and journalists about policy and practice, spanning North American, European, and Latin American markets. Synthesis of this literature supports the themes, trends and overall development of newsroom social media policy discussed below.

Because newsroom social media policy is constantly developing and changing, including while completing this study, we conducted a discourse analysis of current and publicly available newsroom social media policies. Most newsroom social media policies exist only as internal documents (if they are written down at all). Only a few of the largest news organizations make public their newsroom policies on social media. The organizations whose policies could be found published online and were included in this discourse analysis are as follows: *Associated Press, BuzzFeed, The Guardian, Los Angeles Times, The New York Times, NPR, South China Morning Post, USA Today*, and *The Washington Post*. These policies can be idiosyncratic to particular newsrooms or leaders, but our analysis highlights only themes and emphases they share.

The analysis also included articles about newsroom social media work published in *Columbia Journalism Review, The New York Times,* and other media outlets. The goals were to observe what assumptions underlie the formation and implementation of newsroom social media policy, and to observe what values and beliefs are communicated through these policies to the journalists who are expected to follow them. Together, this approach offers a comprehensive view of newsroom social media policies and enumerates their strengths and weaknesses.[15]

Journalist interviews

Journalists were recruited for interviewing using snowball sampling techniques on social media. In all, 37 journalists were interviewed.[16] These individuals are reporters, editors, publishers, freelancers, and social media managers who are current or former employees of print, digital and broadcast news outlets throughout the United States. The interviewees included 22 women and 15 men; half of the respondents identified as journalists of color.

The interviews were semi-structured conversations that drew on a fixed list of questions, but also included frequent follow-up questions meant to provide participants with more opportunities to expand upon their answers. These questions focused on how interviewees felt about social media's benefits and risks, their experiences with their newsroom's social media policies, the opinions about those policies that they formed because of those experiences, and their recommendations for how these policies should be improved. Interviews typically lasted an hour and took place between July and September of 2021. The second author conducted the interviews via Zoom, recorded them as audio files and subsequently had those files transcribed by a professional transcription service. This research was exempted by the second author's university's institutional review board.

Following completion of the discourse analysis and the in-depth interviews, the researchers considered both datasets looking for areas of direct conflict between managerial narratives and journalistic performance. As themes emerged, they were developed inductively while seeking to situate them among the conceptual schema present in existing literature. The first section below describes overarching trends in newsroom social media policies— namely that they privilege public perceptions of newsrooms rather than the journalists working within them. The second section describes journalists' reactions to their newsroom's social media policies, focusing primarily on journalists' frustrations and their recommendations for improving those policies. In short, they hope for more managerial support and increased awareness of how to approach social media in ways that best align with their organization's values.

Organization-Focused Policies

Newsroom social media policies are primarily concerned with reputation management. They teach that corporate identity takes precedence over personal identity for all employees and in all instances online. This is reflected in phrases such as "*Washington Post* journalists are always *Washington Post* journalists," "You must identify yourself as a *Los Angeles Times* employee online," "And always remember, you represent *NPR*."[17] This includes treating personal social media accounts as strongly associated with the organization: "My Twitter account is a Times account," one reporter wrote when explaining the policy.[18] Ownership disputes have led to some lawsuits as journalists try to maintain control of their network.[19] Rather than setting limits on organizational reach such that personal and professional may be separated, newsroom policies convey the supremacy of organizational identity.

Newsroom policies consider opinions to be the worst kind of personal disclosure. *Post* journalists are told not to post anything that could be perceived as reflecting any kind of "bias or favoritism."[20] *NYT* journalists "must not express partisan opinions," "or do anything else" that appears to take sides.[21] The nature and tone of journalist–audience interactions is also prescribed in newsroom social media policies. The policies universally encourage engagement with audiences online but advise journalists not to respond to criticism and complaints. Journalists may not offer their own criticism of their employer, other journalists,[22] and even other companies. Newsroom social media policies suggest discretion in which links are shared, which accounts are followed, which groups are joined, and even when to use humor. Retweets are discouraged. Notably, the policies do not address harassment or other negative interactions from the audience, beyond suggesting that journalists report the offending post to the platform. As the following section reveals, this is a particularly painful point for journalists.

Finally, the policies notify journalists that they should not expect privacy in any form online. Journalists are advised to act as if everything they do on social media is part of the public record, no matter what settings or exclusions social media platforms may allow them to impose. The policies remind journalists that they, and not their organizations, are legally responsible for what they post on social media, and journalists are subject to any terms of conduct the platforms themselves may impose. Overall, newsroom social media policies are consistent in their focus on reputation management, opinion, audience interaction, and privacy.

Journalists' Frustrations and Recommendations

Journalists interviewed consistently observed that newsroom social media policies focus on protecting their institution rather than the institution's employees. Consequently, rather than feel protected by their managers when it came to online harassment, journalists described feeling that using social media carried *two* risks: one from the public in the form of online harassment, and one from their managers in the form of punitive measures if their social media posts were deemed to have violated their newsroom's social media policy. As a male journalist of color explained,

> Either [newsroom social media policies] are extremely vague and lead to punishment, or they're extremely specific and lead to punishment ... There's this double-edged sword of you're not sure if you're going to be punished for using social media, and yet you need to use social media to represent the outlet and the brand.

Because these policies offer no resources or guidance for journalists who face harassment while using social media for their work, journalists felt they had no safety net to protect them when they ran into trouble online. They also feel the policies are unclear on lines that cannot be crossed, and instead leave that judgment largely to the court of public opinion. In short, journalists interviewed felt pushed by newsroom managers to engage with online publics regardless of what personal risk they may incur while doing so.

To improve these policies, journalists suggested clarifying managerial guidance, including journalists in the formation of these policies, and discussing the newsroom's overarching values. Journalists consistently advocated for centering their mental health and well-being, especially in cases involving abuse. "I would like to see a policy that acknowledges that harassment can take a really big toll on your mental health, and that you need care and attention when that happens to you," said a white, female journalist.

Many asked that these policies be part of a larger effort to create support networks within news organizations and journalism at large to help journalists navigate online abuse. As a female journalist of color said,

> I think a lot of the concern and maybe the trauma that some journalists experience could be alleviated by just having a support network and having an institution that is like, "Okay. We are here to protect you if anything does escalate. Let's figure out how our community of newsmakers can support you."

Journalists also recommended that newsrooms more explicitly address how the reality of journalistic practice in a digital environment challenges their current values. Perhaps, some journalists suggested, the pursuit of neutrality is incompatible with journalists' efforts to build and maintain audiences via social media. Instead of newsrooms trying to persuade the public that journalists are bias-free, they might consider a standard of transparency, allowing journalists to share their biases more openly to build more honest and genuine connections with audiences. "There are people who hold these opinions, and they're still reporting these stories. They're just not doing it publicly," said a Black, female journalist. "I'd rather see those biases upfront and out there instead of them being hidden in plain sight." Preserving the veneer of objectivity, or proclaiming it as an ideal value, may be counterproductive in that it invites the very criticisms of bias that anti-opinion policies are intended to avoid.

Finally, journalists consistently asked for a seat at the table when it comes to their news organization's social media policies. One of the main reasons that the views mentioned above are not reflected in newsroom social media policies is that journalists are not consulted when forming them.[23] A collective approach, obviously, would be less likely to privilege only organizational interests or advance incompatible values and vision. This means newsrooms should hire more diverse employees, and then give those employees avenues to influence or serve as leaders. As a female journalist of color said in her succinct summary of journalists' recommendations,

> Managers should listen to our perspective and make a policy where—one, their organizations stand by their journalists who are being attacked right now; that, two, it is very clear on what's biased and what's not biased; and three, that takes into consideration the experiences that we have every day. Because I think we can give them—our managers, who oversee enforcing all of that—a lot of insight of what's going on so they can draft a more comprehensive policy for us that will not only protect the outlet's credibility, but also will protect their journalists.

A Return to Foundational Values

One clear and direct way to increase happiness in journalism is to address the inadequate and contradictory social media policies in newsrooms. We recommend newsrooms revisit their social media policies in connection with the journalists who must live by them, focusing on three key areas of improvement. First, return to foundational values for both organizations and employees, and let these values, rather than fears of losing face, guide policy development. As it stands, the primary value expressed in these policies is damage control, but this need not crowd out all other considerations. A newsroom that values democracy, verification, and independence can uphold these values without usurping all personal expression, and such expression can exist within clearly defined limits that prevent harm to the organization. A focus on newsroom values, rather than a defensive crouch, is also likely to reduce contradictions (e.g., attract attention, but not the wrong kind) and increase clarity (what's the wrong kind?).

Second, newsroom social media policies should include both boundaries and support, for organizational and individual interests. Current policies establish (often vague) organizational boundaries but are unhelpful in clarifying when individual boundaries may be violated and how to respond when that happens. Directions for preventing, reporting, and mitigating online abuse should be part of every social media policy. Furthermore, newsrooms should provide resources to treat and restore journalists' mental health following an incident of abuse.

Finally, newsrooms must include journalists and managers representing the full range of newsroom interests while rebuilding social media policies. Assuming social media continues to play a central role in journalistic practice, then, newsroom managers who find ways to align their organization's values with their journalists' approach to social media will likely find themselves with happier employees. And assuming social media policies allow for this sort of emotional honesty, those journalists might inevitably discuss that newfound happiness with their online audiences, making social media use a positive branding development for newsrooms after all.

Notes

1 Avery E. Holton et al., "'Not Their Fault, but Their Problem': Organizational Responses to the Online Harassment of Journalists," *Journalism Practice*, (2021): 1–16, https://doi.org/10.1080/17512786.2021.1946417; Kaitlin C. Miller and Jacob L. Nelson, "'Dark Participation' Without Representation," *Social Media + Society* 8, no. 4 (2022), https://doi.org/10.1177/20563051221129156.

2 Logan Molyneux, "Social Media as Reporting Tool." In *The International Encyclopedia of Journalism Studies*. (London and New York: Wiley, 2019).

3 Logan Molyneux and Rachel R. Mourão, "Political Journalists' Normalization of Twitter," *Journalism Studies* 20, no. 2 (2017): 1–19, https://doi.org/10.1080/1461670X.2017.1370978.

4 Rasmus Kleis Nielsen and Sarah Anne Ganter, "Dealing with Digital Intermediaries," *New Media & Society* 20, no. 4 (2018): 1600–1617, https://doi.org/10.1177/1461444817701318.

5 Molyneux, Lewis, and Holton, "Media Work, Identity, and the Motivations That Shape Branding Practices"; Nelson, "'Worse than the Harassment Itself.'"

6 Jon Allsop, "Felicia Sonmez and the Tyranny of the Social-Media Policy," *Columbia Journalism Review*, January 29, 2020, https://www.cjr.org/the_media_today/felicia_sonmez_kobe_bryant_washington_post.php.

7 Nicole S. Cohen, Andrea Hunter, and Penny O'Donnell, "Bearing the Burden of Corporate Restructuring," *Journalism Practice* 13, no. 7 (2019): 817–33, https://doi.org/10.1080/17512786.2019.1571937.

8 Logan Molyneux, "A Personalized Self-Image," *Social Media + Society* 5, no. 3 (2019), https://doi.org/10.1177/2056305119872950.

9 Miller and Nelson, "'Dark Participation' Without Representation"; Nelson, "'Worse than the Harassment Itself.' Journalists' Reactions to Newsroom Social Media Policies."

10 Holton et al., "'Not Their Fault, but Their Problem.'"

11 Nelson, "'Worse than the Harassment Itself."

12 Andrew Duffy and Megan Knight, "Don't Be Stupid: The Role of Social Media Policies in Journalistic Boundary-Setting," *Journalism Studies* 20, no. 7 (2019): 932–951, https://doi.org/10.1080/1461670X.2018.1467782; Michaël Opgen-haffen and Leen D'Haenens, "Managing Social Media Use," *International Journal on Media Management* 17, no. 4 (2015): 201–216, https://doi.org/10.1080/14241277.2015.1107570.

13 Miller and Nelson, "'Dark Participation' Without Representation,'" 1.

14 Brooke Erin Duffy et al., "The Nested Precarities of Creative Labor on Social Media," *Social Media + Society* 7, no. 2 (2021), https://doi.org/10.1177/20563051211021368.

15 For an expanded analysis with additional details and dimensions, see Diana Bossio, Valérie Bélair-Gagnon, Avery E. Holton, and Logan Molyneux, "The Paradox of Connection," University of Illinois Press, 2024.

16 The data presented here is part of a larger project examining journalists' experiences with social media.

17 Deirdre Edgar, "L.A. Times Updates Newsroom Ethics Guidelines," *Los Angeles Times*, June 18, 2014, sec. Readers' Representative Journal, https://www.latimes.com/local/readers-rep/la-rr-la-times-updates-newsroom-ethics-guidelines-20140618-story.html; *NPR*, "Special Section: Social Media," accessed October 8, 2021, https://www.npr.org/about-npr/688418842/special-section-social-media; *The Washington Post*, "Policies and Standards."

18 *The New York Times*, "Social Media Guidelines for The Times Newsroom," *The New York Times*, 2017, https://www.nytimes.com/2017/10/13/reader-center/social-media-guidelines.html?_r=0.

19 Jonathan Peters, "Lawsuits over Journalist Twitter Accounts May Become More Common," *Columbia Journalism Review*, September 2018, https://www.cjr.org/united_states_project/roanoke-times-twitter.php.

20 *The Washington Post*, "Policies and Standards."

21 *The New York Times*, "Social Media Guidelines for The Times Newsroom."

22 E.g., Katie Robertson, "Felicia Sonmez Is Fired by The Washington Post," *The New York Times*, June 9, 2022, https://www.nytimes.com/2022/06/09/business/media/felicia-sonmez-washington-post.html.

23 Michaël Opgenhaffen and Harald Scheerlinck, "Social Media Guidelines for Journalists," *Journalism Practice* 8, no. 6 (2014): 726–741, https://doi.org/10.1080/17512786.2013.869421.

10

SUPPORTING DIGITAL JOB SATISFACTION IN ONLINE MEDIA UNIONS' CONTRACTS

Errol Salamon

Trade unions have long been a strong organizational form and for worker resistance and legal defense, providing workers with collective bargaining power to negotiate with employers over working conditions and professional standards.[1] More than 7,400 newsworkers unionized between April 2015 and June 2021 at over 200 internet-only and legacy for-profit and nonprofit media companies in the United States.[2] They have joined the Writers Guild of America, East (WGAE), The NewsGuild (TNG), or Screen Actors Guild-American Federation of Television and Radio Artists (SAG-AFTRA). Newsworkers have unionized within a context marked by chain and hedge fund ownership concentration, reduced advertising revenue and profit margins as Google and Facebook now capture a share of industry revenue, newspaper closures or downsizing, the prevalence of news websites, mobile applications, and social media accounts, and fewer full-time permanent reporting jobs.

Within this context, more research is needed to better understand *what issues digital newsworkers' unions resist and the communicative means through which they articulate solutions to these issues, striving for employee job and life satisfaction*. This chapter analyzes collective bargaining agreements (CBAs) of WGAE union-represented digital newsworkers since 2015. A CBA is a legally binding written contract that sets out the terms and conditions of employment and is negotiated between unions representing employees and the employer. Bringing together critical political economy of media and industrial relations research, this chapter asks, "What language have digital newsworkers' unions incorporated into CBAs, which have constituted and redressed employees' grievances since 2015? How could this CBA language help provide the conditions for employees' digital job and life satisfaction?" This chapter advances two interrelated claims: the CBA is, first, a communicative means through which digital news unions express employee resistance to labor

DOI: 10.4324/9781003364597-12

issues, and second, a legal mechanism articulating solutions to these issues that could provide the basis for employee life satisfaction.

Next, this chapter contextualizes features of digital newsworker unions' CBAs in the U.S. since 2015. It then conceptualizes labor unions' role in facilitating conditions for *job and life satisfaction* through CBAs. Following, it presents a content analysis of all WGAE online news media unions' CBAs ratified between 2015 and 2022 ($N = 22$). The conclusion discusses how CBAs are a legal means through which unions could provide necessary conditions for digital job and overall life satisfaction among newsworkers.

Contextualizing Digital Newsworker Unions' Contracts

This section briefly contextualizes how unions have organized and negotiated digital-era newsworkers' working conditions in CBAs, which arguably have implications for newsworkers' *life satisfaction*. Digital-era newsworkers have won notable gains in CBAs since organizing in 2015 at companies, including Gawker, VICE Media, Salon Media, Vox Media, and MTV News.[3] Their unions have adapted universal labor union gains in CBAs around pay, benefits, equity, and worker control. Some CBAs also establish fair and transparent *pay* scales with salary minimums and guaranteed annual pay increases, and put limits on excessive overwork, introducing compensatory time or overtime pay.[4] Additionally, CBAs formalize monetary and non-monetary *benefits*. Some contracts even establish a process to convert full-time contract workers into employee status, protect against outsourcing, include benefits for part-time workers, and guarantee interns a minimum wage. Some CBAs also safeguard newsworkers' right to do outside employment to earn more income from their derivative works.

Unions negotiate CBAs further to meet another digital newsworker demand: *equity*.[5] They contain language protecting against discrimination and harassment, including online harassment. They also mandate companies to set recruitment criteria, post job openings publicly, circulate job posts to diverse professional networks, and guarantee racial and gender pay equity. Additionally, CBAs affirm the right to a safe and healthy work environment and establish diversity committees to address equity beyond collective bargaining.

Digital newsworkers use CBAs further to leverage *control* over their workplace and working conditions.[6] CBAs importantly establish grievance and arbitration procedures. They also incorporate language mandating transparent communication between union members and management, with access to written job role descriptions, regular staff meetings, and standard performance evaluations. Some CBAs contain successorship language, too, forcing a new company owner to inherit a CBA. Moreover, contracts protect job security, including *just cause*, limiting management to terminate employees for only legitimate reasons. Additionally, they formalize a layoff process, severance, recall rights if a laid-off worker's job reopens, the role of seniority in the process, and sometimes nullify non-compete agreements preventing employees from working for a competitor after their employment ends. Certain CBAs also uphold editorial independence and autonomy, protecting newsworkers' right to decline work on branded advertorial content. Finally, some CBAs establish workplace committees so newsworkers can raise their collective voice beyond contract negotiations.

CBAs are a communicative means through which digital newsworkers' unions express employee resistance to workplace issues and working conditions.[7] They articulate the

> communicative constitution of organizing: contract language is bargaining's terrain of struggle. The negotiated phrasing of the various articles that constitute a collective agreement produce, in aggregate, the normative framework shaping the material conditions of media labor and governing the power relations of the newsroom.[8]

Next, more systematic research is presented to better understand *the prominence of individual protections across digital newsworker unions' CBAs.* More research is also offered to conceptualize *how CBAs could establish conditions for the communicative constitution of digital newsworkers' happiness and subjective well-being* beyond only a "bargaining process to reduce journalists' precarity by raising standards in media work."[9]

Exploring Unions' Role in Life Satisfaction: the case of the Writers Guild of America, East

An interdisciplinary social sciences literature has established a solid empirical basis for happiness studies of subjective well-being and life satisfaction. Sociologist Ruut Veenhoven pioneered them, defining happiness as "the overall appreciation of one's life-as-a-whole."[10] For Veenhoven, "the most comprehensive measure for quality of life is how long and happy a person lives."[11] Informed by this literature, industrial relations researchers suggest unions can increase workers' quality of life and boost union members' life satisfaction.[12]

The CBA is a key mechanism through which unions contribute to citizens' life satisfaction, ensuring job satisfaction and security for union members. Negotiated CBAs can protect workers against arbitrary dismissals and set minimum pay floors, insulating workers from employers' financial bottom-line. CBAs have provided employees with basic workplace rights, including antidiscrimination protections, respect and dignity clauses, discipline and discharge protections, and grievance procedures.[13] Unions' first CBAs could also establish and sustain a "certain quality of life for workers and their families."[14] Key benefits have included health insurance, pension schemes, leaves of absence, pay systems, training, and continuing education. Additionally, CBAs have put restrictions on management rights. However, CBAs have their limits.

They might include key individual clauses but lack comprehensiveness and all core provisions, like antidiscrimination, grievance and arbitration, and seniority in layoffs.[15] Some CBAs, including those of digital newsworker unions, also contain a provision that workers will not strike, forfeiting a vital source of their "counterpower."[16] Further, CBA language is merely that: "language—until and unless the union does what it takes to implement and enforce what it has negotiated in the agreement."[17]

Nevertheless, by limiting the stress and anxiety of unemployment and relatively low pay, the potential benefits of union membership and CBAs could arguably contribute to higher rates of job satisfaction and subjective well-being. Data reveal a positive association between union membership and job satisfaction in the U.S. since the 2000s.[18] Union members have also had higher happiness levels and lower stress levels than non-union members.

Following, this chapter brings to bear newsworker unions' potential role in facilitating job satisfaction by examining WGAE's online media CBAs. A content analysis was conducted of WGAE's online media publications' CBAs based on all bargaining units that unionized and ratified their first CBAs between April 2015 and June 2022 ($N = 22$). Most CBAs cover regular full-time and regular part-time editorial employees only. To determine their potential to facilitate life satisfaction among digital newsworkers, the CBAs were initially analyzed according to the multidimensional research typology of unions' first-CBA provisions.[19] This typology includes three overarching dimensions, each of which is addressed in turn: workplace rights, union restrictions on management rights, and worker benefits, as introduced earlier. Subdimensions were added, accounting for the distinct nature of digital newsworkers' CBAs. This chapter then establishes a new *digital job satisfaction model* for newsworkers.

Securing Digital News Workplace Rights

This section is focused on the workplace rights about which digital news-workers organized and obtained in WGAE's online media CBAs. These rights include antidiscrimination protections, discipline and discharge processes, grievance procedures, and extensions to temporary workers. While many of these rights are already protected under federal and state laws, CBAs *guarantee newsworkers collective representation*.[20] Most CBAs contain common language that sets standards and antidiscrimination protections for digital newsworkers (e.g., union activity, race, color, sex, age, disability, national origin, martial and partnership status, sexual orientation, creed, etc.). Additionally, almost all CBAs include just cause provisions, progressive discipline procedures, and multi-step grievance procedures with third-party arbitration.

Some CBAs also include innovative language for digital era, newswork such as mandating an employer to *protect workers against online harassment*. CBAs mandate employers to create policies against online harassment threatening workers' personal safety (e.g., doxing, and abusive posts). For example, as Salon Media Union puts it, these policies are intended to set "community standards that prohibit online harassment by commenters on the Company's various websites and platforms, reporting procedures for employees experiencing harassment."[21] They also direct the company to take anti-harassment measures (e.g., contract a third-party to take anti-doxing measures), make training on online security and anti-harassment measures accessible to workers, and provide support to workers (e.g., employee assistance program, peer-to-peer counseling, and short paid leave). Additionally, they mandate the company to provide a service like DeleteMe to protect workers' privacy.

Tackling the contingent nature of precarious media work, some CBAs also provide *freelance, temporary contractors, and/or interns with some protection*, despite them typically being excluded from bargaining unit membership. Vox and MTV News are notable exceptions, as temporary contract or project-based workers are bargaining unit members. Another contract innovation is the formation of *special management-union committees* to address contractors: the Slate CBA mandates the company and union create a Contractor Assessment Committee, meeting once per year to "assess and discuss contractors and their contributions" to the publication.[22] In some cases, the employer must pay contractors or project-based workers, at minimum, the rate of an equivalent bargaining unit employee. Many CBAs also provide different employment relationship standards in relation to contractors: after a certain period of contract services, some companies automatically consider contractors part of the bargaining unit; must end a temporary contract employment relationship; give a contractor the option of continuing as a contractor; and/or must convert a contractor into a regular bargaining unit employee, if an open position is available. While interns are typically excluded from bargaining units, Talking Points Memo's CBA uniquely mandates the company to bargain with the union over the use of editorial interns. Such language is intended to discourage short-term, temporary, and flexible employment relationships.

Limiting Digital News Management Rights

This section is focused on language in WGAE's online media CBAs that restricts management from unilaterally making decisions, formalizing a standardized system of workplace rules and procedures. Like other unions' CBAs, WGAE's online media CBAs set restrictions on management rights around the following issues: the filling of vacancies; schedules, hours of work, and workload; overtime; shift and other pay differentials; health and safety; job security; outside employment and freelancing; and reuse of employees' work. While some limits on management rights are specific to a particular bargaining unit, others are common across all or most CBAs: for example, the posting of vacancies; editorial independence and standards; severance packages; and career development and performance review meetings (e.g., to discuss raises and promotions).

In placing restrictions on management rights, some WGAE online media CBAs also recognize unique conditions of digital journalism work. For instance, CBAs include language regarding *remote work* on certain days (e.g., working from home on holidays or Fridays) or multiple days by request, while *minimum workload and productivity goals* are meant to ensure employees have "manageable workloads."[23] Some CBAs, such as CBSN's, also mandate the company to *bargain over the consolidation or merger of business operations and* "notify the Union of its desire to bargain over the effects of the decision."[24] Considering the potential challenges of moving, some CBAs further mandate a company to provide *office relocation notice and (sometimes) paid moving expenses:* for example, "[f]or moves beyond city limits … the [Onion] shall notify the union at least three (3) months in advance of the move. Employees shall receive moving reimbursements to cover the cost for relocation."[25] Finally, acknowledging that digital journalism employment can be transitory and relatively low-paid, CBAs create the potential for employees to leverage their intellectual property and earn extra income: for instance, granting *a nonexclusive license for employees to reuse their work* and/or *a third-party platform derivative works bonus* for producing new content (e.g., books/ eBooks, films, TV, video games, or digital video programs) based on content originally created for the company. A related CBA provision sometimes grants employees *permission to accept outside employment* (e.g., freelance writing).

Codifying Digital Newsworkers' Benefits

This section is focused on benefits about which digital newsworkers organized and secured in CBAs. Like unionized workers in other industries, WGAE's online media CBAs adopt common language that sets standards and establishes monetary and non-monetary benefits for digital newsworkers: health benefits, retirement benefits, leaves of absence, transit and parking plans, pay systems, training and professional development, and employee involvement in company decision making. Such benefits vary for each bargaining unit, demonstrating union members' unique interests, but some benefits are standard across all or most CBAs. They include medical insurance, retirement benefits, parental and family forming leave, annual percentage pay increases, job title salary minimums, and labor-management committees.

Despite similarities with the first CBAs of unions in other sectors, several WGAE online media CBAs include innovative language, recognizing the distinct nature of digital journalism work, setting standards around paid time off (PTO), and establishing unique committees. Many CBAs adopt an *unlimited PTO policy*. For instance, Gizmodo Media Group Union writes,

> Unlimited PTO means taking the time you need for vacation, time off for non-extended illnesses or injury, preventative care, care, diagnosis, or treatment of an existing health condition of either you, a covered family

member or other person under applicable state or local law, time off for being the victim of domestic violence, sexual assault, or stalking, bereavement leave, and to shift your schedule as necessary.[26]

One CBA even establishes provisions for *COVID-19 paid time off*, recognizing the long-term challenges for newsworkers posed by the pandemic. Other CBAs provide clear frameworks for establishing novel committees with employee involvement clauses. For instance, most CBAs provide guidelines for *diversity committees*. While rare, other CBAs (e.g., ThinkProgress) formalize a *workload committee* that speaks directly to employee life satisfaction, the purpose of which was to "improve the quality of life for ThinkProgress employees and increase productivity and the quality of the work produced."[27]

Conclusion

This chapter analyzed CBA content of WGAE-affiliated online media workers' bargaining units to better understand issues digital newsworkers resist within a context of industry instability and precarious work to win workplace rights and worker benefits, while placing limits on management rights. It contributes a new understanding of how newsworkers communicatively constitute their collective voice and redress employees' grievances (RQ1) and the communicative means through which they offer solutions to those issues to secure employees' digital job and life satisfaction (RQ2). It develops a relational model of employees' digital job and life satisfaction CBA language that is attentive to wider industry and workplace conditions.

First, WGAE CBAs illustrate how bargaining units incorporate language on workplace rights, newsworkers' benefits, and limits on management rights, revealing the relative weight of different union solutions to newsworkers' *digital-era* grievances. WGAE CBAs extend to digital newsworkers many language provisions that other unions had won earlier. Yet, WGAE CBAs also secure new digital-era language protecting workers. These findings support a critical political-economic understanding of news industry structures, workplace (re)organization, and CBA language in relation to chain and hedge fund mergers, ownership concentration, and precarious newswork during the COVID-19 pandemic. Such language communicatively constitutes newsworkers' resistance to grievances over pay, benefits, equity, and attempts to gain more *control* over working conditions and the workplace.

Second, in addition to representing struggles against precarity,[28] CBA language communicatively constitutes conditions for *digital newsworkers' happiness and subjective well-being*. My research suggests the following characteristics should be included in a *comprehensive* relational model of CBA language oriented at digital newsworkers' life satisfaction, which arguably align with subjective well-being: *workplace rights* (anti-harassment, including sexual and online harassment, and protections for temporary workers including freelancers, contractors, and interns); *restrictions on management rights* (options to work remotely, clear editorial standards and independence, the right to refuse unsafe work, a contract binding on successors, regular career development and performance review meetings, options to take outside employment, and third-party platform derivative works bonuses); and *benefits* (medical insurance, an unlimited paid time off policy, wellness benefits, training, professional development, and employee involvement through committees in between contract negotiations). This model recognizes that newsworkers have unique demands based on local organizational and industry conditions.

These findings support a focus on not only precarity but also *happiness*, emphasizing CBA language that facilitates an "overall appreciation of one's life-as-a-whole"[29] and "quality of life for workers."[30] Moving beyond only legacy features of CBAs that could facilitate happiness, the above model recognizes CBA language that is unique to editorial newsworkers and the digital-age workplace. By proposing a relational model of digital newsworkers' CBAs, researchers and practitioners could better understand the language that is needed to communicatively constitute and facilitate happiness in newsrooms, supporting digital job and life satisfaction among newsworkers.

Notes

1 Nicole S. Cohen, *Writers' Rights*. (Montreal: McGill-Queen's University Press, 2016), 3–23; Henrik Örnebring, "A Social History of Precarity in Journalism," *Australian Journalism Review* 42, no. 2 (2020): 194–198; Errol Salamon, "Precarious E-Lancers," in *The Routledge Handbook of Developments in Digital Journalism Studies*, eds. Scott A. Eldridge and Bob Franklin, (New York: Routledge, 2018), 186.

2 Nicole S. Cohen and Greig De Peuter, *New Media Unions*. (New York: Routledge, 2020), xiii; Errol Salamon, "Media Unions' Online Resistance Rhetoric," *Management Communication Quarterly* 37, no. 2 (2023): 377, https://doi.org/10.1177/08933189221097067.

3 Nicole Cohen and Greig de Peuter, "'I Work at VICE Canada and I Need a Union'." In *Labour Under Attack* eds. Stephanie Ross and Larry Savage, (Halifax: Fernwood, 2018), 115; Cohen and de Peuter, *New Media Unions*, 19; Nicole S. Cohen and Greig de Peuter, "Collectively Confronting Journalists' Precarity Through Unionization." In *Newswork and Precarity* eds. Kalyani Chadha and Linda Steiner, (New York: Routledge, 2022), 203–204.

4 Cohen and de Peuter, *New Media Unions*, 57–71; Cohen and de Peuter, "Collectively Confronting Journalists' Precarity," 205–212.

5 Cohen and de Peuter, *New Media Unions*, 57–71; Cohen and de Peuter, "Collectively Confronting Journalists' Precarity," 205–212.

6 Cohen and de Peuter, *New Media Unions*, 57–71; Cohen and de Peuter, "Collectively Confronting Journalists' Precarity," 205–212.

7 Errol Salamon, "Communicative Labor Resistance Practices," *Communication Theory* (2022): 7, https://doi.org/10.1093/ct/qtac023.

8 Cohen and de Peuter, *New Media Unions*, 57.

9 Cohen and de Peuter, "Collectively Confronting Journalists' Precarity," 204.

10 Ruut Veenhoven, *Conditions of Happiness*. (Dordrecht: D. Reidel, 1984), 7.

11 Ruut Veenhoven, "The Four Qualities of Life: Ordering Concepts and Measures of the Good Life," *Journal of Happiness Studies* 1, no. 1 (2000): 26.

12 Patrick Flavin and Gregory Shufeldt, "Labor Union Membership and Life Satisfaction in the United States," *Labor Studies Journal* 41, no. 2 (2016): 173; Patrick Flavin, Alexander C. Pacek, and Benjamin Radcliff, "Labor Unions and Life Satisfaction: Evidence from New Data," *Social Indicators Research* 98, no. 3 (2010): 435.

13 Tom Juravich, Kate Bronfenbrenner, and Robert Hickey, "Significant Victories." In *Justice on the Job: Perspectives on the Erosion of Collective Bargaining in the United States* eds. Richard N. Block, Sheldon Friedman, Michelle Kaminski, and Andy Levin, (Kalamazoo: W.E. Upjohn Institute for Employment Research, 2006), 94–95.

14 Juravich, Bronfenbrenner, and Hickey, "Significant Victories," 104.

15 Juravich, Bronfenbrenner, and Hickey, "Significant Victories," 109.

16 Cohen and de Peuter, *New Media Unions*, 68.

17 Juravich, Bronfenbrenner, and Hickey, "Significant Victories," 110.

18 David G. Blanchflower, Alex Bryson, and Colin Green, "Trade Unions and the Well-Being of Workers," *British Journal of Industrial Relations* 60, no. 2 (2022): 258.

19 Juravich, Bronfenbrenner, and Hickey, "Significant Victories," 89.

20 Juravich, Bronfenbrenner, and Hickey, "Significant Victories," 92.

21 "Collective Bargaining Agreement: Salon Media Group And the Writers Guild of America, East," Writers Guild of America, East, accessed October 13, 2022, https://www.wgaeast.org/wp-content/uploads/sites/4/2018/12/Salon_Agreement.pdf.

22 "Agreement Between Slate Magazine and The Writers Guild of America East," Writers Guild of America, East, accessed January 30, 2023, https://web.archive.org/web/20190629183943/https://www.wgaeast.org/wp-content/uploads/sites/4/2019/01/Slate-WGAE-Contract.pdf.

23 "Collective Agreement Between Vox Media, LLC, and the Writers Guild of America, East," Writers Guild of America, East, accessed January 31, 2023, https://www.wgaeast.org/wp-content/uploads/sites/4/2022/11/Now
This-WGAE-CBA-2022-2024.pdf; "Collective Bargaining Agreement," Writers Guild of America, East, accessed January 31, 2023, https://www.wgaeast.org/wp-content/uploads/sites/4/2019/01/WGAE-DODO-CBA-FINAL-ex
ecuted-by-WGAE-12-21-18-1.pdf.

24 "2020–2023 CBSi-CBSN/WGA Agreement," Writers Guild of America, East, accessed January 31, 2023, https://www.wgaeast.org/wp-content/uploads/sites/4/2020/09/CBSN-CBA-signed.pdf.

25 "Collective Bargaining Agreement: Writers Guild of America, East and Onion, Inc.," Writers Guild of America, East, accessed January 31, 2023, https://www.wgaeast.org/wp-content/uploads/sites/4/2021/10/Onion-U
nion-CBA-2021-23-FINAL.pdf.

26 "Collective Bargaining Agreement: Writers Guild of America, East and Gizmodo Media Group, LLC," Writers Guild of America, East, accessed October 12, 2022, https://www.wgaeast.org/wp-content/uploads/sites/4/2022/04/GMG-A
greement-2022-2025.pdf.

27 "Collective Bargaining Agreement Between Writers Guild of America, East, Inc., AFL-CIO and Center for American Progress," Writers Guild of America, East, accessed January 30, 2023, https://www.wgaeast.org/wp-content/uploads/sites/4/2019/01/TP-Contract-2019-2021-Executed.pdf.

28 Cohen and de Peuter, *New Media Unions*, 57.

29 Veenhoven, *Conditions of Happiness*, 7.

30 Juravich, Bronfenbrenner, and Hickey, "Significant Victories," 104.

11

ESTABLISHING INDIVIDUAL, ORGANIZATIONAL AND COLLECTIVE PRACTICES FOR JOURNALISTS' WELL-BEING THROUGH DISCONNECTION

Diana Bossio

For senior business journalist Somesh Jha, reporting news stories isn't just his job, it's his calling. In a thread addressed to his Twitter followers in June 2021, Jha described his love for "digging stories and holding people accountable."[1] The thread seemed like his love letter to journalism, but it was his swan song. Jha admitted that despite his great passion for journalism, the relentless work schedule had made him mentally and physically unwell, and he was leaving the profession.

Jha's announcement would not have come as a surprise to many journalists.

Between covering the COVID-19 pandemic, and near-constant global, political and environmental crises, in an industry constantly impacted by financial instability, job insecurity and technological change, journalists are consistently reporting symptoms of burnout.[2] Research conducted prior to the pandemic has shown that journalists have always been at higher risk of physical and mental burnout,[3] and that a combination of organizational pressure and poor work–life balance were key contributors to this increased risk.[4] This has resulted in reports of journalists' poor online safety and hygiene,[5] with journalists perceiving social media use as a relentless, unsupported, yet non-negotiable part of their role.[6]

There is no doubt that the organizational and institutional structures supporting journalism practices on social media need to change to improve journalists' wellbeing. While Jha's Twitter feed shows that he has returned to freelance journalism and study, he has not pursued another full-time professional role in a news organization. Jha is not alone in pursuing journalism outside the traditional newsroom. An Australian study of journalists who experienced layoffs showed many had suggested that their lives had improved after leaving what they described as "toxic" work cultures.[7] A number of research studies describe journalists' stress levels increasing and following them into their online work

DOI: 10.4324/9781003364597-13

environments, and in personal online interactions.[8] The issue for many journalists is that while they expect negative online interactions will occur, there is no organizational or professional support when it does. Organizational training for online and social media use is focused on increasing audience engagement,[9] social media policies are largely focused on organizational reputation management,[10] and individual self-regulation or disconnection practices are often the only remedy to online abuse or unwanted interactions.[11]

While previous research has called for a systemic approach to improving the well-being of journalists,[12] most have stopped short of explaining how this might be achieved. This chapter provides a conceptual and methodological approach to how this systemic change could occur, using examples of best practice approaches to improving well-being and happiness in journalism. Using case studies and associated interviews, the chapter will conceptualize individual, organizational, and professional forms of social media connection and disconnection practice as part of "caring" practices.

Why Should We Center "Care" in Journalism?

Research about care in journalism largely focuses on journalists' care for others; that is, ethical journalistic practice and how to avoid inflicting pain or trauma about news investigation.[13] An ethics of care turns journalistic practice away from the prioritization of neutrality, objectivity and the provision of facts, towards more contextualized, dialogic, intersectional, and equitable practices. Care in this context means that journalistic practice does not just provide a community service with the provision of facts but contributes to the maintenance of a community defined through professional culture that emphasizes solidarity, mutual concern, and inclusive agential social practices. In this context, research has shown that enacting care for online communities of users includes building both individual and group relationships,[14] intimate and authentic communication,[15] but also building relational boundaries.[16] Caring positioned as labor can be professionally productive because it is reciprocal; it grows connections back to the worker's personal brand and paid work, but it also invites professional and personal participation in communities that provide both individual professional satisfaction and community purpose.

While caring practices can have positive impacts on communities, caring in journalism has rarely been reciprocal. Women, LGBTQIA+ and BIPOC journalists report negative impacts of online interactions with their subjects and audiences, and newsrooms rarely center the experiences of journalists in organizational strategies or policies around online audience engagement and interaction. "The siren call" for creative workers like journalists, of doing "what they love," often obscures the unpaid, and physically and mentally impactful labor that online authenticity, community building and devotion to professional and organizational branding requires.[17]

This chapter aims to focus caring practices back onto journalists and how they both practice and experience digital labor. Caring practices for journalists are defined by dialogic, inclusive, and bounded labor, prioritizing safety, and well-being in online and offline interactions.

Caring as a framework for online connection and disconnection is therefore seen through:

- Individual strategies that foreground productive and pleasurable professional practices.
- Organizational training and policies that center care for journalists and mediation of the impacts of their digital labor.
- A professional community of practice and culture that focuses on using agential and collaborative practices to support and "pays forward" knowledge based on varied experiences of digital labor.

Emphasizing caring connection and disconnection from online and social media labor allows forms of agency and negotiation over the material impacts of the overall pervasiveness of social media's affective bonds in journalists' professional lives.[18]

Caring for the Self through Disconnection

Disconnection strategies have emerged from the negative impacts of social media labor, including increased affective labor, poor communication environments, and social media fatigue or burnout. Disconnection practices are boundaries, defined as strategically and selectively aiming to exert more control and autonomy over online presence and labor.

Research about the individual disconnection strategies used by journalists has shown strategies such as: disconnection from profiles through suspension or avoidance; disconnection from engagement such as muting, blocking, or other technical barriers; and changing the types of interactions occurring.[19] However, research about journalists' disconnection strategies[20] has often overlooked these self-care practices as symptomatic of the development of a more professional, meaningful or even enjoyable interaction with particular platforms, their specific cultures, and communities. Caring, in this context, shows journalists' increasingly curatorial use of social media, including strategies of disconnection, are not just part of maintaining a sustainable online labor practice. It also frames online labor that is both professionally and personally satisfying, as well as safe and manageable over time.

Professionalized forms of disconnection are more often tied to gaining professional purpose and job satisfaction through audience connection, especially for those content creators who have no choice but to be online. Negotiating connection and disconnection practices is not just a way to negotiate this additional labor. It also prioritizes connections that are professionally beneficial and personally rewarding. Thus, journalists use forms of digital connection and disconnection that are rewarding or pleasurable, either because of the connections formed with individuals or groups through shared interest, or through protection of personal and professional time.

Adopting such practices requires time to engage, experiment with, and understand the complex social media practices and literacies required to meet social and professional expectations in these spaces.[21] Selena is a senior fashion and lifestyle journalist for a major metropolitan news organization in Australia. Much of Selena's use of social media focuses on techniques used to bolster audience engagement with her work, however her curation of different platforms over time indicates incorporation of disconnection techniques into online labor. She uses three different social media platforms and has developed her practices on each platform for different purposes. Selena uses Facebook to post links to her own reportage and Twitter to post links to reportage or content that is relevant to her fashion and lifestyle journalism. Selena is most active on Instagram, posting daily images of herself attending fashion and lifestyle events, videos about the fashion she is wearing and reels and images of her life outside of journalism.

Twitter has often been positioned as the platform of choice for journalists, but Selena suggests that this does not fit with her current role or professional enjoyment of media tools. As she developed her career as a fashion and lifestyle journalist, she discovered through both experimentation with posting, and her increased knowledge of the technical and social affordances of Twitter that her fashion reporting "goes into a black hole … I don't find that I'm reaching an audience that is interested in that sort of stuff." From a professional practice perspective, Selena has found that limiting her use of the platform to more occasional posting of generalist content has made managing her digital labor easier, and her professional engagement more strategic.

Another reason Selena limits professional use of Twitter is because the communication culture on the platform does not meet her professional or personal preferences for pleasurable engagement and interaction online: "I've seen people quite damaged by what's happened to them on Twitter simply for expressing an opinion." The limitations she has put on her use of Twitter means that there are stark differences between the content she uses on that platform and others, especially Instagram. Selena posts images of an aspirational and fun professional life, but also posts images of her children, pets, and major life events, like buying a new house, to indicate her authentic, "real" and thus trusted status to her Instagram community. She suggests this kind of posting, though aligning with the posting conventions of the platform, are not contrived or premeditated opportunities to promote content, but rather an opportunity to feel part of a safe community unified by shared interests.

Selena's social media practices were established through her own individual labor, without organizational training or mentorship. Though these long-established practices should be viewed as valuable within the news organization she works for, there is no organizational policy or structure that might encourage sharing of these practices, nor mentorship or training for more junior journalists establishing their professional social media presence and forms of digital labor for the first time. Without structures within organizations to support collaborative allyship around digital labor, many of these practices remain individualized.

Caring Organizations Prioritizing Connection and Disconnection Practices

Prioritizing journalists' well-being in digital labor requires organizational change, including centering the actual online experience of journalists within the frameworks for social media policy, training, and resources. Practices of care within news organizations forward operational strategy, policy and training that center care for journalists and mediation of the impacts of their digital labor through connection and disconnection practices.

An example of how this has occurred in practice is seen in the collaboration between Australia's Office of the eSafety Commissioner and the Australian Broadcasting Corporation (ABC). The eSafety Commissioner is the Australian independent regulator for online safety. The Commissioner has enforcement powers under Australia's online safety legislation and administers the world's first reporting scheme for online harassment targeting adults with the intent to seriously harm and to menace and harass. Journalists being targeted with violent threats or doxing can report to the Commissioner to ensure the content is removed, and that the platforms are acting to remove abusive users.

The eSafety Commissioner also collaborated with Australia's national public service news organization, the ABC to create better resources for journalists experiencing online harassment. Over a year the collaboration allowed for a mix of institutional, legislative, and organizational perspectives to be shared on online safety, professional practice and journalism. The eSafety Commissioner reviewed and approved the resulting guidelines before sharing them with the wider public.

Within these practice guidelines, the ABC's Social Media Well-Being Advisor recommends several disconnection strategies, including:

- Bolstering and regularly assessing security and privacy.
- Proactively limiting interactions such as limiting direct messaging and notifications, and muting content containing certain words or phrases.
- Using the in-app functions to ignore, mute, restrict or block abusive people or accounts after collecting evidence of abusive behavior; and,
- Taking regular offline breaks and setting boundaries with colleagues to ensure notifications or content do not infiltrate the break.[22]

The benefit of the wider collaboration between ABC and the eSafety Commissioner was ensuring these guidelines co-ordinated with organizational team leadership around all-of-newsroom approaches to journalists' safe online connection and disconnection. The guidelines include kits for media organizations to support staff to manage and mitigate the risk of social media abuse, preparing staff for engaging with online audiences, and how organizations should respond to online abuse.[23] The collaboration aimed to reflect individual and team guidelines with a whole-of-organization approach to online safety, including aspects of disconnection in organizational culture and policy guidelines. For example, the advice given to individual journalists to set boundaries with work colleagues around social media breaks, also corresponded with organizational guidelines around ensuring that newsrooms have consent to promote personal social media handles, or specific online content. Managers, editors, and producers were also encouraged to take the onus of responsibility for dealing with online journalism away from individual journalists and deal with negative impacts as a team. Suggestions included providing opportunities for the individual journalist to access support, reporting abuse on their behalf, and talking through options for disconnection from social media in the event of online harassment or abuse.

Anita L'Enfant from the eSafety Commission's Education, Prevention, and Inclusion branch, suggested that this approach aimed to empower individual journalists to stipulate the framework for professional connection and disconnection in online and digital labor, while also ensuring a framework that encouraged all levels of management to take responsibility for the material impacts of digital labor on journalists. As such, organizations were encouraged to "approach the issue from the top down" by taking responsibility for promoting discussion, resources, and feedback about social media safety.[24] The guidelines include initiatives like hosting forums, offering training, hiring social media well-being advisors, and creating resources for staff to signal to journalists that they are supported to maintain their own boundaries online, including disconnection from social media.

More importantly, improving online labor meant not using social media engagement and connection as the only measure of newsroom success. The guidelines are forthright about media organizations reviewing: "whether they prioritize online engagement over staff well-being." The guidelines indicate that social media content can expose journalists to heightened risks and are often not recommended to be part of online engagement strategies. For example, L'Enfant suggests: "one of the things that organizations can do is build an understanding of online safety into the everyday, into weekly team meetings, just to have a spot on the agenda." Creating forms of collaboration or "digital allyship" in experimenting, talking about and then sharing practices is a way of forming consistent online practices. These strategic forms of disconnection from the social affordances of platforms may run counter to the connection and engagement strategies usually recommended within newsrooms, but also articulates a form of digital labor that ensures abusive engagement is not part of an individual journalist's everyday practice.[25]

Caring Professions through Collaborative Agential Practices

Professional cultures in journalism require institutional norms that push away from the seemingly relentless expectations of online connection. Many professional associations and institutional support organizations focusing on journalism are centered on the collaborative practices of building a community of practice; something that has been largely missing from the newsrooms struggling to integrate social media use into the everyday work cultures. Sustainable digital labor can be extended through the collaborative agential practices that develop a community of professional practice within professional associations. They can also support journalists to extend organizational and professional care practices by "paying forward" knowledge based on their experiences of digital labor to more junior colleagues.

A contemporary example of this is the global work of the U.S.-based support organization, Trollbusters to develop and maintain a community of practice focused on the safety of journalists. Trollbusters is an online organization aimed at supporting mostly women journalists to protect themselves from online abuse and provide a reporting mechanism for those experiencing online abuse. The organization was founded by Michelle Ferrier, who had experienced harassment while working as a journalist. Ferrier frames Trollbusters as prioritizing collaboration to forward to agential practices to journalists: "my approach to building [Trollbusters] digitally has always been one that has maintained that communal perspective by, for and with the communities that journalists were reporting in and for." In this context, Trollbusters uses collaborative frameworks to protect individual journalists, and to extend a community of practice that prioritizes the safety and care in the profession itself.

TrollBusters is also unique in that it offers a team available to provide immediate support to those experiencing online violence. This includes mass personal endorsements, coaching and reputation repair when journalists have been exposed to online abuse. For example, the Trollbusters support team uses mass positive messaging on the profiles of journalists experiencing harassment to "create a hedge of protection around targets in online spaces like Twitter," and provides "emotional, technological and other support to help targets rebuild their digital identity and reputation."[26] Ferrier suggests: "[Trollbusters] starts with making sure you feel safe in your own home and then making sure that you have people around you that know what's going on and support you. I think that's important for your own self-care as well as to let those around you know that something's going on."

Building a community of practice around safe digital labor is part of letting others "know what is going on." This means not only raising awareness within organizations, but also providing broad reaching education focused on how to safely connect, and the ways that disconnection practices can be formulated as part of digital labor. For example, the Trollbusters team offers digital hygiene lessons that focus on online safety through boosting privacy and avoiding leaving digital traces online. Avoiding inadvertent online connection is key to Trollbusters' training including removing possibilities for online contact, curating digital labor and reclaiming personal space both online and offline.

The apparent universality of women's experiences online has also motivated Trollbusters to share their resources globally, including mapping global support for journalists and partnering with global organizations like The DART Center to promote online safety techniques for media workers. As Ferrier suggests, collaborative work to create online agential practices attempts to stem the exploitative frameworks of individualism that have framed newsroom cultures of digital labor.

An Approach of Care

The focus on this chapter has been to call for more work within organizations and within the industry more broadly to explore the potential for more collaborative practices of defining connection and disconnection practices as part of sustainable and safe digital labor for journalists. Focusing on individual practices of autonomy is important, but also risks reinforcing the lone wolf mythology of journalistic practice that ultimately alienates journalists at the level of everyday practice. This chapter has argued that one way to do this is to reflect journalists' shift towards an ethics of care in their digital labor within their own organizational and professional cultures. Caring practices emerge from prioritizing dialogic and agential creation of bounded labor, prioritizing safety, and well-being in both online and offline interactions. This means:

1. Encouraging self-care through disconnection as part of individual journalists' curation of a professional space online.
2. Organizational policy, training and resourcing should prioritize journalists' well-being and safety in online environments.
3. Development of a community of practice that includes new professional norms in journalists' digital labor.

Notes

1 Somesh Jha (@someshjha7), *Twitter*, June 6, 2021: https://twitter.com/som eshjha7/status/1401411855638171648.
2 Maja Šimunjak, "Pride and Anxiety," *Journalism Studies* 23, no. 3 (2022): 320–337; Gretchen Hoak, "Covering COVID," *Journalism & Mass Communication Quarterly* 98, no. 3 (2021): 854–874.
3 Jasmine B. MacDonald et al., "Burnout in Journalists," *Burnout Research* 3, no. 2 (2016): 34–44.
4 Fredric F. Endres, "Stress in the Newsroom at Ohio Dailies," *Newspaper Research Journal* 10, no. 1 (1988): 1–14.
5 Jennifer R.Henrichsen, Michelle Betz, and Joanne M. Lisosky, *Building Digital Safety for Journalism*. (UNESCO Publishing, 2015); Fiona Martin, "Tackling Gendered Violence Online," *Australian Journalism Review* 40, no. 2 (2018): 73–89.

6 Annina Claeeson, "'I Really Wanted Them to Have My Back, but They Didn't'—Structural Barriers to Addressing Gendered Online Violence against Journalists," *Digital Journalism* (2022): 1–20.

7 Nick Mathews, Valérie Bélair-Gagnon, Matt Carlson, "'Why I Quit Journalism:' Former Journalists' Advice Giving as a Way to Regain Control," *Journalism*, 2021. DOI: 10.1177/1464884921106195.

8 Gina Masullo Chen, Paromita Pain, Victoria Y. Chen, Madlin Mekelburg, Nina Springer, and Franziska Troger, "'You really Have to Have a Thick Skin'," *Journalism* 21, no. 7 (2020): 877–895; Silvio Waisbord, "Mob Censorship," *Digital Journalism* 8, no. 8 (2020): 1030–1046.

9 Vittoria Sacco and Diana Bossio, "'DON'T TWEET THIS!'" *Digital Journalism* 5, no. 2 (2017): 177–193.

10 Logan Molyneux, Seth C. Lewis, and Avery E. Holton, "Media Work, Identity, and the Motivations that Shape Branding Practices among Journalists," *New Media & Society* 21, no. 4 (2019): 836–855.

11 Sadia Jamil, "Suffering in Silence: The Resilience of Pakistan's Female Journalists to Combat Sexual Harassment, Threats and Discrimination," *Journalism Practice* 14, no. 2 (2020): 150–170.

12 Diana Bossio, Valérie Bélair-Gagnon, Logan Molyneux, Avery E. Holton, *The Paradox of Connection*. (University of Illinois Press, 2024). Digital disconnection in journalism is conceptualized further in this forthcoming book.

13 Garry Pech and Rhona Leibel, "Writing in Solidarity," *Journal of Mass Media Ethics* 21, no. 2–3 (2006): 141–155; David A.Craig and John P. Ferré, "Agape as an Ethic of Care for Journalism," *Journal of Mass Media Ethics* 21, no. 2–3 (2006): 123–140.

14 Avery E. Holton, Seth C. Lewis, and Mark Coddington, "Interacting with Audiences," *Journalism studies* 17, no. 7 (2016): 849–859.

15 Diana Bossio and Vittoria Sacco, "From 'Selfies' to Breaking Tweets," *Journalism Practice* 11, no. 5 (2017): 527–543.

16 David Wolfgang, "Taming the 'Trolls'," *Journalism* 22, no. 1 (2021): 139–156.

17 Brooke Erin Duffy, "The Romance of Work," *International Journal of Cultural Studies* 19, no. 4 (2016): 441–457.

18 Karppi Tero, *Disconnect*. (U of Minnesota Press, 2018).

19 Diana Bossio and Avery E. Holton, "Burning Out and Turning Off: Journalists' Disconnection Strategies on Social Media," *Journalism* 22, no. 10 (2021): 2475–2492.

20 Bossio and Holton, "Burning Out and Turning Off."

21 Amparo Lasén and Edgar Gómez-Cruz, "Digital Photography and Picture Sharing," *Knowledge, Technology & Policy* 22 (2009): 205–215.

22 "New Resources to Promote Safer Online Working Environments for Journalists," *eSafety Commissioner*, accessed December 1, 2022, https://www.esafety.gov.au/newsroom/media-releases/new-resources-promote-safer-online-working-environments-for-journalists.

23 See: "Supporting Journalists to Engage Safely Online," *eSafety Commissioner*, accessed December 1, 2022, https://www.esafety.gov.au/educators/corporate-and-community-education/supporting-journalists-engage-safely-online.

24 L'Enfant, Anita, "Personal Interview."

25 See also: Diana Bossio, Valérie Bélair-Gagnon, Logan Molyneux, and Avery E. Holton, *The Paradox of Connection*. (University of Illinois Press, 2024).

26 Kristen Hare, "Meet the Woman Drowning Out Trolls that Harass Female Writers," *Poynter*. March 28, 2016, http://www.poynter.org/2016/meet-the-woman-drowning-out-trolls-that-harass-female-writers/.

12

CHAMPIONING A SECURITY-SENSITIVE MINDSET

Jennifer R. Henrichsen

The world is awash with rising populism and authoritarianism, democratic backsliding, and increasing political polarization. Within this environment, journalists are facing a variety of threats and challenges to their journalistic livelihood and role in a democratic society. In the United States, rhetoric against the media dramatically increased following the 2016 election of Donald Trump. Although Trump was no longer president as of 2021, "Trumpism," —a phenomenon that embodies the characteristics of nativism, populism, celebrity, and the outsider—continues to hold significant sway across the population[1] and has contributed to political enmity against the media. Journalists are also operating within a capitalistic system that provides additional challenges, such as precarious labor conditions, the ongoing commercialization of the media, and decreased trust in the media. The COVID-19 pandemic has exacerbated these concerns and has further entrenched inequalities of power and privilege.

Amidst this deleterious backdrop are intensifying digital challenges facing journalists and journalism. Digital threats like surveillance can operate passively or actively, implicating journalists' workflows, communications, and contacts. Digital attackers, including mobs, state, and parastate actors, can target journalistic accounts and devices through malicious software and hardware, exposing secrets and identities. Online harassers can overwhelm and traumatize journalists through mob censorship,[2] doxing, and other technical means. Digital attacks can also intersect with or contribute to offline harm, from threatening in-person messages to stalking and physical violence.

Tied to these concerns, but less overtly acknowledged or systematically studied by scholars and practitioners until recently, is a reduction in happiness among journalists working in the news industry. This chapter places happiness in journalism into the larger socio-political context that has garnered more

DOI: 10.4324/9781003364597-14

interest over the past years from scholars within journalism studies.[3] This chapter examines the intersection of journalist security and safety with the condition of happiness to proffer solutions at the individual and organizational levels, including vis a vis boundaries, mental models, and security champions, with the ultimate aim of contributing to journalistic happiness, safety, and security.

Attacks Against Journalists and their Repercussions for Journalistic Roles and Democracy

Digital and physical attacks have significant consequences for journalists and the practice of journalism in a democratic society. Online and offline harm can result in self-censorship among journalists,[4] limited digital publicity,[5] and self-censorship among journalistic sources who may be more hesitant to share.[6] Journalists broadly, and not only those covering traumatic events, are experiencing psychological trauma,[7] which can lead to decreased well-being, burn out, and "quiet quitting" or the idea of doing the bare minimum to keep one's job.[8] In some situations, online harm can lead to a complete departure from the profession—a dramatic escalation of censorship.[9] Online harm, such as harassment, can also affect journalistic autonomy, a necessary component of journalistic practice; implicating journalists' abilities to carry out their roles—which are often contested—in democratic societies.[10] Although often constrained in certain ways and under particular conditions, decreased journalistic autonomy alongside increased censorship negatively impacts journalism's role of holding powerful people and interests to account and contributes to an impoverished information society.[11] Violence against journalists also uncovers more widespread issues in democratic societies, such as weakened institutions that cannot guarantee rule of law or the right to free expression.[12]

The intensity and pervasiveness of attacks against journalists will likely continue to deepen and proliferate as technologies become more pervasive, intrusive, and inexpensive,[13] and as increased swaths of society engage with digital infrastructure and participate in political polarization.[14] In recent years, for example, harassment has spread its tentacles to ensnare journalists who write about innocuous subjects rather than traditionally polarizing political topics,[15] reflecting an expansion of digital reach and the immediacy of harms.

Reimagining Journalist Safety and Security to Contribute to Happiness

As the psychologist Abraham Maslow theorized in his 1943 paper, "A Theory of Human Motivation,"[16] people require certain basic needs to be met before higher needs can be pursued or achieved. Physiological needs like sleep and food need to be met before safety and personal security needs can be pursued. Once these two levels of basic needs have been fulfilled, humans are able to experience the third level of Maslow's hierarchy, which comprises love, belonging, and connection. Following this, they can experience respect, recognition, strength, and freedom. It is at this fourth level, the esteem level, that happiness can be experienced. At the final level, individuals achieve self-actualization or the desire to become the best version of oneself. Despite these concrete levels initially proposed by Maslow, the levels can overlap and are not completely discrete from one another.[17] Safety and security are needed in some capacity before individuals can reliably experience connection, esteem, and the closely associated phenomenon of happiness.

The phenomenon of happiness is not new. For centuries, numerous philosophers, from Plato to Bertrand Russell and Thoreau have examined the question of happiness. Religious figures like the 14th Dalai Lama, positive psychologists like Dr. Martin Seligman, and in recent years popular media figures like Oprah have expounded on and expanded our understanding of happiness.[18]

Happiness can take many forms and, in many cases, may feel complex, lofty, or intangible as a goal.[19] Happiness is dynamic and often ephemeral. It may be conceived of as an individual task, made possible by changing or adopting certain behaviors and mindsets, such as cultivating gratitude or being present. Happiness is subjective and idiosyncratic—what brings one individual (or journalist) happiness, may be anathema to another, and the ingredients for happiness may or may not be readily available or accessible. Despite these competing or overlapping characteristics present within the concept of happiness, it seems that nearly everyone, regardless of language or culture, aspires to happiness, aims to avoid suffering, and can cultivate happiness with purpose, practice, and effort.[20] Individuals are motivated to be happy, as evidenced by the growing field of positive psychology, the numerous books about happiness, and even college classes focused on happiness and well-being. Happiness not only generates benefits for individuals, but for families, communities, and society. Studies reveal that happy workers tend to be better workers and bring in higher profits, are more loyal, take fewer sick days, and generate greater customer satisfaction.[21] Happiness is also contagious and can lead to societal benefits because personal happiness can lead to kindness and compassion for others.[22]

Journalists, like the rest of us, aspire to be happy, and greater happiness among journalists could benefit communities and society. Following Maslow's Hierarchy of Needs, concerns related to safety and security must be addressed in advance or in tandem with concerns about happiness. Additionally, security and safety need to be addressed at the individual and organizational levels because organizations are composed of individuals who have practices and habits. Individual behavior also overlaps and intersects with organizational cultures and structures and must be considered within these contexts and confines. This chapter proposes specific recommendations to help improve journalist security, safety, and well-being, including developing spatial and temporal boundaries amidst context collapse, adopting a "security-sensitive" mindset, and deepening and expanding the roles of "security champions" in newsrooms.

Developing Spatial and Temporal Boundaries Amidst Context Collapse

As with other professions, the personal and professional worlds of journalists overlap, with *context collapse*, meaning when a social network site flattens multiple audiences into one, routinely occurring in the online environment.[23] Such context collapse has important implications for the safety and security of journalists, their connections, and their sources. Journalists may provide information about their personal lives, including photos, names of loved ones, or routinely visited locations on social media sites like Twitter or Facebook. Such sharing of personal information may humanize the individual journalist and contribute to their online persona and popularity, but it also can offer a roadmap for nefarious actors who wish to target journalists with harassment or release their personal information online through practices such as doxing.

One way to address this context collapse is by encouraging journalists to set boundaries temporally, such as by only engaging with social media channels during specific hours. Journalists could limit their engagement with their professional social media accounts when they are not working on or promoting a story, although they would likely need the support from their news organization to disengage (see also Chapter 8 on the concept of disconnective practices in journalism labor). Doing so could help to silo the pressures of continuous online engagement notorious within the norms of the journalism profession. To be successful at such temporal limits, however, journalists need the support of their news organizations, including those in management roles, to ensure they aren't intentionally or unintentionally penalized for setting such boundaries.

Journalists could also place limits on how they engage spatially in the digital arena. Harassers can leverage public information about journalists to attack them in private ways, including sending them misogynistic and racist threats through direct messages, text messages, or phone calls. To mitigate this hate and vitriol, journalists could use tools like BlockParty (a suite of anti-harassment tools that allow users to mute, block, and report vitriol on Twitter) or the TRFilter (an application which recognizes and flags harmful comments on Twitter), to set spatial boundaries around the content that they receive on social media platforms.

By archiving the hate and making a digital repository, journalists can be less distracted and distressed in the moment, but still access the content for prosocial means. For example, journalists can use a tool like BlockParty to create a boundary around the hate and separate it from their daily experience yet retain the messages in a digital archive for future examination and extraction. Doing so would allow journalists to continue using platforms like Twitter for its benefits (e.g., publicizing new stories and finding new sources), while keeping the barrage of hate-filled messages separate from their daily journalistic experience. Journalists could then create reports from the archive and share them with their news organization to raise awareness of the harassment and obtain the support they need to mitigate or prevent future abuse.

Adopting a "Security-Sensitive" Mindset

In addition to constructing temporal and spatial boundaries around harassment and doxing, journalists can adopt tools and practices that help to secure their online accounts, devices, and communications. These mechanisms include foundational, yet critical, tools and techniques like password managers, multi-factor authentication, and encrypted communication channels. These tools must fit journalists' workflows and be supported by management to be comprehensively adopted and integrated into news organizations.

More difficult, perhaps, is changing journalists' mindsets to be more attuned to security concerns.[24] Scholars have found two primary mental models among journalists and journalism educators that limit their engagement with digital security tools and techniques. McGregor and Watkins found that journalists have a "security by obscurity" mental model, where they believe security practices are irrelevant to them unless they are reporting on high profile national security stories.[25] I found that journalism educators and journalism students adhere to a "security by insularity" mental model, or a belief that journalism students' reporting is innocuous and not focused on sensitive topics; thereby rendering security practices irrelevant. Both mindsets are problematic because they contribute to the belief that security knowledge is not necessary in newsrooms or classrooms, despite increasing numbers of professional journalists[26] and now student journalists experiencing harassment[27] and the general lack of on-the-job anti-harassment or security training in news organizations.

To combat this reality, we need a "security sensitive" mindset in which journalists understand that they will be targeted online in myriad ways and for various reasons, including their background, their stories, their gender, and their sexual orientation. This mindset proposes that they need to take proactive steps at the individual and organizational levels to mitigate these harms. Such steps at the individual level could include becoming more open and curious about security and integrating specific security tools into their workflow, such as password managers, multi-factor authentication, and encryption by default.

A security sensitive mindset can be fostered and facilitated within news organizations by individuals known as "security champions" or individuals who believe security is important to journalistic practice and advocate for it in newsrooms.[28] Such security champions can live across news organizations, but they are often found initially among the investigative and national security desks, as reporters writing about sensitive stories traditionally have done the leg work of learning how to keep their communications and their sources confidential. Security champions help to foster the cross-pollination of security knowledge across the newsroom through knowledge sharing, advocacy, and by bringing external actors into the newsroom to share security-related expertise.

Expanding and Deepening the Roles of "Security Champions" in Newsrooms

To foster a "security culture" within a newsroom, it is important to have security champions throughout the organization, including at different levels of leadership. Doing so also requires a stronger commitment to diversity, equity, inclusion, and belonging because journalists who most frequently experience harassment tend to be journalists of color, female-identifying journalists, and journalists who are not hetero-normative.[29] Having champions at different levels allows a security sensitive mindset to be infused into policies, guidelines, and more general knowledge sharing.[30] When leaders within a newsroom have such a mindset, resources related to security needs are more likely to be allocated accordingly, contributing to a security culture. This, in turn, can benefit newsrooms, including by attracting and retaining diverse talent and by limiting financial repercussions from security-related incidents, such as ransomware.

Technological solutions for journalistic safety, security, and well-being

As efforts to improve diversity in newsrooms continue to build slowly and unevenly, newsroom leaders could take immediate steps to implement practical and technological solutions that could increase journalistic safety and security. There are many simple steps news organizations could take including offering informational and technological resources and partnering with technology companies to improve journalists' security, safety, and well-being.

One such step would be offering resources like DeleteMe, a service that removes personal content online, to journalists and if necessary, their immediate family members. Doing so could help reduce the information available to entities eager to harass journalists and their families and provide them more safety and security.[31] If a newsroom does not have the resources to provide this service to its reporters, it could offer a brown-bag lunch session that teaches reporters to do it themselves using open-source information from *The New York Times*.[32] A second step could involve news organizations providing password managers to their employees to encourage unique and complex passwords across devices and accounts. A third step could involve news organizations partnering with technology organizations that offer security services and tools to journalists for free or at a reduced price. Journalists wary or concerned about state-level attackers could sign up for Google's free Advanced Protection Program (APP) that helps protect journalists from sophisticated phishing attacks, malware, malicious downloads, and unauthorized access to their account data.[33] Google has also provided journalists with security keys to help them secure their online accounts from cybersecurity threats. The cybersecurity organization, CloudFlare, provides security to vulnerable groups like news organizations that are targets of distributed denial of service (DDoS) or other cyber-attacks through its service Project Galileo.[34]

Journalists and news organizations rely on technology companies' infra-structure and tools to carry out their day-to-day work. It is thus important that platforms are part of the solution when conceptualizing ways to improve journalists' security, safety, and well-being. In addition to content moderation tools like BlockParty and TRFilter, social media platforms could create automated tools to comprehensively identify trends in harassment which then necessitate human review.[35] Technology companies could strengthen outreach to news organizations and provide training on multi-factor authentication and other techniques to secure journalistic accounts. Some of the tensions that prevent news organizations from working toge-ther with technology companies may include a lack of awareness and prior-itization around journalistic security needs, limited resources (e.g., time, money, staff) for such engagement, and the desire to maintain autonomy (perceived or otherwise) from technology platforms. These obstacles could be overcome by internal and external actors highlighting the importance of security considerations to journalistic workflows and newsrooms' financial bottom lines and by organizations providing sliding scales for services to mitigate costs from shuttering conversations before they begin.

Policy solutions for journalistic safety, security, and well-being

Tools and technologies are not the only components of a more secure news-room. Policies related to digital security and social media are also important elements of a holistic security culture in newsrooms and security champions need to have a stronger role in creating and advocating for such resources. Policies related to digital security in newsrooms appear scarce, although empirical data on this topic is also lacking in scholarly and practitioner circles. More information is known about social media policies in newsrooms, but even these have come under fire in recent years. Nelson found that U.S.-based journalists feel that social media policies are not designed to mitigate harass-ment of journalists, but rather to maintain organizational credibility of the news organization.[36] Journalists reported that their organizations' social media policies provided little guidance and support to them after they experienced harassment and that the social media policies themselves were ambiguous and unequally enforced.

Despite this, journalists said they were encouraged to be genuine and active on social media platforms, but they were also discouraged from sharing any information that would affect the perception of the outlet's objectivity. Addi-tionally, women journalists and journalists of color said that despite being targets of harassment on social media, they were not sufficiently protected from abuse, and they were unfairly identified for using social media in ways that were supposedly contrary to an organizations' position of objectivity.[37] Therefore, there is a need among news organizations to account for this rea-lity in their social media policies. One way to do so is to conduct surveys about harassment in the newsroom and then use this data to inform policies, from content moderation guidelines to strategies for wellness.[38] Another way is to have newsroom leadership and security champions support the development and deployment of digital security policies in the newsroom and articulate the importance of these policies to their fellow journalists to ensure robust buy-in and utilization.

The Road Forward

The road ahead is a difficult one for journalists and news organizations. Both are facing unprecedented threats within a context of rising populism and nationalism, democratic backsliding, and political polarization. Adding to the struggle are macro-conditions facing newswork, including labor precarity, commercialization of the media, and decreased trust in journalism. Digital and physical attacks, from surveillance, spyware, and harassment to physical violence, have significant consequences for journalism, implicating journalists' role in a democratic society.

Despite these difficulties, journalists, news organizations, and platforms can take specific and concrete steps at the individual and organizational levels to mitigate the deleterious consequences of such a challenging environment. Developing spatial and temporal boundaries amidst context collapse, adopting tools, technologies, and a "security-sensitive" mindset, and fostering newsroom security cultures through "security champions," resource allocation, and policy development, are necessary components when reimagining journalist safety and security, and contributing to happiness in journalism.

These proposed solutions and their implementation will differ based on newsrooms' contexts and characteristics, including location, ethos, available resources, and mandate, among other considerations. Organizations facing more acute restrictions on press freedom will have more specific and immediate concerns to consider that need to reflect their socio-political contexts. At the same time, tools and technologies change and security considerations evolve. Just as there is no one-size-fits-all approach to security, the phenomenon of happiness is complex and multifaceted. Despite these considerations and limitations, there is significant room and need to improve journalist safety, security, and well-being.

Notes

1 David Edward Tabachnick, "The Four Characteristics of Trumpism," *The Hill*, January 5, 2016, http://thehill.com/blogs/congress-blog/presidential-campa ign/264746-the-four-characteristics-of-trumpism.
2 Silvio Waisbord, "Mob Censorship," *Digital Journalism* 8, no. 8 (2020): 1030–1046.
3 Valérie Bélair-Gagnon, Diana Bossio, Avery E. Holton, and Logan Molyneux, "Disconnection," *Social Media + Society* 8, no. 1 (2022), doi: 10.1177/ 20563051221077217.
4 Silvio Waisbord, "Antipress Violence and the Crisis of the State," *The Harvard International Journal of Press/Politics* 7, no. 3 (2002): 90–109.

5 Silvio Waisbord, "Trolling Journalists and the Risks of Digital Publicity," *Journalism Practice* 16, no. 5 (2022): 1–17.

6 FDR Group and PEN America, "Chilling Effects," 2013, http://www.pen.org/chilling-Effects; FDR Group and PEN America, "Global Chilling: The Impact of Mass Surveillance on International Writers," 2015, http://pen.org/global-chill; Human Rights Watch and American Civil Liberties Union, "With Liberty to Monitor All: How Large-Scale US Surveillance is Harming Journalism, Law, and American Democracy," 2014, https://www.hrw.org/sites/default/files/reports/usnsa0714_ForUPload_0.pdf.

7 Julie Posetti et al., "The Chilling," UNESCO, 2021,https://en.unesco.org/publications/thechilling.

8 Bélair-Gagnon, Bossio, Holton, and Molyneux, "Disconnection"; Jo Constantz, "Everyone is Talking about 'Quiet Quitting,' But is it a Good Idea?" *Seattle Times*, August 21, 2022, https://www.seattletimes.com/business/everyone-is-talking-about-quiet-quitting-but-is-it-a-good-idea/; Taylor Telford, "'Quiet Quitting' isn't Really about Quitting. Here are the Signs," *The Washington Post*, August 21, 2022. https://www.washingtonpost.com/business/2022/08/21/quiet-quitting-what-to-know.

9 Michelle Ferrier, "Attacks and Harassment," International Women's Media Foundation and TrollBusters, 2018, https://www.iwmf.org/wp-content/uploads/2018/09/Attacks-and-Harassment.pdf; Freedom House, "Chasing Stories, Women Journalists are Pursued by Trolls," 2017, https://freedomhouse.org/article/chasing-stories-women-journalists-are-pursued-troll.

10 Monica Löfgren Nilsson and Henrik Örnebring, "Journalism under Threat: Intimidation and Harassment of Swedish Journalists," *Journalism Practice* 10, no. 7 (2016): 880–890.

11 Grant Penrod, "A Problem of Interpretation," *The News Media & the Law* 28, no. 4 (2004): 4. https://www.rcfp.org/journals/the-news-media-and-the-law-fall-2004/problem-interpretation/.

12 Waisbord, "Antipress Violence and the Crisis of the State," 90–109.

13 Ron Deibert, "Digital Threats against Journalists." In *Journalism After Snowden* eds. Emily Bell and Taylor Owen, (New York: Columbia University Press, 2017), 240–257. doi: 10.7312/bell17612.

14 Henrichsen and Shelton, "Expanding the Analytical Boundaries of Mob Censorship," *Digital Journalism* 14 September (2022). https://doi.org/10.1080/21670811.2022.2112520.

15 Patrick Egwu, "In a Nation Polarized by COVID-19, Canadian Women Journalists Suffer Online Abuse," Reuters Institute, July 26, 2022, https://reutersinstitute.politics.ox.ac.uk/news/nation-polarised-covid-19-canadian-women-journalists-suffer-online-abuse.

16 Abraham H. Maslow, "A Theory of Human Motivation," *Psychological Review* 50, no. 4 (1943): 370–396. doi: 10.1037/h0054346.

17 Louis Tay and Ed Diener, "Needs and Subjective Well-Being around the World," *Journal of Personality and Social Psychology* 101, no. 2 (2011): 354–365. doi: 10.1037/a0023779.

18 Gretchen Rubin, *The Happiness Project*. (New York: HarperCollins, 2018).

19 Rubin, *The Happiness Project*.

20 Dalai Lama XIV Bstan-Ḍdzin-rgya-mtsho and Howard C. Cutler, *The Art of Happiness* (10th anniversary). (New York: Riverhead Books, 2009).

21 Bstan-'dzin-rgya-mtsho and Cutler, *The Art of Happiness*.

22 Bstan-'dzin-rgya-mtsho and Cutler, *The Art of Happiness*.

23 Danah m. Boyd, "Why Youth <3 Social Network Sites," in *Youth, Identity, and Digital Media* ed. David Buckingham. (Cambridge, MA: MIT Press, 2008), 119–142.

24 Jennifer R. Henrichsen, "Breaking through the Ambivalence," *Digital Journalism* 8, no. 3 (2020), 328–346: doi: 10.1080/21670811.2019.1653207.

25 Susan E. McGregor and Elizabeth Anne Watkins, "'Security by Obscurity'" *International Symposium on Online Journalism* 6, no. 1 (2016). https://isojjournal.wordpress.com/2016/04/14/security-by-obscurity-journalists-mental-models-of-information-security/.

26 Jennifer R. Henrichsen, Michelle Betz, and Joanne M. Lisosky, *Building Digital Safety for Journalism* (Paris: UNESCO Publishing, 2015); Henrichsen and Shelton, "Expanding the Analytical Boundaries of Mob Censorship;" Julie Posetti et al., "The Chilling."

27 Meg Heckman, Myojung Chung, and Jody Santos, "'This isn't what the Industry Should Look Like Anymore'," *Teaching Journalism & Mass Communication* 12, no. 2 (2022): 14–24. http://www.aejmc.us/spig/journal.

28 Jennifer R. Henrichsen, "Understanding Nascent Newsroom Security and Safety Cultures," *Journalism Practice* 16, no. 9 (2021): 1829–1848. doi: 10.1080/17512786.2021.1927802.

29 Julie Posetti et al., "The Chilling."

30 Henrichsen, "Understanding Nascent Newsroom Security and Safety Cultures."

31 Henrichsen and Shelton, "Expanding the Analytical Boundaries of Mob Censorship."

32 Kristen Kozinski and Neena Kapur, "How to Dox Yourself on the Internet," The NYT Open Team, February 27, 2020, https://open.nytimes.com/how-to-dox-yourself-on-the-internet-d2892b4c5954.

33 Google, "Google's Strongest Security Helps Keep Your Private Information Safe," 2022, https://landing.google.com/advancedprotection/.

34 Cloudflare, "Cloudflare Cyber Security Protection for At-Risk Sites," 2022, https://www.cloudflare.com/galileo/.

35 Henrichsen and Shelton, "Expanding the Analytical Boundaries of Mob Censorship."

36 Jacob L. Nelson, "A Twitter Tightrope Without a Net," *Columbia Journalism Review* (2021). https://www.cjr.org/tow_center_reports/newsroom-social-media-policies.php.

37 Nelson, "A Twitter Tightrope Without a Net."

38 Susan E. McGregor, *Information Security Essentials.* (New York: Columbia University Press, 2021).

13

JOB CONTROL AND SUBJECTIVE WELL-BEING IN NEWS WORK

Víctor Hugo Reyna

Over the course of the last decade, journalism scholars globally explored job satisfaction, burnout, and turnover in journalism.[1] Through their work, the field of journalism studies acknowledged the centrality of journalists' subjective well-being and sought to identify new ways of enhancing it. This edited volume on happiness in journalism is part of that trend. This chapter proposes to move away from the question "what drives the job dissatisfaction, burnout and turnover of news workers?" and instead ask "what drives or could drive their happiness and overall well-being?"

A number of journalism researchers use the notion of control to explain the nature of news work in organizational settings and the reasons for the rise in turnover intentions and actual turnover in journalism.[2] Despite the theoretical differences between their studies, these academics offer us a strategy for addressing subjective well-being in news work: if a lack of control over the labor process and career paths is a factor in news workers' job dissatisfaction, burnout and turnover, perhaps its opposite—a surplus of control—could contribute to their happiness.

This chapter establishes a relationship between the concepts of job control and subjective well-being to explore the question of journalists' happiness. Defined as the "workers' ability to actually influence what happens in their work environment,"[3] job control is widely studied and measured as a factor in the psychological and physiological well-being of workers in different industries. In this chapter, we theorize job control as a precondition of the subjective well-being of news workers, as it could contribute to job satisfaction and work–life balance, allowing these professionals to recover from their workday and to engage in whichever activities that make them happy (leisure and recovery).

The chapter is organized into two sections. The first section reviews the literature on job satisfaction in journalism to identify factors that contribute to

DOI: 10.4324/9781003364597-15

journalists' subjective well-being. The second develops a conceptual framework for the study of happiness in journalism from a labor perspective, with job control as an independent variable. The purpose of this framework is to rethink the well-being of news workers beyond the notions of journalistic autonomy and job satisfaction. This could help news workers and concerned decision-makers to introduce a process of change in their news organizations as part of efforts to nourish the subjective well-being of those who make the news.

Job Satisfaction in Journalism Studies

Job satisfaction and subjective well-being are not synonyms. The former refers to "the degree to which employees are contented with their job,"[4] and the latter is defined as "[p]eople's assessment of the overall quality of their lives."[5] This means that while one is restricted to contentment in the labor sphere, the other refers to happiness in life in a broader sense. Nevertheless, as work occupies one third of a person's day, spillover theory has linked job satisfaction to subjective well-being under the premise that contentment in the labor sphere could have a positive or spillover effect on the overall quality of a worker's life.[6]

Although job satisfaction in news work has been researched since the 1960s,[7] our literature review has not identified a single study on the subjective well-being of journalists. We found a master's thesis centered on professional identities and boundary work titled *Satisfaction and Journalism: A Study of Newsroom Happiness and its Implications in Print Design*[8] and an edited volume that proposes the development of mindful journalism from a Buddhist perspective in order to bring "amity and sanity in the world community."[9] However, we were unable to find studies focused on the well-being of news workers beyond the labor sphere.

As spillover theory suggests that job satisfaction can contribute to the subjective well-being of workers,[10] in this section we briefly review recent studies on journalists' job satisfaction to identify factors that could enhance their psychological and physiological well-being. As Table 13.1 shows, journalism scholars have identified several factors that produce job satisfaction in news workers. These range from journalistic autonomy[11] to job stability[12] and work–life balance.[13]

Factors specific to journalism such as the business and professional goals and priorities of news organizations,[14] reporting for their communities,[15] and performing the adversarial role of the press[16] have also been included in surveys to measure what makes journalists in particular content with their jobs. Likewise, leadership,[17] being part of a process of change,[18] scooping the competition[19] and even emotional intelligence[20] have been studied as predictors of job satisfaction in news workers.

This trend acknowledges that the enactment of professional ideals is key for journalists, and can encompass not one, but several variables. Previous studies

TABLE 13.1 Job Satisfaction in Journalism Studies

Author(s)	Findings
Beam (2006)	The business and professional goals and priorities of news organizations matter as journalists tend to be more satisfied with their jobs if they perceive that their employers value good journalism.
Beam and Spratt (2009)	Leadership and empathy can be predictors of job satisfaction in news workers and can help them stay committed to their organizations and careers even after traumatic experiences.
Chan, Pan, and Lee (2004)	Having a clear role, either against or in favor of economic and political elites, drives job satisfaction in journalists because it erodes ambiguity and produces job autonomy within a specific social function.
Chen, Chang, Cheng, and Ma (2011)	Emotional intelligence can help news workers to manage stress at work and can produce job satisfaction and organizational commitment by helping them to put problems in perspective.
Deprez and Raeymaeckers (2012)	Job stability is a predictor of job satisfaction in journalists as both the type of contract (freelance or employed on a permanent basis) and the job function stand out in a context of ambiguity and uncertainty.
Ireri (2016)	Job security and job autonomy are the main predictors of job satisfaction in journalism as news workers tend to prioritize having a job and the opportunity to put their ideals into practice over salaries.
Lim (2013)	Authority, scooping the competition and the perceived quality of the news organization that they work for drive job satisfaction among journalists by giving them a daily sense of accomplishment.
Lucht (2015)	Organizational factors play an important role in news workers' attitudes towards and perceptions of their work because job satisfaction is triggered both by working conditions and the opportunities for growth.
Massey and Elmore (2011)	For female freelance journalists, work–life balance is more important than income. Those who leave traditional employer-based news jobs for freelancing tend to prioritize raising their children.
Massey and Ewart (2012)	Being part of a process of organizational change can produce job satisfaction in news workers by making them part of a process of change of values and routines that aims at improving the quality of the news output.
Powers (2006)	Leadership behaviors are related to job satisfaction and openness to organizational change because they provide a sense of certainty in a process of uncertainty.
Reinardy (2011)	Job security, job quality and organizational commitment are significant, positive predictors of job satisfaction in journalism, while new roles and new responsibility might create an uncertain environment.

Author(s)	Findings
Reinardy (2014)	Job autonomy, organizational support and the quality of journalism influence journalists' job satisfaction because, altogether, they make them feel that they are backed in the production of the news that they consider relevant.
Ryan (2009)	Autonomy and freedom usually produce job satisfaction in news workers even if they have to develop adaptive strategies to react to the temporary or per diem labor patterns emerging in the news industry.
Stephens and Natoli (2022)	Community service, understood as reporting for their communities, contributes to journalists' job satisfaction by giving them authority and responsibility and making their work more meaningful.
Xiaoming, George and Lang (2013)	Autonomy and the adversarial role of the press drive job satisfaction in countries with high political parallelism while monetary reward and job security are not as relevant for their news workers.

on the job satisfaction of news workers have been limited to applying standardized questionnaires without including variables specific to the nature of work in the field of journalism. This explains, at least partially, why most of the studies find that autonomy is what regulates the job satisfaction of journalists. However, they do not discuss what having or not having autonomy implies in an organizational setting. Hence, broader theorizations are needed.

Job Control and Subjective Well-Being in News Work

Journalistic autonomy—the "professional principle among journalists that they should not be swayed by interested parties,"[21] —is restricted to the occupational sphere of journalism, to the sphere of collegial power among news workers.[22] Given that it sits outside of the organizational sphere of journalism, where news is actually made, and refers to the right to publish without the intrusion of actors external to journalism (as guaranteed by political constitutions and professional statutes), it can be quite limited as a predictor of job satisfaction or subjective well–being. This is because a number of factors such as working conditions and work–life balance mediate these variables beyond freedom of the press.

By contrast, the notion of job control, meaning a worker's capacity of influence in their workplace,[23] is organizational and has more to with how things are done in the newsroom than with occupational ideals and collegian power. Also, it is not limited to the right to publish without the intervention of interested parties and includes the analysis or measurement of a variety of methods and tasks, quality, quantity and pace of work, methods of supervision, salaries and schedules, and other variables.[24]

Thus, studying job control as a predictor of journalists' subjective well-being makes much more sense than addressing it through journalistic autonomy. This is due to its organizational character and because it comprises several variables that stem from the worker's perceived capacity of influence. This does not mean that job control makes journalistic autonomy irrelevant. Rather, it suggests that the former regulates the latter, among other variables, by describing influence over decision-making.

In journalism, journalistic autonomy,[25] community reporting,[26] scooping the competition,[27] performing the adversarial role of the press,[28] organizational priorities,[29] job stability,[30] and work–life balance[31] have been identified as drivers of job satisfaction. These drivers fit under the theoretical umbrella of job control, as their organizational enactment depends on the capacity of influence of those who perform them.

In an ideal world, a journalist can publish whatever they consider relevant. No organizational news values are opposed to their vision. It all depends on their criteria. They can define their own methods and tasks, as well as the quality, quantity, and pace of their work, not to mention their salaries and schedules. In the real world, however, a news worker must always negotiate what is and what is not news, their contract and working conditions, and the organization of work. Given that news is not produced in an ideal world, we must study its workers from real world anthropological, psychological, and sociological perspectives.

Following spillover theory's premise, in this chapter we describe a model for examining the relationship between job control and subjective well-being in news work. Within this model, job control is the independent variable, while job satisfaction, work–life balance and leisure and recovery are the dependent variables. We are aware that job satisfaction, work–life balance and leisure and recovery have diverse validated scales for research and diagnosis that would make this model too complex for empirical analysis, but we also believe that the intersection of these variables drives or could drive journalists' subjective well-being.

Our argument is built upon an extensive review of studies on job satisfaction in journalism and our fieldwork in Mexico. As previous studies have stressed, news work is unique because it has an idealistic component that mediates job satisfaction. Regardless of the degree of contentment that professionals may have with news production, work–life balance and leisure and recovery are important for the overall quality of news workers' lives. These professionals are not only news makers. They are individuals with various identities and life contexts who need time to perform other social roles or to do whatever makes them happy.

If the variety of methods and tasks and the quality, quantity and pace of work can be related to job satisfaction, giving journalists some leverage over how their labor is conducted, supervision, salaries and schedules can be associated with work–life balance, as they would enable news workers to have more free time. These professionals continuously report that they are overworked and underpaid, particularly in emerging democracies.[32] This suggests that they do not have a work–life balance or the means to change the conditions of their field. Even those who are happy in the labor sphere,[33] lack equilibrium in the private sphere.

Passion,[34] community reporting,[35] and performing the adversarial role of the press[36] can produce job satisfaction, but they can also wear out if they are not supported by boundaries—making it the achievement of a certain form of work–life balance. As work and stress scholars remark, work–life balance is relevant not only because it allows workers to carry out other social roles, but because workers need time to recover from after–work fatigue.[37]

How can news workers include work–life balance in their lives and ensure that they have sufficient time for leisure and recovery? Job control is a key factor. If concerned decision-makers, journalists and even journalism scholars become aware of the centrality of the capacity to influence overall decision-making as a predictor of job satisfaction and subjective well-being, they can collectively push for its increase. However, if what persists is the idea that the psychological and physiological well-being of journalists depends only on the right to publish without the intrusion of external actors, they and we will contribute to the social reproduction of adverse working conditions.

Gaining or conceding job control does not necessarily imply a dramatic change in news organizations. Rather, it involves modifying the hierarchical chains of command and strict division of labor that still characterize many of these outlets around the world. If those who make the news feel that they are included in decision-making and that their well-being is important beyond their productivity, they will feel content in their jobs and become happier.

What makes journalists happy beyond their occupation? Is it spending time with their loved ones? Hobbies? Random acts of kindness? Is it scrolling through pictures of cats and dogs? Or is it brunching spicy *chilaquiles* on Sundays? As happiness scholars have suggested, we may need to move from the quantitative study of subjective well-being and embrace a more holistic approach to happiness.[38] Perhaps what we need is not a standardized questionnaire, but an opportunity to observe precisely what makes news workers happy. The task is arduous but will be worthy if we can achieve a new understanding of the well-being of those who make the news.

Conclusion

This chapter established a relationship between job control and subjective well-being to delve into the issue of happiness among journalists. In doing so, it proposes a shift away from the notions of journalistic autonomy and job satisfaction in the interests of gaining conceptual precision. Unlike journalistic autonomy, job control is not limited to the right to publish without the intrusion of interested parties, and it involves variables related to labor relations, working conditions and the organization of work.[39] This makes it an overarching concept that can help us study and push for the well-being of news workers beyond satisfaction with their news output.

In future studies, we will refine the model outlined in this chapter to address the scope and the limitations of job control as a precondition of journalists' subjective well-being and happiness. Some questions that we did not tackle in this chapter include: Which factors enhance or inhibit the development of this ability? How can news workers, concerned decision-makers and even journalism scholars push for an increased capacity of influence of those who make the news? And what would a quest for a work–life balance imply in a culture of work overload? These and other questions must be answered if researchers want to contribute more significantly to the subjective well-being and happiness of journalists.

Notes

1 Roei Davidson and Oren Meyers, "Should I Stay or Should I Go?" *Journalism Studies* 17, no. 5 (2016): 590–607, https://doi.org/10.1080/1461670X.2014. 988996; Scott Reinardy, "Newspaper Journalism in Crisis: Burnout on the Rise, Eroding Young Journalists' Career Commitment," *Journalism* 12, no. 1 (2011): 3–50, https://doi.org/10.1177/1464884910385188.

2 Nick Mathews, Valérie Bélair–Gagnon and Matt Carlson, "'Why I Quit Journalism'," *Journalism*, https://doi.org/10.1177/14648849211061958; Henrik Örnebring, "The Two Professionalisms of Journalism," accessed September 25, 2022, https://reutersinstitute.politics.ox.ac.uk/sites/default/files/2017–11/The %20Two%20Professionalisms%20of%20Journalism_Working%20Paper.pdf; Víctor Hugo Reyna, "'This is my Exit Sign': Job Control Deficit, Role Strain and Turnover in Mexican Journalism," *Journalism Practice* 15, no. 8 (2021): 1129–1145. https://doi.org/10.1080/17512786.2020.1776141.

3 Daniel C. Ganster, "Autonomy and Control," accessed January 6, 2022. https:// www.iloencyclopaedia.org/part–v–77965/psychosocial–and–organizational–factors/ factors–intrinsic–to–the–job/item/18–autonomy–and–control.

4 Andrew M. Colman, "Job Satisfaction." In *A Dictionary of Psychology* ed. Andrew M. Colman, (Oxford: Oxford University Press, 2015).

5 Andrew M. Colman, "Subjective Well–Being." In *A Dictionary of Psychology* ed. Andrew M. Colman, (Oxford: Oxford University Press, 2015).

6 Glenn Medallon Calaguas, "Satisfied and Happy," *Asia Pacific Journal of Multidisciplinary Research* 5, no. 1 (2017): 104–111.

7 Neil V. McNeil, "The Washington Correspondents," *Journalism Quarterly* 43, no. 2 (1966): 257–263, https://doi.org/10.1177/107769906604300206.

8 Rachel Schallom, "Satisfaction and Journalism" (Master's thesis, University of Missouri, 2012).

9 Shelton A. Gunaratne, "Introduction." In *Mindful Journalism and News Ethics in the Digital Era* eds. Shelton A. Gunaratne, Mark Pearson, and Sugath Senarath, (New York: Routledge, 2015), 1–17.

10 Calaguas, "Satisfied and Happy," 104–111.

11 Kioko Ireri, "High Job Satisfaction Despite Low Income," *Journalism and Mass Communication Quarterly* 93, no. 1 (2016): 164–186. https://doi.org/10.1177/ 1077699015607334.

12 Joseph Man Chan, Zhongdang Pan, and Francis L. F. Lee, "Professional Aspirations and Job Satisfactiondia," *Journalism & Mass Communication Quarterly* 81, no. 2 (2014): 254–273, https://doi.org/10.1177/107769900408100203; Annelore Deprez and Karin Raeymaeckers, "A Longitudinal Study of Job Satisfaction among

Flemish Professional Journalists," *Journalism and Mass Communication* 2, no. 1 (2012): 235–249.

13 Tracy Lucht, "Female Employees find Iowa Newspaper Jobs Satisfying," *Newspaper Research Journal* 36, no. 4 (2015): 426–440, https://doi.org/10.1177/0739532915618410; Scott Reinardy, "Autonomy and Perceptions of Work Quality Drive the Job Satisfaction of TV News Workers," *Journalism Practice* 8, no. 6 (2014): 855–870, https://doi.org/10.1080/17512786.2014.882481.

14 Randal A. Beam, "Organizational Goals and Priorities and the Job Satisfaction of U.S. Journalists," *Journalism and Mass Communication Quarterly* 83 no. 1 (2006): 169–185, https://doi.org/10.1177/107769900608300111.

15 Elizabeth Jane Stephens and Rosanna Natoli, "Pressure, Compromise and Overwork," *Journal of Applied Journalism & Media Studies*, 2022, https://doi.org/10.1386/ajms_00076_1.

16 H. Xiaoming, Cherian George and Shi Cong, "Job Satisfaction of Journalists: Professional aspirations, newsroom culture and social context" *Media Asia* 40, no. 1 (2013): 73–84,. https://doi.org/10.1080/01296612.2013.11689952.

17 Randal A. Beam and Meg Spratt, "Managing Vulnerability," *Journalism Practice* 3, no. 4 (2009): 421–438, https://doi.org/10.1080/17512780902798653.

18 Brian L. Massey and Jacqui Ewart, "Sustainability of Organizational Change in the Newsroom," *International Journal on Media Management* 14, no. 3 (2012): 207–225, https://doi.org/10.1080/14241277.2012.657283.

19 Jeongsub Lim, "The Relationships of Online Journalists' Emotional Responses to Competitors with Job Satisfaction, Workload, and Perception of the Quality of the News," *Asian Journal of Communication* 23, no. 2 (2013): 209–224, https://doi.org/10.1080/01292986.2012.725177.

20 Chun–Hsi Vivian Chen et al., "Emotional Intelligence in the Workplace," *Furen Management Review* 18, no. 3 (2011): 1–18, https://doi.org/10.29698/fjmr.201109.0001.

21 Daniel Chandler and Rod Munday, "Journalistic Autonomy." In *A Dictionary of Media and Communication* eds. Daniel Chandler and Rod Munday, (Oxford: Oxford University Press, 2020).

22 Julia Evetts, "The Sociology of Professional Groups: New Directions," *Current Sociology* 54, no. 1 (2006): 133–143, https://doi.org/10.1177/0011392106057161.

23 Ganster, "Autonomy and Control."

24 Deborah J. Dwyer and Daniel C. Ganster, "The Effects of Job Demands and Control on Employee Attendance and Satisfaction," *Journal of Organizational Behavior* 12 (1991): 595–608, https://doi.org/10.1002/job.4030120704.

25 Ireri, "High Job Satisfaction Despite Low Income," 164–186.

26 Stephens and Natoli, "Pressure, Compromise and Overwork."

27 Lim, "The Relationships of Online Journalists' Emotional Responses," 209–224.

28 H. Xiaoming, Cherian George and Shi Cong, "Job Satisfaction of Journalists," 73–84.

29 Beam, "Organizational Goals and Priorities," 169–185.

30 Chan, Pan, and Lee, "Professional Aspirations and Job Satisfaction," 254–273.

31 Lucht, "Female Employees find Iowa Newspaper Jobs Satisfying," 426–440.

32 Evelyn Daniela Caminos, "El Mundo del Trabajo y la Precariedad Laboral de los Comunicadores y Periodistas," *Revista de Estudio de Derecho Laboral y Derecho Procesal Laboral* 2, no. 2 (2020): 27–38, https://doi.org/10.37767/2683-8761(2020)002.

33 Ireri, "High Job Satisfaction Despite Low Income," 164–186.

34 Carl–Gustav Lindén et al., "Journalistic Passion as Commodity," *Journalism Studies* 22, no. 12 (2021): 1701–1719, https://doi.org/10.1080/1461670X.2021.1911672.

35 Stephens and Natoli, "Pressure, Compromise and Overwork."

36 H. Xiaoming, Cherian George and Shi Cong, "Job Satisfaction of Journalists," 73–84.

37 Achim Elfering et al., "Cortisol on Sunday as Indicator of Recovery from Work," *Work & Stress* 32, no. 2 (2018): 168–188, https://doi.org/10.1080/02678373.2017.1417337.

38 Sunny Jeong and Orneita Burton, "Happiness on Your Own Terms." In *The Routledge Companion to Happiness at Work*, ed. Joan Marques, (New York: Routledge, 2020), 23–36.
39 Dwyer and Ganster, "The Effects of Job Demands and Control," 595–608.

PART III

STEPS AND PRACTICES TOWARD HAPPINESS

14

COGNITIVE DISSONANCE IN JOURNALISTIC TRAUMA

Danielle Deavours

Previous research suggests workplace happiness can be conceptualized and measured at multiple levels, including stable individual, subjective-level attitudes, and collective memory of events, and with respect to multiple foci, such as discrete events, the job, and the organization.[1] At the individual level, happiness is subjective feelings about well-being. Subjective well-being is "an umbrella term used to describe the level of well-being people experience, according to their subjective evaluations of their lives."[2] These evaluations can be positive or negative, and they affect how satisfied individuals feel about "work, relationships, health, recreation, meaning and purpose, and other important domains."[3] Individuals with high subjective well-being tend to enjoy their work more, and are better evaluated by supervisors for productivity, dependability, creativity, and overall work quality.[4]

At the organizational level, workplace happiness, which is conceptualized as pleasant employee emotions, personal and organizational well-being, and positive attitudes about the workplace, is critical for individual employee and organizational health.[5] Failure to address discontent, negative emotions, and poor sense of well-being often leads to individual work inefficiency, organizational disruption and turnover, and disinterest in a particular organization or even an entire industry. Organizational policy changes and attention to systemic issues are often keys to addressing cognitive dissonance experiences at work.[6] This chapter seeks to understand how journalists cognitively work to regain individual and organizational happiness, despite encountering deeply negative experiences regularly.

Journalistic work is demanding, not only physically with long shifts, heavy equipment, and potentially dangerous or even life-threatening fieldwork, but also mentally as journalists experience trauma and harassment in daily practice. Many studies suggest repeated exposure to crises and harassment are among

DOI: 10.4324/9781003364597-17

the leading causes for burnout and turnover in the newsroom.[7] Broadcast journalists experience crises in a realistic way, getting closer to scenes for visuals and watching footage continually while editing;[8] broadcasters face more frequent and severe harassment cases compared to print journalists.[9] As more news operations require crisis coverage and participation in online forums exposing individuals to harassers, researchers and practitioners need to better understand how journalists are able to continue their work with professional happiness perceptions and well-being while experiencing trauma.

Through the concept of cognitive dissonance—the process by which individuals reconcile internally inconsistent perspectives to existing belief systems to perform more effectively and efficiently—this chapter outlines the ways journalists are utilizing dissonance resolution techniques to cope with workplace harassment and trauma to create a subjective sense of workplace happiness. The chapter proposes solutions for unhealthy coping techniques, such as ignoring, only positive focus, and diminishing negatives, and encourages change through collaboration of individual journalists, newsroom leadership, owners, and professional associations.

Happiness at Work

Trauma as routine

The journalism maxim, "if it bleeds, it leads," suggests media reliance on trauma and crisis in everyday work. As a result, many experience vicarious traumatization, when crisis workers feel empathetic connections to clients and their traumas,[10] experiences that not only diminish workplace happiness but can have lasting mental health effects.

Vicarious traumatization has been widely studied among first responders, such as police, firefighters, and EMS. However, journalists who arrive on disaster scenes at the same time as other first-responders and witness the same levels of tragedy also experience vicarious traumatization, "a form of post-traumatic stress response experienced by people who are indirectly exposed to traumatic events."[11] Research suggests between 80 to 100 percent of journalists have been exposed to a work-related traumatic event. Journalists, particularly broadcasters, report often witnessing these traumas first-hand, rewatching them continuously in the editing and playback process, and reading traumatic, unredacted official reports.[12]

Trauma theory from psychology suggests first responders who experience vicarious traumatization experience a decrease in their efficiency and effectiveness while working, such as not following police protocol when working a scene.[13] While trauma theory typically centers around counselors and first responders and does not typically recognize journalists, researchers suggest they experience the same roles, witnessing, and routines as first responders because of their exposure to the same scenes, victims, and aftermath of crises.[14] Like first responders, research suggests journalists experiencing vicarious traumatization may suffer in professional practices, from not following journalistic routines, breaking objectivity,[15] losing nonverbal neutrality control,[16] and/or not being able to continue work at all. These findings suggest real impacts on news products, a threat organizationally. While most trauma research has focused on how crises affect journalists' practices, little research has been done on how socio-political contexts may contribute.[17]

Journalists aren't recognized as first responders, thus not receiving the same resources for trauma and recognition despite having similar experiences. Research shows newsrooms are often not supporting journalists' mental health after disasters, meaning many are left without training or resources when affected. Yet, few journalists report trauma, discuss it, or visit mental health professionals. Without proper ways to deal with trauma consequences, journalists may be forced to continually experience trauma without utilizing healthy coping mechanisms.[18]

Harassment as commonplace

Journalists also regularly experience trauma first-hand through violence (physical injury done to a person or their property), intimidation (verbal or physical threats focused on a person's work as a journalist), and harassment (aggressive verbal or physical actions because of personal characteristics).[19] Reporters Without Borders reports, "Never before have U.S. journalists been subjected to so many death threats or turned so often to private security firms for protection."[20] Previous studies have found journalists are regularly subjected to online abuse when interacting with audiences on social media, especially women, Black, indigenous and BIPOC, LGBTQIA+, and younger journalists.[21] Researchers have found journalists routinely do not report harassment, do not feel trained to do so, and do not feel protected by their organizations through prevention policies.[22]

Cognitive dissonance of trauma-based journalistic experiences

Cognitive dissonance, the process by which individuals reconcile internally inconsistent perspectives to existing belief systems in order to perform more effectively and efficiently,[23] creates cognitive discomfort through neural activity in the left frontal cortex, where anger is centered, when beliefs about a subject do not align.[24] Professionally, unresolved cognitive dissonance can lead to issues with mental health and worker efficiency.[25] When a person is forced to keep doing something conflicting with their previous ideology, psychosociological discomfort results,[26] and dissonance must be resolved.[27] Common dissonance resolution tactics include changing behaviors, increasing the value of the desired belief while diminishing the rejected belief's value, adding new belief systems, and avoiding the trigger.[28] Dissonance is manageably reduced or resolved when the coping strategy allows the individual to have aligning belief systems.[29] Once alignment is perceivably and subjectively achieved, even temporarily, journalists' happiness is more likely to occur.[30]

With colleagues, I explored journalists' experiences of cognitive dissonance after experiencing harassment online with audience members, and found journalists report psychological discomfort after experiencing online harassment while having to continue reciprocal journalism practices at work.[31] Journalists reported extreme cases of audience harassment, including stalking, death threats, and sexual threats being sent to reporters. Yet, participants, including those who had recently left the industry, resolved dissonance in favor of continuing the practice, deciding reciprocal journalism benefits outweighed their experiences with harassment. If left unresolved, the journalists may not be able to do basic job functions. Journalists felt they had very little efficacy to resolve the situation except to accept harassment as normal, and all journalists noted there was little to no organizational resources available for them to utilize.[32]

Researchers also found journalists uphold potentially trauma-inducing routines and practices, such as getting too close to a crisis event to get visuals, interviewing victims about their traumatic experiences, ignoring or normalizing trauma as integral to journalist's work.[33] This is both conscious and learned behavior.[34] Journalists actively ignore trauma feelings because they don't want to deal with emotional and professional challenges regularly or seem weak. It is also learned behavior, where fellow journalists display this tough exterior, don't ask for help, and treat these negative experiences as a "badge of honor." As scholars and practitioners seek to understand how journalists can continue working in trauma-filled environments, they must explore the motivations behind the dissonance resolution strategies and why certain strategies for dealing with harassment may be favored over others.

Common Resolution Tactics

Media studies find common dissonance resolution tactics from psychology also apply to journalism. Across trauma studies,[35] common themes emerge for resolution strategies used by journalists who experience trauma or harassment, including modifying the interactions, added belief systems, focusing on the positives, and ignoring the pain.

Modifying the interactions

Research suggests journalists tend to react to trauma by making slight alterations to their behaviors to prevent future instances. This is also a common coping strategy in cognitive dissonance, such as cutting back on smoking or quitting altogether after learning the health risks.[36] Some researchers find journalists who experience recurring trauma will experience burnout and leave the industry,[37] modification stopping exposure, resulting in fewer journalists working. Others report they change beats, most common among war correspondents and political reporters.[38] Yet, studies show journalists often don't stop the traumatic practice altogether, showing resilience despite the experience.[39] Instead, journalists make smaller adjustments, such as setting up stronger social media privacy settings or taking breaks from an activity (usually one or two days) to "clear their head," although journalists are hesitant fearing seeming incapable or unprofessional.[40]

These practices[41] have chilling effects on press freedom, including "mob censorship," a hesitancy to cover certain topics or to continue reporting as normal due to fear of trauma or harassment.[42] It puts resolution onus on the individual without organizational help. Disconnective practices help the individual remove triggering trauma or harassment stimuli; research shows it is not effective long term, particularly when only enacted by the individual without organizational support, since the stimulus can't be removed as professional expectations don't change.[43]

Added belief systems

Another common tactic is adding a new belief system to rationalize the action's negative impacts.[44] For instance, smokers may add a belief that a short life filled with smoking's pleasures is better than a long life without it. Journalists used this coping strategy by believing trauma and harassment are normal, expected aspects of journalistic work. Participants in previous studies describe laughing about seeing dead bodies, threatening messages, or even having guns pointed at their heads because these traumas are so commonplace. Others describe it as a "badge of honor," a way to distinguish one's service.[45] Trauma is often considered a taken-for-granted journalistic practice,[46] and by adding this normalization belief, journalists diminish trauma's personal impact.

Another added belief is rationalization of harassers' actions and victim blaming. Many journalists describe online harassers' actions as acting out or 'silly talk,' essentially justifying harassment through perspective-taking.[47] Other journalists suggest journalists make themselves vulnerable to attack by what they say, wear, and how they present themselves to viewers, a form of victim blaming.[48] These added rationalization belief systems allow individuals to diminish negative trauma effects. They're operating at individual levels, however, not having organizational or industry level support.

Focusing on the positives or purpose

Journalism studies literature cites a sense of purpose or focusing on journalistic work's positives as coping tactics. An example from cognitive dissonance is a smoker who focuses on the stress-relieving benefits, while diminishing the health risks of tobacco use. Novak and Davidson found while journalists experience negative traumas, journalists with a strong sense of meaning and purpose workwise were more likely to perceive those traumas as less negative.[49] Research shows journalists report not reflecting on trauma because they are focusing on getting work done and their work's importance. This often fosters a false sense of workplace happiness, as the employee is ignoring the issue. It can help with mental cognition and trauma perceptions, but if those traumas compound and increase severity, positive focus falters as a dissonance tool.[50]

Beyond a purpose-driven, positive outlook, journalists cited benefits of experiencing trauma. Some say trauma experiences are "worth it" when recognized by newsroom leaders, colleagues, and professional associations with praise, higher ratings, and awards for crisis coverage,[51] all forms of fostering workplace happiness. By focusing on these benefits to trauma, journalists diminish negatives and thus resolve dissonance. The industry and society often help formulate what purpose, meaning, and benefits would be perceived as professionally important, but it must be enacted and believed on an individual level to be effective.

Ignoring the pain

A common journalistic dissonance tactic is ignoring issues, consciously or subconsciously. Cognitive dissonance scholars suggest ignoring the contrary belief works temporarily but is ineffective long-term.[52] For example, pretending the health warnings about smoking aren't there won't prevent a smoker from developing lung cancer. Journalists report consciously ignoring trauma's negative effects. One journalist in my study on crisis reporting described purposefully pretending to perceive the dead body at a scene as a mannequin to continue working.[53] Mostly it is an unconscious action, the unwillingness to deal with the psychological discomfort it creates, pushing it deeper down instead of dealing with it head-on. Research shows journalists would describe harassment as "no big deal," "silly," or "meaningless," while recounting minute details about incidents that happened a decade ago.[54] Even if the journalist has decided to ignore the pain, it does not mean it does not have an impact.

This coping is heavily influenced by industry expectations. Journalists describe dealing with traumas and harassment as wearing a mask, having to hide their feelings to appear strong and unaffected because they believe that's what the industry expects. Journalists say it was easier to brush aside those feelings the longer they were in the industry. Veteran journalists may have an easier time developing the "thick skin" some journalists describe when it comes to trauma because they have had more strategy implementation. As researchers and practitioners consider solutions, it is important to consider ways to protect younger, novice journalists and how to overcome veteran journalists' built-up resiliency. This is particularly nuanced as older generations are less likely to openly discuss and even be aware of mental well-being.[55] Ignoring the pain is not a healthy way of fostering workplace happiness because it involves ignoring the issues threatening happiness by diminishing their perceived value.

Moving Beyond Unhealthy Coping Patterns

Current cognitive dissonance resolution tactics seen in journalism studies are unhealthy and unmaintainable coping mechanisms, according to psychologists. Festinger notes ignoring the dissonance, focusing only on positives, adding belief systems that diminish the negatives, and modifying only the dissonance-inducing behavior are not long-term solutions.[56] Cognitive dissonance and sociological research on workplace happiness suggest that until the dissonance-inducing issue reduces or disappears, individuals will have to continually go through the mental processing of discomfort, which can lead to issues including burnout, perceived work inefficiency, and mental health issues.[57] For instance, smokers do not stop having cognitive dissonance struggles until they fully quit tobacco use, and the more they are around tobacco, the harder it will be for them to stop its use. The emotional labor this takes to create workplace happiness will eventually outweigh its outcome, and true discontent will surface.

Instead, psychologists suggest dissonant beliefs must be examined and modified to create lasting change. For smokers, these resolution tactics aren't likely to help them quit. Instead, reconciling dissonance requires acknowledging serious smoking risks, while simultaneously recognizing the challenges of abruptly stopping tobacco use, thus using nicotine patches, weaning, etc.[58] Similarly, the most common dissonance resolution tactics for journalistic trauma are too short-sighted and focused on individuals creating protection, rather than organizational change.[59]

Systemic cooperation of individuals, organizations, and the industry is critical to solving dissonance. For instance, journalists speaking out against using one-man-bands, where a single person is reporter, camera operator, engineer, etc. When there is no other person with the multimedia journalists, the danger and exposure to traumatic or harassing events increases. While cost-efficient for newsrooms, recent events (such as WSAZ's Tori Yorgey being hit by a car on live television) are causing individuals and organizations to re-examine policies.[60] Professional associations like the non-profit media institute and newsroom Poynter, the Dart Center for Journalism & Trauma, and the Society of Professional of Journalists provide safety guidelines for owners and newsrooms to balance individual safety, organizational duty for protection, and efficient work. Being able to contribute to solutions also fosters workplace happiness perceptions, allowing individuals, collectives and organizations to strive.

Civil society actors like Trollbusters and others are calling for organizations to take more responsibility in protecting journalists from online vitriol. After recent incidents of journalists speaking out about harassment by viewers as well within their newsrooms, particularly in the wake of #MeToo, many advocacy groups like PEN America, Freedom Forum, and others are calling for organizations to provide more cybersecurity training, support, legal and mental health counseling. Others like Poynter and Freedom Forum critique journalism educators for remaining silent on industry prevalent problems, encouraging academics to bring awareness and solutions in the classroom as it may bleed subsequently in newsrooms. To create lasting changes, individuals, newsrooms, and industry organizations must work together to find online work that also protects individuals from harm collectively.

Journalists can be resistant to change. Just as the smoker is initially resistant to giving up what they may consider their small pleasure, journalists often feel reluctant to support organizational policies they perceive as threatening their rights to a free press.[61] Collaborative solutions are thus necessary. Journalists should not be worried about normative repercussions of speaking out against online harassment, allowing the false veil of happiness to come down so true workplace happiness can be rebuilt in its place.

Research shows the best dissonance resolution happens through organizational interventions. Novak and Davidson suggest newsrooms and academic classrooms must provide training facilitating social support networks and meaningful coping mechanisms with mental health professionals.[62] Others suggest journalists need to feel management's support to seek mental health resources, challenge the status quo, and look for safer practices.[63] Currently journalists report receiving little to no training in coping with trauma or harassment, and they are not hopeful such change will ever happen in newsrooms.[64]

Journalists believe newsrooms are too finance-focused, considering the bottom line more important than the individual's safety. Yet, organizations suffer economically and culturally when dissonance resolution is not prioritized, as it leads to employee burnout, poor attitude, and resignation. Replacing and training new employees is expensive, financially, and culturally, and research suggests newsrooms that hosted workshops on mental health had a 40 percent decline in turnover.[65] Findings suggest budgetary investments in workplace happiness may be worth it.

Despite hopelessness expressed by some journalists, there are many ongoing conversations in professional and academic associations around the world about the need for trauma response in journalism fields. The Dart Center hosts training on trauma.[66] The Freedom Forum created workplace integrity training to build newsroom cultures free from harassment, discrimination, and incivility.[67] More academic researchers are seeking to better understand how to help journalists, meaning increased awareness and available solutions to improve the status quo, such as increased attention to mental health, a key goal of this chapter and textbook at large. Even if change may be possible, the road there may be long and rocky.

Notes

1 Cynthia D. Fisher, "Happiness at Work," *International Journal of Management Reviews* 12, no. 4 (2010): 384–412, https://doi.org/10.1111/j.1468-2370.2009.00270.x.
2 Ed Diener and Kathryn Ryan, "Subjective Well-Being," *South African Journal of Psychology* 39, no. 4 (2009): 391, https://doi.org/10.1177/008124630903900402.
3 Diener and Ryan, "Subjective Well-Being," 391.
4 B.M. Staw, R.I. Sutton, and L.H. Pelled, "Employee Positive Emotion and Favorable Outcomes at the Workplace," *Organization Science* 5 (2004): 51–71, https://doi.org/10.1287/orsc.5.1.51.
5 Fisher, "Happiness at Work," 384–412.
6 Lyumbomirsky S., L. King, and E. Diener, "The Benefits of Frequent Positive Affect," *Psychological Bulletin* 131, no. 6 (2005): 803–855.
7 Nilsson, M. L. and H. Örnebring, "Journalism Under Threat," *Journalism Practice* 10, no. 7 (2016): 880–90, DOI: 10.1080/17512786.2016.1164614; Natalee Seely, "Journalists and Mental Health," *Newspaper Research Journal* 40, no. 2 (2019), 239–259, https://doi.org/10.1177/0739532919835612.
8 Jasmine B. MacDonald, Rachel Fox, and Anthony J. Saliba, "Contextualizing Psychological Outcomes for TV News Journalists," *Journal of Constructivist Psychology* 35, no. 1 (2022): 255–279, https://doi.org/10.1080/10720537.2020.1809579.
9 Kaitlin C. Miller and Seth C. Lewis, "Journalists, Harassment, and Emotional Labor," *Journalism* 23, no. 1 (2022): 79–97, DOI:10.1177/1464884919899016.
10 Kathleen M. Palm, Melissa A. Polusny, Victoria M. Follette, "Vicarious Traumatization," *Prehospital and Disaster Medicine* 19, no. 1 (2014): 73–78, DOI: 10.1017/s1049023x00001503.
11 Palm et al., 73–78.
12 Isobel Thompson, *The Dart Center Style Guide for Trauma-Informed Journalism.* (New York: Dart Center, 2021): https://dartcenter.org/resources/dart-center-style-guide.
13 Andrew Phipps and Mitchell Byrne, "Brief Interventions for Secondary Trauma: Review and Recommendations," *Stress and Health* 19 (2003): 139–147, https://doi.org/10.1002/smi.970.
14 S. Collins and A. Long, "Too Tired to Care? The Psychological Effects of Working with Trauma," *Journal of Psychiatric and Mental Health Nursing* 10 (2003): 17–27, DOI: 10.1046/j.1365-2850.2003.00526.x.
15 R. Coleman and D. Wu, "More Than Words Alone," *Journal of Broadcasting & Electronic Media* 50, no. 1 (2006): 1–17.
16 Danielle Deavours, "Nonverbal Neutrality Norm: How Experiencing Trauma Affects Journalists' Willingness to Display Emotion," *Journal of Broadcast and Electronic Media* 67, no. 1 (2023): 112–134, https://doi.org/10.1080/08838151.2022.2151600.
17 Pamela J. Shoemaker, and Steven D. Reese, *Mediating the Message in the 21st Century: A Media Sociology Perspective.* (New York, NY: Taylor & Francis, 2014).
18 Deavours, "Nonverbal Neutrality Norm," 112–134.
19 Susan Drevo, "The War on Journalists," (Doctoral dissertation, University of Tulsa, 2016).
20 Reporters without Borders, *Worldwide Round-up of Journalists Killed, Detained, Held Hostage, or Missing in 2018,* (Paris: Reporters Without Borders, 2018), https://rsf.org/sites/default/files/worldwilde_round-up.pdf.

21 Gina M. Chen et al., "'You Really Have to Have a Thick Skin'," *Journalism* 21, no. 7 (2018): 877–895, https://doi.org/10.1177/1464884918768500.
22 Deavours et al., "Reciprocal Journalism's Double-Edged Sword," *Journalism* (2022): 1–20.
23 Leon Festinger, *A Theory of Cognitive Dissonance.* (Redwood City, CA: Stanford University Press, 1957).
24 Eddie Harmon-Jones, "Contributions from Research on Anger and Cognitive Dissonance to Understanding the Motivational Functions of Asymmetrical Frontal Brain Activity," *Biological Psychology* 67, no. 1 (2004): 51–76, DOI: 10.1016/j.biopsycho.2004.03.003
25 Amanda S. Hinojosa et al., "A Review of Cognitive Dissonance Theory in Management Research," *Journal of Management* 43, no. 1 (2016): 170–199, https://doi.org/10.1177/0149206316668236
26 Harmon-Jones, "Contributions from Research on Anger and Cognitive Dissonance," 51–76.
27 L. Festinger, *Conflict, Decision, and Dissonance.* (Redwood City, CA: Stanford University Press, 1964).
28 Festinger.
29 Joan Lindsey-Mullikin, "Beyond Reference Price," *Journal of Product & Brand Management* 12, no. 3 (2003): 140–153, DOI:10.1108/10610420310476906.
30 Fisher, "Happiness at Work," 384–412.
31 Deavours et al., "Reciprocal Journalism's Double-Edged Sword," 1–20.
32 Avery E. Holton et al., "Not Their Fault but Their Problem."
33 Deavours, "Nonverbal Neutrality Norm," 112–134.
34 Deavours, 112–134.
35 Deavours et al., "Reciprocal Journalism's Double-edged Sword," 1–20.
36 Festinger, *Conflict, Decision, and Dissonance.*
37 Nilsson, and Örnebring, "Journalism under Threat," 880–90.
38 Waisbord, 2000.
39 Deavours, "Nonverbal Neutrality Norm," 112–134; Deavours et al., "Reciprocal Journalism's Double-Edged Sword," 1–20; Smith, Newman, Drevo, and Slaughter, *Covering Trauma.* (2015). https://dartcenter.org/content/covering-trauma-impact-on-journalists.
40 Deavours et al., "Reciprocal Journalism's Double-Edged Sword," 1–20.
41 Diana Bossio, Valérie Bélair-Gagnon, Avery E. Holton and Logan Molyneux, *The Paradox of Connection* (2024, University of Illinois Press).
42 Waisbord, S. "Mob Censorship," *Digital Journalism* 8, no. 8 (2020): 1030–1046. DOI: 10.1080/21670811.2020.1818111.
43 Hinojosa et al., "A Review of Cognitive Dissonance Theory," 170–199.
44 Festinger, *Conflict, Decision, and Dissonance.*
45 Deavours et al., "Reciprocal Journalism's Double-Edged Sword," 1–20.
46 Deavours, "Nonverbal Neutrality Norm," 112–134.
47 Renae M. Hayward, and Michelle R. Tuckey, "Emotions in Uniform: How Nurses Regulate Emotion at Work via Emotional Boundaries," *Human Relations* 64, no. 11 (2011): 1501–1523, https://doi.org/10.1177/0018726711419539.
48 Deavours et al., "Reciprocal Journalism's Double-Edged Sword," 1–20.
49 Novak, R. J. and S. Davidson, "Journalists Reporting on Hazardous Events," *Traumatology* 19, no. 4 (2013): 1–10. https://doi.org/10.1177/1534765613481854.
50 Deavours, "Nonverbal Neutrality Norm," 112–134; Hinojosa et al., "A Review of Cognitive Dissonance Theory," 170–199.
51 Deavours, "Nonverbal Neutrality Norm," 112–134.
52 Festinger, *Conflict, Decision, and Dissonance.*
53 Deavours, "Nonverbal Neutrality Norm," 112–134.
54 Deavours et al., "Reciprocal Journalism's Double-Edged Sword," 1–20.

55 American Psychological Association, 2018. Stress in America. https://www.apa.org/news/press/releases/stress/2018/stress-gen-z.pdf.
56 Festinger, *Conflict, Decision, and Dissonance.*
57 Harmon-Jones, "Contributions from Research on Anger and Cognitive dissonance," 51–76.
58 Festinger, *Conflict, Decision, and Dissonance.*
59 Holton and Bélair-Gagnon, Bossio and Molyneux, "'Not Their Fault, but Their Problem.'"
60 Brian Stelter, "Local TV Journalists Voice Concerns about One-Man-Band Reporting," *CNN*, January 27, 2022, https://www.cnn.com/2022/01/27/media/local-tv-journalists-concern-reliable-sources/index.html.
61 Deavours et al., "Reciprocal Journalism's Double-Edged Sword," 1–20.
62 Novak and Davidson, "Journalists Reporting on Hazardous Events," 1–10.
63 Beam, R. A. and M. Spratt, "Managing Vulnerability," Journalism Practice 3, no. 4 (2009): 421–438. DOI: 10.1080/17512780902798653.
64 Deavours, "Nonverbal Neutrality Norm," 112–134.
65 Michelle McLellan, and Tim Porter, "Newsroom Training," *Nieman Reports* 61, no. 3 (2007): 90–91.
66 Dart Center, "Resources," Dart Center for Journalism and Trauma, n.d. https://dartcenter.org/resources.
67 Freedom Forum, "Workplace Integrity Training."

15

SAFER VOX POPS AND DOOR KNOCKING

Kelsey Mesmer

Vox pop interviews and door knocking are common reporting techniques used by journalists. They are also stressful and dangerous, because little is known about the person being approached.[1] With vox pops, a reporter either approaches people on the street[2] in hopes of interviewing them about a topic of broad interest to gauge public opinion or shows up unannounced to a potential source's home and knocks on their door. These techniques can be problematic given their impromptu nature and the lack of prior knowledge about the potential source, allowing for more frequent interactions with people who might vilify the news media or otherwise pose a threat to reporters because of their sexist, racist, homophobic or other harmful beliefs. Thus, these reporting practices have become a source of stress for journalists, especially for women and Black, indigenous and journalists of color (BIPOC), LGBTQIA+ journalists, younger journalists, journalists who speak English as a second language, and those who hold other (or multiple) non-dominant identities.[3] This uncertainty and the possibility of hostility that can arise when utilizing these reporting methods are therefore adding to declines in the subjective well-being and happiness of journalists.[4] More stringent organizational policies regarding these practices can help erase or greatly ease that stress. Prior research has found journalists are already finding creative—but sometimes problematic—ways to mitigate hostility when tasked with vox pop interviews,[5] so it stands to reason that being proactive by assigning less of these interviews and putting safety measures in place when vox pops and door knocking are necessary would decrease reporters' stress and promote more happiness overall.

Happiness is broadly described as the feeling of positive emotions, such as joy and contentment, with a "happy person" being "a person who frequently experiences positive emotions relative to negative ones."[6] When happiness is

DOI: 10.4324/9781003364597-18

conceptualized in the workplace, those positive or negative experiences are connected to workplace experiences, job roles, and routines. These experiences may be related to the overarching organization and its culture, the job itself, or discrete events,[7] such as a particular journalist–source interaction.

Building on scholarship regarding hostility in journalism and toward journalists, this chapter outlines the problematic nature of vox pop interviews and door knocking and seeks to establish safer reporting strategies. While acknowledging that these reporting practices are sometimes necessary, best practices are discussed for individual reporters and newsroom editors to ensure reporters' safety and increase overall well-being on the job. These reporting techniques are important to reconsider in climates of media distrust and hostility not only from a safety perspective, but also from an organizational standpoint. Research suggests that career success is often correlated and preceded by higher levels of employee happiness,[8] making happiness essential for journalists' productivity and retention.

Hostility and Impromptu Sourcing as a Problematic Practice

Hostility toward journalists and the news media in general has increased globally over the last decade,[9] both online and offline,[10] and many recent studies have documented frequent and salient hostility toward journalists in the United States.[11] Hostility is broadly defined as "unwanted abusive behaviors,"[12] including verbal abuse and threats, physical assault, sexual harassment and sexual assault, and other behaviors perceived by the journalist as threatening, dangerous or making them feel uncomfortable. It can occur online or offline, with online hostility often having tangible offline consequences, such as online doxing, the practice of publicizing someone's personal information, including addresses and phone numbers, which can lead to stalking and threats made at reporters' homes and/or directed at their loved ones.

Scholars have created typologies to describe the various forms of hostility journalists may experience. Focusing on harassment stemming from people outside of the newsroom, defined as "readers, viewers, and strangers," Miller identified three categories of harassment:[13]

1. Incivility and disruptive harassment, including a journalist having their appearance made fun of, having someone trying to embarrass them or rudely interrupt an interview or stand-up
2. Sexual harassment, including being touched inappropriately, sent graphic sexual photos and being stalked
3. Personally, attacking harassment, including being threatened, physically attacked or doxed.

In this chapter I examined hostility from sources and potential sources (people approached for an interview, whether or not they agreed to participate in a news story) and identified four forms of hostility experienced by journalists:[14]

1. General distrust of the news media, including anti-media rhetoric and accusations of being biased
2. Boundary crossing, in which sources would break professional norms by contacting reporters at all hours, incessantly and via non-work channels, or would post about the journalist online, often to berate the reporter
3. Safety-violating hostility, including sexual harassment and assault, physical threats, and assault
4. Microaggressions, which are subtle offensive statements made during otherwise normal conversations that attack aspects of the reporter's identity.

Approaching someone unannounced at their home or on the street increases the chance that a reporter unknowingly approaches someone who is armed or someone who may harass them. That harassment can often be racial and/or gendered, so that journalists of color and/or women are more likely to be harassed by people who hold racist and sexist beliefs. Also, there are often few or no onlookers during these types of journalist–source interactions, especially when door knocking, creating opportunities for hostility and related safety concerns. In interviews with journalists who had experienced hostility from sources, research found:

> [R]eporting door-to-door or, for that matter, any type of person-on-the-street reporting was often problematic and led to potentially dangerous interactions. [A journalist] explained, "You just never know who's on the other side of the door, which is why I really don't know why they keep telling us to go out and do them, because I think it's dangerous." Nevertheless, many journalists engaged in this common reporting practice, usually at the request of their editors.[15]

The journalist found herself temporarily locked in a source's house while door knocking. The man had been pleasant and agreed to do an interview on camera with her when it started raining, so he invited her in. Immediately his demeanor changed, and he locked his door, standing between her and the exit. Although the reporter was able to leave unharmed, she said she was terrified and thought about the encounter when embarking on similar assignments.

Journalists have also been threatened when knocking on people's doors. One case made national news in 2014 when a man pulled a gun on a reporter working for a news station in Houston, Texas.[16] The intended source was a crime suspect, and a producer had asked the reporter to show up at his house to try to get a statement for a sound bite. Afterward, the station's news director issued an order stating that reporters would no longer be asked or allowed to door-knock on crime suspects seeking comment and that door knocking for other sources is also strongly discouraged because of the associated risks.

Without connecting their reasoning to hostility, Beckers found journalists generally despise conducting vox pop interviews and don't believe they add value to news stories.[17] Rather, they include vox pops when no other sources are available or when asked to by an editor or producer. The job of collecting vox pops is therefore often handed to newer reporters and interns, meaning those with the least amount of experience might be put in more hostile situations with sources. Furthermore, hostility is largely normalized in journalistic work[18] and journalists rarely report hostility to their supervisors. If they do report hostility, they often find their supervisors and the organization at large does not provide adequate support or know how to help them in tangible ways.[19]

Hostility and intersectionality

Miller and I argue that hostility is an intersectional issue, as it is largely context-based. Aspects of journalists' identity, such as their perceived gender, race, and age,[20] as well as their professional identity as journalists, locate them at the center of multiple sites of oppression.[21] As such, the potential for hostility is increased for women journalists and men and women journalists of color, especially when reporting on contentious topics. In Mesmer's study, she heard stories from an Indian American woman who found herself in an unsafe situation when she asked a man on the street about his views on former U.S. President Trump's immigration ban, and a Black woman who encountered hostility while reporting on a business owner who had hung a caricature of former U.S. President Barack Obama from a noose in their storefront. However, hostility isn't always tied to story topics and can arise not only for politized topics, but also for human interest stories. In many cases, the reporter's identity has the potential to create unique opportunities for hostility when the journalist is reporting in the field alone.[22]

Young women found themselves in situations where they were alone with men who cornered them, temporarily blocking them from the exit, making them feel unsafe and sometimes sexually harassing or assaulting them. A Black reporter said the police were regularly called on him when he had to door-knock for assignments.[23] While these examples didn't always result in physical harm, they did produce psychological harm, causing fear and anxiety that often manifested in subsequent reporting scenarios.[24] Both Miller and I found journalists thought about or intended to quit the journalism field because, at least in part, of their experiences with hostility.[25]

Alternative Reporting Strategies

Since hostility cannot be avoided in the journalism field, reporters and news-room leaders can take steps to mitigate or better prepare for hostile encounters. Strategies range from small changes in sourcing habits, to more sustained efforts to gain control during hostile encounters.

Sourcing through social media

One solution that can improve reporters' safety and increase their happiness in the profession is to use informed sourcing practices by utilizing the affordances of social media. While using social media to find sources is by no means a new practice,[26] using it in lieu of vox pop interviews would lessen the chance that a reporter encounters hostility in a face-to-face source interaction. Since vox pop interviews are usually conducted as a means of including community members' opinions on a topic, reporters can utilize online spaces such as Facebook groups, Twitter, Snapchat and TikTok to connect with people who are already talking about the topic they are reporting on. Hostility can still be—and often is—encountered by journalists online in social media spaces,[27] but by *strategically* joining and connecting with groups and leaders in their own communities, reporters can ensure they are still finding local sources in lieu of roaming the streets to talk with community members.

While an exchange over social media or a phone call with a source found online may be all a reporter working for a print or online news outlet needs, journalists working for broadcast or radio stations will likely still need to meet sources face-to-face to record audio and video interviews. This is why vox pop interviews are more commonly used by radio and broadcast reporters.[28] In those cases, reporters using social media to find sources who are interested in talking with them will have to set up a time and place to hold the interview, but they would have already started building rapport with a source and connected with someone who has agreed in advance to do an interview, two things that would lessen the chance for hostility in the following face-to-face journalist–source interaction. If looking to do vox pop interviews at an event, such as a protest or festival, reporters can utilize Facebook and Instagram Live, or utilize hashtags on Twitter, to find people nearby who may be interested in talking with them. These tactics are commonly used by journalists already,[29] however they should be considered as ideal from a safety standpoint when given the choice between online sourcing and conducting traditional vox pop interviews.

Preparing scripts in response to hostility

Inevitably, reporters are going to encounter a source who doesn't like or trust the news media and uses hostile, anti-media rhetoric toward them. This may occur during door knocks, vox pop interviews or other reporting methods. To prepare for this hostility, journalists can create hypothetical scenarios that they might find themselves in and practice responses for each scenario. Rather than simply disengaging or getting frustrated in the moment, reporters can prepare short "scripts" that they can draw from to work through hostility, a common tactic used by journalists who have learned to overcome anti-media rhetoric from sources.[30] Items to add to these scripts may include an explanation of how interviews are recorded, how facts are verified and why it is important to include the source's full name in the story. Reporters might also prepare to share more information about the story they are working on, such as why it is newsworthy and the other types of sources they are including in the article. Illuminating these "rules of engagement" may make untrusting sources feel more comfortable about being included in a story, since most people have never interacted with a journalist and do not understand what the job entails.[31]

Learning when to abandon the scene and how to protect yourself

Hypothetical scenarios to practice working through, like those mentioned above, should also involve more serious forms of hostility, such as verbal threats or safety violations. It would not be unreasonable for journalists to seek out basic self-defense courses, and recommendations have been made for newsrooms to sponsor safety trainings for their staff.[32] After finding them-selves in one unsafe situation, some reporters started carrying pepper spray to give them peace of mind.[33] Safety trainings stress the importance of having situational awareness, not only when approaching potentially unsafe situations, but as a constant practice. Rather than sticking with a story, "If you feel something isn't right, make a decision [to escape] and don't second guess."[34] However, since journalists are often instilled with the idea that the story matters above all else, they may be hesitant to walk away from a story for fear of losing their editor's respect and trust.

This may require a conscious reframing of priorities so that reporters put their well-being above getting a quote or visuals for a story. Journalists may also seek out safety resources from organizations such as the Dart Center for Jour-nalism and Trauma, Society of Professional Journalists (SPJ), Investigative Reporters and Editors (IRE), Committee to Protect Journalists (CPJ), and United Nations Educational, Scientific and Cultural Organization (UNESCO), which all provide free, online resources as well as virtual courses and workshops. The Radio Television Digital News Association provides safety training specifi-cally for broadcast journalists, who face specific challenges related to their heightened visibility and equipment.[35]

A Call to Newsroom Leadership

Since individual reporters may not feel empowered to turn down an assign-ment or to walk away from a story that proves to be unsafe, it is the respon-sibility of newsroom editors and producers to explain that journalists should prioritize their safety and well-being at all costs, even when a story is on the line. Based on the literature, this point is not emphasized—enough but sometimes at all—and therefore many journalists feel obligated to compro-mise their safety in the pursuit of news and future career success. Indeed, many journalists said they felt compelled to take on story assignments they were uncomfortable with because they feared there would be negative career-related consequences if they turned it down or came back empty handed.[36]

This mentality is dangerous and needs to shift, and one place where that shift can begin is with newsroom managers telling new staff members on day one—making it overtly clear—that no story is worth a journalists' safety, happiness, and well-being. Safety should be a routine topic of discussion when story planning, so reporters and photographers have an opportunity to voice their concerns before going out into the field. Editors who believe door knocking or vox pops are necessary for a story should prioritize reporters' well-being by ensuring journalists report in pairs, so they have support. Sending a reporter to knock on someone's door on their own can be a recipe for disaster.

There has been a recent, and much needed, push to create structural and cultural change within newsrooms at the organizational level to address sys-temic problems, one of which is harassment and hostility.[37] Given the nor-malization of hostility[38] and tensions surrounding the discussion of hostility with supervisors and a lack of attention to employees' long-term mental health,[39] editors and other members of newsroom and station leadership should work to change the culture of their organizations so that support is available and journalists feel comfortable discussing concerns with their supervisors. This is easier said than done and will likely take time, but one step toward this goal would be for editors and producers to embody a feminist ethic of care within the newsroom, which promotes a culture of mutual sup-port and caring for others.[40] This perspective would normalize things like mental health check-ins, regular access to therapists, and open, routine dialo-gue about safety, well-being, and staff members' overall happiness. And much like policies on how to handle online harassment would be strengthened and more useful if younger, more diverse people were writing those policies,[41] so too would be policies on risky reporting scenarios, since those are the repor-ters more likely to be affected by those policies. Moreover, as discussed in Chapter 11 of this volume, these systemic changes would help fulfill "the 'duty of care' that news organizations have considering those challenges."[42]

While there have been applications of the ethic of care in the study of journalism, with calls for it to be enacted when reporters and photographers are interacting with sources and communities, when choosing stories to pursue,[43] and in private, online groups among women journalists with communal motivations offering others gendered professional support,[44] the ethic of care has not been explored at the newsroom level. There is reason to believe that the enactment of feminist ethics would improve workplace satisfaction overall, whether a journalist is dealing with hostility, trauma, or mental health issues. For example, open communication and teamwork increased in a newsroom when women were installed as leaders.[45] Departing from the masculine values and communication practices embedded within most U.S.-based newsrooms[46] would promote more open and empathic dialogue about the harsh realities and challenges associated with journalism, potentially making it less likely that early-career journalists will leave the profession, and foster happiness throughout their career.

In sum, individual reporters and newsroom leadership need to find strategic and supportive ways to prioritize reporters' safety in the field. Hostility toward journalists shows no signs of lessening, and the job can be dangerous.[47] Therefore, to retain staff and attract new journalists to the profession, more risky reporting strategies need to shift accordingly so reporters feel safer on the job. Vox pop interviews and door knocking are just two examples of reporting practices that cause reporters stress and compromise their safety. Adopting policies and protocols with safety and journalistic well-being in mind can have positive effects on reporters' overall job satisfaction and happiness in the field.

Notes

1 Kelsey Mesmer, "An Intersectional Analysis of U.S. Journalists' Experiences with Hostile Sources," *Journalism and Communication Monographs* 24, no. 3 (2022): 181.
2 Kathleen Beckler, "Vox Pop in the News," *Communications* 43, no. 1 (2017).
3 Mesmer, "An Intersectional Analysis," 157.
4 Mesmer, "An Intersectional Analysis," 199.
5 Kelsey Mesmer, "An 'Assumption of Bad Faith'," *Journalism Practice*. DOI: 10.1080/17512786.2022.2086158.
6 Lisa C. Walsh, Julia K. Boehm, and Sonja Lyubomirsky, "Does Happiness Promote Career Success?" *Journal Of Career Assessment* 26, no. 2 (2018): 200.
7 Cynthia. D. Fisher, "Happiness at Work," *International Journal of Management Reviews* 12, no. 4 (2010): 384.
8 Walsh, Boehm, and Lyubomirsky, "Does Happiness Promote Career Success?" 207.
9 Julie Posetti et al., "Online Violence Against Women Journalists," United Nations Educational, Scientific And Cultural Organization, 2020; International Press Institute, "Rising Violence Against Reporters in the U.S," January 29, 2021.
10 Michelle Ferrier, "Attacks and Harassment," International Women's Media Foundation, September 2018, 11.
11 Gina Masullo Chen, "'You Really Have to Have a Thick Skin'," *Journalism* 21, no. 7 (2020): 884; Kaitlin C. Miller, "Harassment's Toll on Democracy," *Journalism Practice* 17, (2021); Kaitlin C. Miller, and Seth C. Lewis, "Journalists, Harassment, and Emotional Labors," *Journalism* 23 no. 1 (2022): 93.
12 Kaitlin C. Miller, "Hostility Toward the Press," *Digital Journalism* 4 (2021).
13 Miller, "Harassment's Toll on Democracy," 9.
14 Mesmer, "An Intersectional Analysis," 173–174.
15 Mesmer, "An Intersectional Analysis," 182.

16 Al Tompkins, "No-Knock Policy Bars TV Station Staff From Rapping On Crime Suspects' Doors," Poynter, April 7, 2014.
17 Beckers, "Vox Pop in the News," 9.
18 Kaitlin C. Miller, "The 'Price You Pay' and the 'Badge of Honor'," *Journalism and Mass Communication Quarterly*, (2022): 17.
19 Danielle Deavours et al., "Reciprocal Journalism's Double-Edged Sword," *Journalism* 0, no. 0 (2022): 13–14, https://doi.org/10.1177/14648849221109654; Avery E. Holton, Valérie Bélair-Gagnon, Diana Bossio, and Logan Molyneux, "'Not Their Fault, But Their Problem': Organizational Responses to the Online Harassment of Journalists," *Journalism Practice*, (2021): https://doi.org/10.1080/17512786.2021.1946417: 11.
20 Mesmer, "An Intersectional Analysis," 157.
21 Miller, "Hostility Toward the Press," 13.
22 Mesmer, "An Intersectional Analysis," 182.
23 Mesmer, "An Intersectional Analysis," 181.
24 Mesmer, "An Intersectional Analysis," 181–182.
25 Miller, "Hostility's Toll on Democracy," 10.
26 Yonghwan Kim, Youngju Kim, Yuan Wang, and Na Yeon Lee, "Uses and Gratifications, Journalists' Twitter Use, and Relational Satisfaction with the Public," *Journal of Broadcasting and Electronic Media* 60, no. 3 (2016): 509; Christoph Neuberger, Christian Nuremberg, and Susanne Langenohl, "Journalism as Multichannel Communication," *Journalism Studies* 20 no. 9 (2019): 1262–1263.
27 Posetti et al., "Online Violence Against Women Journalists," 2.
28 Beckers, "Vox Pop in the News," 8.
29 Kim, Kim, Wang, and Lee, "Uses and Gratifications, Twitter Use," 509.
30 Mesmer, "An Assumption of Bad Faith," 14–15.
31 Mesmer, "An Assumption of Bad Faith," 11.
32 Council Of Europe, "How to Protect Journalists and Other Media Actors?" June 2020, 18.
33 Mesmer, "An Intersectional Analysis," 181.
34 Radio Television Digital News Association. "Safe Training Part 1," January 13, 2021.
35 Miller and Lewis, "Journalists, Harassment, and Emotional Labor," 80.
36 Mesmer, "An Intersectional Analysis," 176.
37 Kaitlin C. Miller, and Jacob L. Nelson, "'Dark Participation' Without Representation," *Social Media + Society* 8, no. 4 (2022): 7–8.
38 Miller, "Journalists, Gender, and Harassment," 14.
39 Holton, Bélair-Gagnon, Bossio and Molyneux, "Not their Fault, but their Problem," 11.
40 Mary Jeanne Larrabee, *An Ethic of Care: Feminist and Interdisciplinary Perspectives.* (New York: Routledge, 1993).
41 Miller and Nelson, "Dark Participation," 6–7.
42 Seth C. Lewis, Rodrigo Zamith, and Mark Coddington, "Online Harassment and its Implications for the Journalist–Audience Relationship," *Digital Journalism* 8, no. 8 (2020): 1064.
43 Linda Steiner and Chad M. Okrusch, "Care as a Virtue for Journalists," *Journal of Mass Media Ethics* 21, no. 2–3 (2006): 102–122.
44 Kelsey Mesmer, and M. Rosie Jahng, "Using Facebook to Discuss Aspects of Industry Safety," *Journalism Studies* 11, no. 8 (2021): 1097.
45 Tracy Everbach, "The Culture of a Women-Led Newspaper," *Journalism and Mass Communication Quarterly* 83, no. 3 (2006): 487.
46 Jenkins, Joy, and Finneman, "Gender Trouble in the Workplace," *Feminist Media Studies* 18, no. 2 (2018): 170.
47 The National Press Club, "National Press Club Statement on Shooting of Florida TV Journalists," February 22, 2023.

16

TEACHING STUDENT JOURNALISTS TO REFILL THEIR HAPPINESS TANKS

Alexandra Wake and Erin Smith

On any given day, journalists can be directly or indirectly exposed to trauma and moral injury. Student journalists are not immune from the emotional impact of these experiences,[1] with cumulative exposure associated with more severe mental health impact including anxiety, depression, and post-traumatic stress disorder (PTSD).[2]

This nexus between journalism and trauma is important for journalism students to understand. Many young people begin studying journalism at university without fully appreciating the impact that trauma and moral injury can have on them, their loved ones, and their future career. Eager to join the profession, journalism students start with a strong sense of purpose, hoping to produce breaking news and make a difference. While this purpose can be protective against trauma exposure,[3] it can be tested after bearing witness to trauma or experiencing moral injury while simultaneously working under unrelenting stress and deadlines. Research shows that 80 to 100 percent of journalists will experience a potentially traumatic event during their career[4] with many attending traumatic events during their student journalism internships.[5] Students may also initially underestimate the scope of the trauma they will experience as a journalist.

Trauma can occur in brutal, unexpected ways, even when covering journalism beats like sports or fashion. Football stadiums collapse, crowds stampede, and seemingly healthy and active young sports men and women die in accidents on the field or pitch. Others have noted that the September 11, 2001, terrorist attacks that happened in the United States occurred during Fashion Week. Many of the journalists who were in town to cover the fashion beat suddenly found themselves well outside their comfort zone documenting one of the most traumatic events the world has ever witnessed.[6]

Bearing witness to trauma can cause post-traumatic stress reactions that can last a lifetime if they are not appropriately mitigated or managed.[7] One key

DOI: 10.4324/9781003364597-19

protective factor against the development of serious post-traumatic injuries like PTSD is the promotion of happiness as a key component of overall well-being. As human beings, we need happiness. Without it, we may not develop the sense of agency that enables us to assertively establish what we believe in, what we stand for, and which profession we will devote ourselves to. Happiness is also integral to students' ability to understand their values and achieve their purpose.

What is Happiness?

What is happiness? There are references to the concept everywhere, and indeed nuanced explanations throughout this book. As of January 2023, a quick Google search offers nearly two billion results and searching two of the most important online databases in the field of psychology (PsycINFO and PsycARTICLES) produces over 40,000 results from academic and other journals, books, dissertations and more. We know:

1. Happiness is a state, not a trait. It is not a long-lasting, permanent feature or personality trait. It is changeable.
2. Happiness is associated with feelings such as pleasure or contentment, meaning that happiness is not to be confused with more intense feelings like joy or bliss.
3. Happiness can be felt or shown, which means that happiness is not necessarily an internal or external experience but can be both.

Happiness has increasingly been aligned with the concept of well-being. Some believe that happiness is one of the core components of well-being, while others believe being happy *is* well-being.[8] In any case, well-being is frequently used as a shorthand for happiness in the literature.

Modern Problems

Student journalists are under increasing pressure in modern society. They must be prepared to work across all mediums (text, audio, video and social) in multiple deadline-driven environments, knowing that they may not attain a much sought-after job in a mainstream newsroom if they do not perform well on their student placements. They are bombarded by headlines about cuts to newsrooms and hateful online comments from the public about issues related to news gathering and reporting. Like all news professionals, student journalists face growing and changing threats to press freedom. They can find themselves sitting outside the support of newsrooms and can be overlooked for support by universities.

Furthermore, teens and young adults who experienced the global pandemic, were as of 2023, dealing with an acceleration of problems such as climate change which can also impact their very existence. Even talking about the impact of climate change (and the resulting fires, floods, and storms) is so unsettling that Professor Tim Flannery, Chief Councillor of the Climate Council, provides a trauma trigger warning before speaking publicly to audiences that include young people about climate change.[9] Climate change poses a unique threat to the happiness of student journalists who live in communities that are directly impacted by the phenomenon and related severe weather events.

This is not the only modern problem that challenges student journalists. They are increasingly required by the nature of their work to bring their whole selves to their jobs as interns and then journalists, openly disclosing their race, class, gender, and religion. Although some employers are not telling journalists that they do not need to be on social media, others insist upon it as a way of further distributing news content to audiences. This can leave student journalists vulnerable to online trauma, particularly on social media, where one poorly phrased post can invoke fierce reactions online. Religion and race are still tricky topics to navigate inside newsrooms in which long-held overt and covert prejudices—and even microaggressions—can be problematic.

Even before they chose to study journalism, students have likely seen headlines about the closure of newspapers and other news outlets. Barely a day goes by without someone, often an experienced journalist, telling them on Twitter to try another career. Twitter and other social media platforms are an important part of a student journalist's media diet in the same way they are for working journalists. Journalists in training are encouraged to engage in social media to find stories, connect with working journalists and potential sources, promote their own work, and even find a job or work opportunities. Like working journalists who are encouraged to be "always on" students also need to learn how to balance what can become an overlap between the professional and the personal. Each day there is a deluge of information across social media and email, and much of it can bring personal attacks, as well as fresh reports of the loss of trust in journalism and journalists.

Many young people are taught by a generation of former journalists who may have developed a range of maladaptive coping strategies throughout their career. These experienced journalists often share stories of award-winning pieces written in newsrooms fuelled by excessive drinking, but they are not always conscious of the realities of social media etiquette particularly for those seen as "other," and the modern challenges of managing multiple completing deadlines. In Australia, for example, journalism educators tend to have significant newsroom experience, but can lack a nuanced understanding of power dynamics. Gender research found that Australia needed more academically astute journalism educators who understood how issues of gender and power were implicated at every level of society—including in newsrooms and in the content[10] journalists produce.[11]

In the context of the ongoing COVID-19 pandemic, students who worry about dire predictions of more to come thanks to climate change must dodge and weave to stay healthy, despite their often insecure, part-time work and inconsistent access to campuses. All these issues point to the need for educators to embrace new styles of journalism where well-being and happiness are at the centre of the story. Australian educators are increasingly experimenting with constructive and solutions journalism, which encourage journalists to consider potential solutions in addition to problematic issues.[12] Even without those frames, educators can encourage students to produce engaging storytelling on complex environmental issues that contributes to efforts to enhance the legitimacy of climate change in a hyper-politicized and polarized world.[13]

Adapting and Recovering

Although a little bit of stress and adrenaline is good for many parts of a journalist's deadline driven profession, educators can prepare students for that moment when the constant stream of little zips and zaps all finally land a punch. We need to prepare students to question the concept of resilience: the notion of "bending" but "not breaking." It is normal to break sometimes, even several times in a single day. That does not mean that we are not resilient. This is a key message for students that can help them to protect their well-being and happiness.

A successful career should not be measured by how much we can bend, adapt to, or endure. We need to define success based on how much we can recover and refill our happiness tanks. We don't drive around with our cars' fuel tanks empty or batteries uncharged, so why would we go around our daily lives with our happiness tanks running on fumes? Having some fuel in the tank gives us the ability to rest and recover in between all the zips and zaps that life throws at us. In fact, inadequate rest and recovery hold us back from being resilient.[14] We need rest. It may sound simple, but it is getting harder and harder for journalists and other professionals to do so in our fast-paced, complex, and challenging world.[15]

Educators must ask ourselves, when was the last time we had a good night's sleep? Uninterrupted rest? "Taking a break from work" is not the same as "recovering." We must power down our bodies. This involves more than switching off the computer. We need to switch "us" off as well. Bélair-Gagnon et al.[16] argue that disconnecting from social media is particularly challenging due to the nature of journalism, but vital for thorough rest. Educators can help students recognize the need to routinely switch off from social media and email, so that they can refill their happiness tanks and increase their overall resilience. They can also play an important role in helping students learn how to negotiate time off social with news bosses.

The Importance of Purpose

It's not just about resting and recovering. As discussed in Chapter 6 of this volume, journalism educators can help by actively teaching their students that journalism is important, that telling stories is important and that journalism is and can be important to social changes. Democratic societies rely on journalists to tell stories. It is a privilege and an honour to write the first draft of history, visit places that others cannot travel to, and share the survivor's stories. By telling stories that otherwise will not be told, journalists have an opportunity to solve problems and change the world. Journalists write stories and present them in a way that encourages or allows others to act, informing the collective behavior of society.

Equally as important as understanding their own sense of purpose is aligning themselves with news publishers and broadcasters who share similar senses of purpose. While it is often tempting for graduate journalists to accept the first job offered, particularly in a difficult job market, it may be the wrong decision if the employer's values clash with those of the journalist. This clash can cause moral injury.

This is not to say that young journalists should turn down all the assignments that they disagree with or avoid engaging with some of the more difficult parts of journalism, such as knocking on the door of a bereaved family. Looking after one's mental health does not mean avoiding trauma. Afterall, reporting on trauma is a core part of a journalist's job, and no journalist can avoid covering trauma at some point in their career. There is even the possibility of growth from trauma.[17]

Moral Injury

The evidence has shown the importance for journalists to see value in the stories they produce or find themselves at risk of significant moral injury. If their work is repeatedly overlooked, downplayed, or rejected, journalists suffer harm, though this may not occur immediately. Many newsworthy matters can disturb a journalist's moral compass. These include the plight of refugees, climate change, animal rights abuses, domestic violence, child abuse, torture, rape, murder, graphic court, and commission hearings. It's even potentially more damaging when the story the journalist is covering is focused on the journalist's own sense of self or identity, say perhaps as a First Nations and Indigenous person, a person of colour or as a member of the LGBTQIA+ community.

Educators can play a key role here in showing student journalists how to support each other by actively teaching them the value of staying connected and engaged for promoting happiness and preventing burnout, moral injury, and subsequent mental health injury. Educators can hold regular meetings with their students during internships, and model understanding and compassion. Maintaining contact with students via social media, group chats, email, or slack channels on internships using humour and empathy can help build a culture of happiness and the feeling that "we are in this together."

One such intervention being trialled by Australian educators has been the introduction of Listening Circles where students can talk about their experiences during internships and feel validated but appropriately challenged by peers and university staff. The facilitators who run the circles also offer referrals to professional counsellors when necessary.[18] These small informal gatherings of journalism students mirror the process undertaken by medical doctors who gather regularly to discuss patients and to learn from others' mistakes. By creating small supportive group discussion during internships, educators seek to normalize talking and help seeking within trusted communities.

Digital disruption and the stress of modern news practices being felt (and passed on) by permanent staff have been a key theme of the Listening Circles held before the pandemic. Student journalists, who usually complete unpaid internships as part of their studies, used the Circles to discuss the difficulties they had to finish their internships at the same time as continuing to work in their self-supporting jobs. Interns can be often expected by managers to work fully as a journalist, going above and beyond for the story regardless of the hours or emotional toll, in the same way staff are required to behave when employed in a call centre.[19] There are often no or low wages for journalism interns, high stress, often rigid and unsupportive management, draining emotional labour and electronic surveillance through social media and newsroom systems which record how many "clicks" a story has received.

Listening Circles also provide a space for students to discuss traumatic events such as shootings, car accidents, suicides, and drive-by killings. Some student journalists become intimately involved in the production of deeply distressing stories during their work placements, have reported that they were at the centre of major traumatic events and being asked to find, for example, the best camera angle to film murdered women and/or children.[20] As one student noted, "these listening circles are good because we come in and we talk to each other. And I think that's what we really need."[21]

Sharing lived experience is a powerful educational tool; knowing that others have struggled with the same issues can protect against moral and mental health injury and helps to break down stigma and normalize conversations around mental health. Using real examples and discussing difficult ethical issues in the classroom before students experience it in the world can help them prepare for the moral injuries caused by the guilt and shame of tough moral dilemmas in the field.[22]

Help Seeking

While all student journalists need to learn the skills of communicating their own boundaries and taking some responsibility for the development of healthy habits, there are times when they may need professional support. Student journalists can generally access psychological support in an ad hoc manner at their universities but there are often long wait lists for free services. Student interns are not offered the same support as other news workers, and seeking self-help is not without its issues because of time, cost, and stigma. Breaking down this self-stigmatization continues to be an urgent priority for newsrooms and media organizations the world over, as it remains a barrier for journalists—both new and veteran—to seek potentially life-saving mental health support services.

For journalists who are lucky enough to work for major news outlets, mental health support will likely be available at no or little cost. However, such support is rarely offered to freelance or casual journalists and is often under-utilized by career journalists due to lack of awareness and the toxic "It's just part of the job" workplace culture. Journalists who seek professional help may face challenges, particularly if they have been medicated for psychological issues.

Some journalists are fortunate enough to work for organizations that offer formal peer support processes for staff. The Australian Broadcasting Corporation (ABC) has trained senior journalists using techniques developed by the Dart Centre for Journalism and Trauma for more than a decade. This allows veteran reporters to identify and support colleagues who may be struggling after covering traumatic stories. This peer support process allows journalists to seek help without the intervention of management. Sometimes all a journalist needs is someone who understands the profession to listen with an empathetic ear.

Legal Requirements

The Australian court system has recently recognized the need for news outlets to take trauma among journalists more seriously and has put the onus on employers to ensure that news organizations proactively manage a journalist's mental health, even if the journalist does not act on their own.[23] Student journalists are taught in their law and ethics classes about the employers' responsibilities in this area, but such assistance does not typically extend to casually employed and freelance journalists. These journalists are the most vulnerable in this regard because they do not always have an employer to support them. Many of them work from home without colleagues and cannot separate home life from work life.

Australian employers are also now expected to protect staff from psychological trauma.[24] A government solicitor successfully argued in Australia's High Court that her job contributed to her PTSD over the course of several years because she was tasked with prosecuting serious sex offenses. Due to the nature of the cases, she was forced to view graphic images and meet with children and adults who had been abused. Journalists often deal with the same kinds of events and evidence as legal professionals, and the educational and professional scaffolds of journalism also have a responsibility to ensure that reporters are prepared for this and given a psychologically safe workplace.

Curricula and Happiness

It may seem out of place for university educators to discuss happiness and well-being within the curricula, but these are essential for the health of future journalists. Many universities with strong journalism programs have embedded trauma education as part of the Australian journalism education system,[25] but it is rarely extended further into psychosocial education which includes positive mental health initiatives and even meditation.[26] Journalism majors are offered a range of training opportunities around reporting mental health and are given resources designed to help them manage difficult subject matters such as suicide and domestic abuse. The Dart Centre for Journalism and Trauma, Asia Pacific, offers workshops to university level journalism students on how to protect their mental health and to support peers. Mindframe for Journalists has for more than 20 years provided specific classroom support and a curriculum for reporting on mental health and suicide.[27] Our Watch provides guidelines for media covering domestic and family violence. There are also specific guides on reporting on the use of drugs and alcohol. Stigma Watch also provides resources for help seeking as well as media monitoring of best practice reporting.

Despite these resources and the long association of some of these groups in the Australian journalism education system, educators have recently reported that they feel under-prepared to teach about these issues.[28] Although all acknowledge that trauma is part and parcel of the job of a journalist, educators can be uncomfortable talking about such issues fearing that students may over disclose or put the educator in a difficult position.

One thing that can easily be done with students without much preparation is to discuss the habits of happy people. In 2023, *Time* magazine[29] published the results of a survey of 18 happiness experts and reported on the percentage of time each week dedicated to getting enough sleep, spending time in nature, playing sport or exercising, participating in a hobby, meditating, or praying. Overwhelmingly what worked, according to all those experts, was spending time with family outside the house and with friends in a non-professional setting. The experts agreed on the need to acknowledge negative emotions rather than avoiding them.

A Long and Happy Career

In this chapter, we have posited that journalists can experience long and successful careers whilst also living happy healthy lives despite the challenges associated with the ever-evolving profession of journalism. We argue educators should build psychosocial education into their journalism curricula, which reinforces the importance of well-being as well as the centrality of rest. It is vital that student journalists graduate knowing the importance of their role to society, as well as the need to look after their own mental health. This does not necessarily mean avoiding reporting on traumatic stories, but rather reporting in a way that is trauma-informed and supported by line managers and employers. Educators can use supportive discussion groups for journalism students, which help build positive life-long habits where the discussion of mental health and help seeking is normalised and that taking time for rest and recovery is prioritised.

In sum, a key to a happy and resilient student—and subsequently career—journalist, is access to early psychosocial education and support that embeds well-being and happiness into the journalism curriculum. As educators, we have a unique and privileged opportunity to instil in students an awareness of trauma, promote mental health literacy, build a community of support, and encourage healthy ways to fill our happiness tanks. As educators we can model best practice to student journalists, encouraging them to build good protective habits and understand their own value. We can demonstrate how to safely support each other and normalize conversations about well-being and mental health. We can also work together as peers to advocate for student journalists and to call out work practices that do harm.

Notes

1 Desiree Hill, Catherine A. Luther, and Phyllis Slocum, "Preparing Future Journalists for Trauma on the Job," *Journalism & Mass Communication Educator* 75, no. 1 (2020): 64–68, https://doi.org/10.1177/1077695819900735.
2 Anthony Feinstein, Blair Audet, and Elizabeth Waknine, "Witnessing Images of Extreme Violence," *JRSM open* 5, no. 8 (2014): 2054270414533323–23. https://doi.org/10.1177/2054270414533323.
3 Stacey M. Schaefer et al., "Purpose in Life Predicts Better Emotional Recovery from Negative Stimuli," *PloS one* 8, no. 11 (2013): e80329-e29. https://doi.org/10.1371/journal.pone.0080329.
4 "Covering Trauma: Impact on Journalists," Dart Center, Updated July 1, 2015, https://dartcenter.org/content/covering-trauma-impact-on-journalists.
5 Alexandra Wake, "Listening Circles Provide Model for Students in Disrupted Journalism Industry." In *Enriching Higher Education Students' Learning through Post-Work Placement Interventions* eds. Stephen Billett, Janice Orrell, Denise Jackson, and Faith Valencia-Forrester, (Cham: Springer International Publishing, 2020), 247–266.
6 Jill Radsken, "New York Minute," *The Harvard Gazette*, September 8, 2021, https://news.harvard.edu/gazette/story/2021/09/fashion-writer-finds-herself-in-the-middle-of-9-11-mayhem/.
7 Kerrie O'Brien, "PTSD for 30 Years: ABC's Eric Campbell on the Highs and Lows of the Best Job in the World," *Sydney Morning Herald*, July 23, 2022. https://www.smh.com.au/culture/tv-and-radio/ptsd-for-30-years-abc-s-eric-campbell-on-the-highs-and-lows-of-the-best-job-in-the-world-20220711-p5b0rh.html.
8 Kai Ruggeri et al., "Well-Being is More than Happiness and Life Satisfaction," *Health and Quality of Life Outcomes* 18, no. 1 (2020): 192. https://doi.org/10.1186/s12955-020-01423-y. https://doi.org/10.1186/s12955-020-01423-y.
9 Tim Flannary, Kyle Pope, Desi Anwar, and Anna Rose, "Reporting the Climate Crisis and Ethical Journalism," Kerry O'Brien. *Antidote Conference*. Sydney Opera House Talks and Ideas, September 20, 2019. https://www.youtube.com/watch?v=1DbeYNPmTDk.

10 Louise North, "The Gender 'Problem' in Australia Journalism Education," *Australian Journalism Review* 32, no. 2 (2010): 103–115. http://dx.doi.org/10.2139/ssrn.2015844.
11 Lisa French, Claudia Padovani, and Aimée Vega Montiel (eds.). *Gender, Media and ICTs*. Paris, France: UNESCO, 2019.
12 Tanja Aitamurto, and Anita Varma, "The Constructive Role of Journalism," *Journalism practice* 12, no. 6 (2018): 695–713. https://doi.org/10.1080/17512786.2018.1473041.
13 Robert E Gutsche Jr, and Kristy Hess, *Reimagining Journalism and Social Order in a Fragmented Media World*. (Routledge, 2020).
14 Judith K. Sluiter, "The Influence of Work Characteristics on the Need for Recovery and Experienced Health," *Ergonomics* 42, no. 4 (1999): 573–583, https://doi.org/10.1080/001401399185487.
15 Shawn Achor, and Michelle Gielan, "Resilience is About How You Recharge, Not How You Endure," *Harvard Business Review*, June 24, 2016.
16 Valérie Bélair-Gagnon, Diana Bossio, Avery E. Holton, and Logan Molyneux, "Disconnection," *Social Media + Society* 8, no. 1 (2022): 205630512210772. https://doi.org/10.1177/20563051221077217.
17 Cait McMahon and Trina McLellan, "Journalists Reporting for Duty." In *The Phoenix of Natural Disasters: Community Resilience* eds. Kathryn Gow and Douglas Paton, (New York: Nova Science Publishers, 2008), 101–121.
18 Wake, "Listening Circles Provide Model for Students in Disrupted Journalism Industry," 247–266.
19 Edna Brophy, "The Subterranean Stream," *Ephemera Theory and Politics in Organization* 10, no. 3/4 (2010): 470–483.
20 Wake, "Listening Circles Provide Model for Students in Disrupted Journalism Industry," 247–266.
21 Wake, "Listening Circles Provide Model for Students in Disrupted Journalism Industry," 247–266.
22 Clothilde Redfern, "There's a Bigger Risk to Journalists' Mental Health Than PTSD," *New Statesman* (newstatesman.com), July 14, 2022.
23 Alexandra Wake and Matthew Ricketson, "Trauma in the Newsroom: Lessons on the Importance of Australia's Yz Case," *Ethical Space* 19, no. 1 (2022): 10. http://www.abramis.co.uk/ethical-space/feature.php#.
24 Anna Kelsey-Sugg and Damien Carrick, "Zagi Kozarov Sued after Her Job Gave Her PTSD," *The Law Report*, May 22, 2022. https://www.abc.net.au/news/2022-05-25/zagi-kozarov-psychiatric-injury-at-work-law-report/101081728.
25 Marla Buchanan and Patrice Keats, "Coping with Traumatic Stress in Journalism," *International Journal of Psychology* 46, no. 2 (2011): 127–135, https://doi.org/10.1080/00207594.2010.532799.
26 Shelton Gunaratne, Mark Pearson, and Sugath Senarath, *Mindful Journalism and News Ethics in the Digital Era: A Buddhist Approach*. (United States: Routledge, 2017).
27 "Mindframe for Journalism and Public Relations Education," Mindframe National Media Initiative, 2022, https://mindframe.org.au/.
28 Alexandra Wake, Erin Smith, and Matthew Ricketson. "Embedding Trauma Literacy into Curriculum," *Journalism and Mass Communication Educator* (forthcoming 2023).
29 Angela Haupt, "The Daily Habits of Happiness Experts," *Time* (time.com), January 5, 2023. https://time.com/6241099/daily-habits-happiness-experts/.

17

SELF-EMPLOYMENT IN THE NEWS INDUSTRY

Sarah Van Leuven and Hanne Vandenberghe

Many journalism schools are increasingly stressing entrepreneurialism in their programs.[1] A 2018 survey of Belgian journalists showed the need to address entrepreneurialism as it indicated that most young journalists find their way into the news industry as independent or self-employed journalists.[2]

Like in many other jobs, these junior profiles first need to gain experience and demonstrate their journalistic skills before they can move up the professional ladder. But even if after some time they acquire a stable and valued position in the newsroom, they are not always rewarded with a permanent staff position. In Belgium, self-employed journalists are well represented in all age groups across the journalistic workforce, and their number has increased over the years.[3] This is not an isolated finding. Studies in other countries and contexts have documented a sharp increase of freelance journalists in recent years, which has sped up following the 2008 global financial and economic crisis.[4]

Because of this outsourcing of news work and the decentralization of newsrooms, several authors draw attention to the fact that academic research should pay more attention to atypical journalist profiles such as freelancers but also part-time workers, temporary contracts, or internships.[5] Therefore, the aim of this chapter is first, to explain why the working conditions of many freelancers can be precarious. Second, we will see that it is not all doom and gloom, and happiness can be found if we follow a less newsroom-centered approach and consider entrepreneurial efforts in the news industry. Finally, we will map out how the position and happiness of freelancers, entrepreneurial journalists, and other atypical workers in the news industry can be further supported by different stakeholders.

DOI: 10.4324/9781003364597-20

Freelancers as Members of the Precariat

Freelancers are "self-employed journalists who take on assignments for several employers."[6] Yet, the European Federation of Journalists (EFJ)[7] called them "forced lancers" because research[8] showed that many journalists who were laid off during and after the 2008 financial and economic crisis "moved from full-time, secure, and well remunerated work to more precarious forms of employment in and out of journalism, including freelance, contract and part-time." Media companies do not need to invest in training or benefits for freelancers such as social security and legal support, nor take the risk for periods of reduced activity.[9] As a result, they can reduce costs and responsibilities and gain more flexibility.[10] The fact that this seems to be a well-considered strategy is demonstrated by the fact that one in three Belgian freelancers in 2018 admitted to work for only one client in the media sector, which is considered bogus self-employment.[11]

A shift of responsibilities to the individual workers is observed: "much of the risk previously born by employers is now the responsibility of the individual worker, something Fleming calls the 'radical responsibilization' of employment." Studies of precarious work often refer to the hegemonic position of neoliberal economic thought in the globalized society to understand why workers (need to) accept that long-term career possibilities and work-related benefits are replaced with short-term contracts and high demands. Following this argument, "freelance journalists are molded into ideal neoliberal workers: agile, self-commodifying, and shrewdly working to survive in the marketplace."[12] Freelancers under conditions of fierce competition internalized ideas of "enterprise" in such a way that financial and entrepreneurial considerations dominated their work.[13] The lack of steady employment and the benefits that come with it can have a detrimental effect on the well-being of independent journalists.[14] When compared to permanent staff, freelancers report lower levels of extrinsic job satisfaction. They are less satisfied with work-related aspects such as job security, income, social status, or promotion prospects.[15] In addition to low incomes, inability to plan for the long term, a daily struggle to secure future work, and limited access to social protection, they report high levels of stress and burnout problems.[16]

Research shows that these precarious working situations vary between different groups of freelancers. First, young journalists are often pushed into freelance positions when they enter the journalistic field as a gateway to a more permanent position in a newsroom after they have demonstrated their value.[17] Second, female journalists with children often choose a freelance position to buy time for their family.[18] Third, a report of the European Federation of Journalists[19] raised concern about the many freelance journalists in regional reporting. In Belgium, the proportion of freelancers in the regional beat increased from 22.1 percent in 2013 to 30.6 percent in 2018.[20]

In Belgium, The Flemish Association of Journalists (VVJ) reported that freelancers in the regional beat endure being treated like slaves. In 2022, when hired by a newspaper, they received a remuneration of €5 for a short piece; up to €125 for an in-depth news piece. Freelancers who did the same job with exactly as much effort but in relation to national news coverage in newspapers receive between €110–1,200. On top of that, the number of regional beat reporters is decreasing. The remaining journalists need to cover multiple cities or municipalities, creating local news deserts.[21]

The situation was aggravated by the COVID-19 pandemic starting in 2020 which hit freelance journalists substantially more than journalists with a permanent contract. During the COVID-19 lockdowns, freelancers reported a decrease in or, temporarily during the lockdowns, even a complete drop in assignments and income.[22] Australian freelance journalists reported how the pandemic had aggravated their already insecure financial situation, and how they had to resort even more than normal to jobs outside journalism.[23] COVID-19 magnified pre-existing disparities among journalists, as freelancers and those associated with small media startups were very concerned about job security and felt a lot of financial stress.[24] Moreover, they had to deal individually with stressors such as isolation, working from home, and eroding of work–life boundaries, in contrast to journalists in permanent positions who struggled also but felt sufficiently supported by their news organizations.[25]

In the next section we present a different take on the position of self-employed journalists by focusing less on their dependence on media employers. Instead, we celebrate their independence and agency as they are running their own business and can take control of their own professional success, well-being, and happiness. Therefore, we turn to the concept of entrepreneurial journalism and what freelancers can learn from these journalist-entrepreneurs.

Between Journalism and Entrepreneurship

Entrepreneurial journalists have increased since the emergence of online news websites and social media which have democratized the means of news production and distribution, and thus lowered the entry barriers to the news market. Journalistic entrepreneurs are defined as "designating stand-alone enterprises that have a journalistic mission yet are dissociated from legacy media."[26] They have connotative links to business and innovation whereas freelancers are associated with "piecemeal journalistic work."[27] Whereas many freelancers are forced or pushed into a self-employed position (marginalization model), entrepreneurial journalists value self-employment as an opportunity for independence, empowerment, autonomy and self-realization instead of a burden (portfolio model).[28]

Instead of seeing them as two opposing groups who have nothing in common, a middle-way is also possible, as illustrated by talking to freelancers who work for a limited (or even just one) legacy news employer. Even though they are not entrepreneurial journalists in a strict sense, as they do not necessarily aim to start a new, innovative journalistic project, they nonetheless take care of their own business and are really satisfied with their autonomy and self-realization. They may work for a limited number of employers, but they enjoy the feeling of overseeing their professional lives. Research confirms that freelancers may be less satisfied with job-extrinsic factors such as job security and remuneration, but they are generally more satisfied about job-intrinsic factors such as individual freedom and the multitude of new contacts.[29] In addition to the group of entrepreneurs and "forced lancers," it might be needed to add at least one additional category of "idealists," referring to freelancers who "are more driven by the opportunity to work with the kind of journalism they find important, even if it does not always pay well."[30]

Whether journalists deliberately choose to be self-employed or not, freelancers, much like entrepreneurial journalists, need to have a set of skills and competencies beyond the traditional skills in journalism such as critical thinking or writing such as accounting and budgeting skills to run a business.[31] Despite the fact that journalism curricula increasingly address entrepreneurialism, it is often still in small or lower ranked courses,[32] and the fact remains that most journalists are not born entrepreneurs. These "journalists-turned-entrepreneurs"[33] may struggle to make a realistic assessment about the economic viability and demand for their work.[34] Self-employed journalists also need to be better aware of the importance of individualized branding.[35] Instead of the traditional approach of presenting oneself as a detached observer and assuming that people will be interested in the quality of their work no matter what, in brand journalism it is important to develop a more audience-facing identity in order to gain a strong reputation and attention for one's work.[36] In order to gain a stronger and more personalized engagement with their audiences, some (especially younger) journalists start to show more of their personality and their own opinion in their work.[37] This tendency can also be placed under the umbrella of the emotional turn in journalism.[38]

Consequently, it is vital that journalism schools make financial, personnel and research management skills central in their programs such as design thinking, product development, community engagement, problem-solving, resilience, or value creation.[39] Journalism schools should be preparing their students to be able to provide innovative oriented skills such as data literacy and storytelling skills that add value to traditional media organizations.[40] In today's innovative digitally oriented journalistic context, these skills are not or insufficiently present in the newsrooms and therefore outsourced to freelancers.[41] In the Estonian case, the editors' views on freelancers evolved from unemployed journalists offering journalistic pieces for publication on commission in 2014 to entrepreneurial journalists whom they are more keen to cooperate with as they are able to provide highly valued, multimedia-rich, and/or investigative and fact-checked productions in 2019.[42]

Creating a Supportive Environment for Self-Employed Journalists

In the last part of this chapter, we will focus on how journalists as well as other stakeholders in addition to journalism schools, can improve the happiness and well-being of freelance journalists. A vital strategy for self-employed journalists to cope with work-related stressors and to improve their professional opportunities, is to set up a broad social network to rely on. This implies freelance journalists need to invest in building up resilient relationships both with potential clients such as editors or other employed journalists in news organizations and other freelancers.[43] Freelancers cooperating instead of competing with each other creates a supportive community which impacts both well-being and income security.[44] Swedish freelancers experienced working in shared office space with other freelancers as advantageous on an emotional level by reducing loneliness and bringing order and structure in working days, as well as on a professional level by asking for advice for instance who to interview for an article they are working on or which editors should be contacted first to pitch a specific idea for a story.[45] Moreover, being part of an office collective generates work as it is possible to set up a team of freelancers to pitch powerful ideas to news organizations or to exchange assignments with other freelancers when the workload is too high.[46]

A second coping strategy includes adaptation to the market.[47] To make ends meet financially, freelancers must specialize in defined areas where the competition is lower, and/or produce content directly for clients in the public relations and advertising sectors. Self-employed journalists are drawn to work for public relations (PR) and advertising companies who are asking for similar journalistic competencies, but offering higher incomes compared to the journalistic organizations.[48] The combinations of employment in PR and journalism lead to conflicting roles.[49] While for journalists it is important to work independently from their social environments in order to be able to act as a watchdog and serve the public interest (communicative mode), PR is driven by commercial goals and wants to create an advantage for private interests (strategic mode).[50] As such, a conflict of interest may appear when a freelance journalist is asked to produce a critical news story about a PR client. Concerns are raised about lower adherence to journalistic standards and role conceptions, as well as about decreased autonomy from commercial interests.[51] Evidence from Belgium supports these worries as perceived autonomy is highest among political beat reporters (mainly staff employees), and lowest among lifestyle beat reporters (high proportion of freelance journalists).[52]

Therefore, in Belgium for instance, it is not allowed to combine the status of professional journalist with commercial secondary activities, which means that freelance journalists need to make the choice between either not being able to make ends meet because of the loss of income from commercial assignments or accept commercial jobs and relinquish the recognition as a professional journalist. For almost two decades, the VVJ have been advocating for a relaxation to make it possible to combine the status of professional journalist with a commercial side activity, insofar as it does not jeopardize the independence of the journalist. In academia, scholars likewise have been criticizing the normative emphasis on a "wall" or "curtain" between journalists and commercial interests. Contemporary news industry lacks the financial stability to maintain this dogma and therefore the wall has been replaced with a curtain, which is also exemplified by the development of new hybrid types of PR-journalism such as native advertising or sponsored content.[53] This is not necessarily problematic if new norms come to the fore such as transparency and integrity.[54] These boundaries have become "porous and often meaningless, particularly for media users."[55]

Although a smaller group of freelancers is in a sufficiently strong market position to be able to negotiate solid payment terms for a job or even reject underpaid offers, being part of a collective supportive community increases the chance to negotiate for better fees or contracts. Instead of focusing on individual solutions or coping mechanisms, measures can be taken to improve the terms and conditions of freelance journalism in a more structural way through unionizing or associating.[56] In the Swedish context, the journalist union has protested against the so-called "rights-grabbing" contracts in which "publishers are allowed to republish material in all their owned outlets without consent from the journalists or participating parties (such as persons interviewed and portrayed in the material), and without additional remuneration to the producer of the material."[57]

Self-regulatory bodies such as journalistic unions or media policy and regulation at both national, and most preferable, at the supra-national level, can play a crucial role in setting the scene in the contractual regimes in the journalistic labor market to create better working conditions for self-employed journalists. There is a need for more in-depth studying of the impact of employment regimes components on journalists' precarity. In the most ideal situation, business-to-business agreements ensure low risks for both self-employed journalists and news companies as clients.[58]

Governments can also contribute to creating better working conditions by subsidizing journalism without exerting any influence on the substantive implementation. In Belgium, independent news start-ups condemn the government for disrupting the news market because of the reduced rates for newspaper distribution, resulting in a massive amount of €175-million indirect subsidies each year,[59] which leads to the expansion of the already strong media conglomerates like DPG Media and Mediahuis. Instead, the financial means donated by national and international governments to independent non-profit organizations such as journalismfund.eu (supporting unique or innovative projects of self-employed journalists) remain very limited.

The importance of creating a supportive working environment for freelance journalists, with sufficient safeguards for their happiness and well-being, cannot be underestimated. Especially in a time where big media groups provide more of the same kind of "vanilla flavor" news, self-employed journalists can be the ones adding other flavors to our news diet and stimulating innovation in the sector.

Notes

1 Tim Vos, and Jane Singer, "Media Discourse About Entrepreneurial Journalism," *Journalism Practice* 10, no. 2 (2016): 143–159.
2 Sarah Van Leuven, Bart Vanhaelewyn, and Karin Raeymaeckers, "From One Division of Labor to the Other," *Journalism Practice* 15, no. 9 (2021): 1203–1221.
3 Van Leuven, Vanhaelewyn, and Raeymaeckers, "From One Division of Labor to the Other," 1203–1221.
4 Cristian-Ramón Marín-Sanchiz, Miguel Carvajal, and José-Luis González-Esteban, "Survival Strategies in Freelance Journalism," *Journalism Practice* (2021): 1–24, DOI:10.1080/17512786.2021.1929414; Maria Norbäck, "Glimpses of Resistance: Entrepreneurial Subjectivity and Freelance Journalist Work," *Organization* 28, no. 3 (2021): 426–448; Hanne Vandenberghe, and Leen d'Haenens, "The Netherlands. On Media Concentration and Resilient Freelance Journalists," in *The Media for Democracy Monitor 2021* (Göteborg: Nordicom, 2021), 257–296.
5 Beate Josephi, and Penny O'Donnell, "The Blurring Line between Freelance Journalists and Self-employed Media Workers," *Journalism* 24, no. 1 (2023): 139–156.
6 Emma Walters, Christopher Warren, and Mike Dobbie, *The Changing Nature of Work.* (Switzerland: International Federation of Journalists, 2006), 6.
7 Andreas Bittner, *Managing Change.* (Brussels: European Federation of Journalists, 2011), 1–32.
8 Nicole Cohen, Andrea Hunter, and Penny O'Donnell, "Bearing the Burden of Corporate Restructuring," *Journalism Practice* 13, no. 7 (2019): 817–833.
9 Salamon, E., "Freelance Journalists and Stringers." In The International Encyclopedia of Journalism Studies eds Tim P. Vos and Folker Hanusch, (New York: Wiley, 2019), 1–9; Mirjam Gollmitzer, "Precariously Employed Watchdogs?" *Journalism Practice* 8, no. 6 (2014): 826–841.
10 Birgit Røe Mathisen, "Entrepreneurs and Idealists-," *Journalism Practice* 13, no. 8 (2019): 1003–1007.
11 Gerd Nies, and Roberto Pedersini, *Freelance Journalists in the European Media Industry.* (Brussels: European Federation of Journalists, 2003), 1–41.
12 Norbäck, "Glimpses of Resistance: Entrepreneurial Subjectivity and Freelance Journalist Work," 426–448.
13 John Storey, Graeme Salaman, and Kerry Platman, "Living with Enterprise in an Enterprise Economy: Freelance and Contract Workers in the Media," *Human Relations* 58, no. 8 (2005): 1033–1054.
14 Kathleen Ryan, "The Performative Journalist: Job Satisfaction, Temporary Workers and American Television News," *Journalism* 10, no. 5 (2009): 647–664.
15 Annelore Deprez, Sarah Van Leuven, Sara De Vuyst, Rebeca De Dobbelaer, and Karin Raeymaeckers, "Het Veranderende Medialandschap en Jobtevredenheid bij Vlaamse Beroepsjournalisten," *Tijdschrift voor Arbeidsvraagstukken* 31, no. 1 (2015): 46–61.
16 Nicole Cohen, "Entrepreneurial Journalism and the Precarious State of Media Work," *South Atlantic Quarterly* 114, no. 3 (2015): 513–533.
17 Kathryn Hayes, and Henry Silke, "Narrowing the Discourse? Growing Precarity in Freelance Journalism and its Effect on the Construction of News Discourse," *Critical Discourse Studies* 16, no. 3 (2019): 363–379.
18 Sara De Vuyst, and Karin Raeymaeckers, "Gender as a Multi-Layered Issue in Journalism: A Multi-Method Approach to Studying Barriers Sustaining Gender

Inequality in Belgian Newsrooms," *European Journal of Women's Studies* 26, no. 1 (2019): 23–38.

19 Bittner, *Managing Change: Innovation and Trade Unionism in the News Industry*, 1–32.

20 Van Leuven, Vanhaelewyn, and Raeymaeckers, "From One Division of Labor to the Other: The Relation Between Beat Reporting, Freelancing, and Journalistic Autonomy," 1203–21.

21 Penelope Muse Abernathy, *The Expanding News Desert*. (Center for Innovation and Sustainability in Local Media: University of North Carolina at Chapel Hill, 2018); Michelle Ferrier, Gaurav Sinha, and Michael Outrich, "Media Deserts: Monitoring the Changing Media Ecosystem," in *The Communication Crisis in America, And How to Fix It* eds. Mark Lloyd and Lewis A. Friedland, (New York: Palgrave Macmillan, 2016).

22 Josephi, and O'Donnell, "The Blurring Line between Freelance Journalists and Self-employed Media Workers," 139–156; Vandenberghe, and d'Haenens, "The Netherlands", 257–296; Sarah Van Leuven, et al. *Corona als kantelpunt in de Vlaamse journalistieke sector*. (Gent: Universiteit Gent, 2020).

23 Josephi, and O'Donnell, "The Blurring Line between Freelance Journalists and Self-employed Media Workers," 139–156.

24 Edson C. Tandoc Jr., Lydia Cheng, and Matthew Chew, "Covering COVID," *Journalism Studies* 23, no. 14 (2022): 1740–1757.

25 Tandoc Jr., Cheng, and Chew, "Covering COVID," 1740–1757.

26 Jane Singer "Entrepreneurial Journalism," in *Handbooks of Communication*, ed. Tim Vos (Berlin: De Gruyter Mouton, 2018), 349.

27 Singer, "Entrepreneurial Journalism," 349–350.

28 Maria Edstrom, and Martina Ladendorf, "Freelance Journalists as a Flexible Workforce in Media Industries," *Journalism Practice* 6, no. 5–6 (2012): 711–721.

29 Deprez, Van Leuven, De Vuyst, De Dobbelaer, and Raeymaeckers, "Het Veranderende Medialandschap en Jobtevredenheid bij Vlaamse Beroepsjournalisten," 46–61.

30 Mathisen, "Entrepreneurs and Idealists," 1003–1010.

31 Marju Himma-Kadakas, and Mirjam Mõttus, "Ready to Hire a Freelance Journalist," *Central European Journal of Communication* 14, no. 28 (2021): 27–43.

32 Vos and Singer, "Media Discourse About Entrepreneurial Journalism," 143–159.

33 Vos, and Singer, "Media Discourse About Entrepreneurial Journalism," 143–159.

34 Lucia Naldi, and Robert G. Picard, "Let's Start an Online News Site," *Journal of Media Business Studies* 9, no. 4 (2012): 69–97.

35 Josephi, and O'Donnell, "The Blurring Line between Freelance Journalists and Self-employed Media Workers," 139–156.

36 Avery E. Holton, and Logan Molyneux, "Identity Lost?" *Journalism* 18, no. 2 (2017): 195–210.

37 Josephi, and O'Donnell, "The Blurring Line between Freelance Journalists and Self-employed Media Workers," 139–156; Markus Ojala, Mervi Pantti, and Jarkko Kangas, "Professional Role Enactment amid Information Warfare," *Journalism* 19, no. 3 (2018): 297–313.

38 Karin Wahl-Jorgensen, "An Emotional Turn in Journalism Studies?" *Digital Journalism* 8, no. 2 (2020): 175–194.

39 Jeremy Caplan, Rachele Kanigel, and Betty Tsakarestou, "Entrepreneurial Journalism," *Journalism & Mass Communication Educator* 75, no. 1 (2020): 27–32.

40 David Baines, and Ciara Kennedy, "An Education for Independence" *Journalism Practice* 4, no. 1 (2010): 97–113; Marcel Broersma, and Jane B. Singer, "Caught between Innovation and Tradition," *Journalism Practice* 15, no. 6 (2021): 821–838.

41 Rozane De Cock, and Hedwig De Smaele, "Freelancing in Flemish News Media and Entrepreneurial Skills as Pivotal Elements in Job Satisfaction" *Journalism*

Practice 10, no.2 (2016): 251–265; Mark Deuze and Tamara Witschge, *Beyond Journalism* (Cambridge, UK: Polity, 2020), 11.

42 Himma-Kadakas, and Mõttus, "Ready to Hire a Freelance Journalist," 27–43.

43 Himma-Kadakas, and Mõttus, "Ready to Hire a Freelance Journalist," 27–43; Marín-Sanchiz, Carvajal, and Luis González-Esteban, "Survival Strategies in Freelance Journalism," 1–24.

44 Marín-Sanchiz, Carvajal, and González-Esteban, "Survival Strategies in Freelance Journalism: An Empowering Toolkit to Improve Professionals' Working Conditions," *Journalism Practice* 17, no. 3 (2023): 450–473. DOI: 10.1080/17512786.2021.1929414.

45 Norbäck, Maria and Alexander Styhre, "Making it Work in Free Agent Work: The Coping Practices of Swedish Freelance Journalists," *Scandinavian Journal of Management* 35, no. 4 (2019): 1–11. DOI: 10.1016/j.scaman.2019.101076.

46 Norbäck, and Styhre, "Making it Work in Free Agent Work: The Coping Practices of Swedish Freelance Journalists," 1–11.

47 Norbäck, and Styhre, "Making it Work in Free Agent Work: The Coping Practices of Swedish Freelance Journalists," 1–11.

48 Bittner, *Managing Change*, 1–32; Gollmitzer, "Precariously Employed Watchdogs? Perceptions of Working Conditions among Freelancers and Interns," 826–41; Marín-Sanchiz, Carvajal, and Luis González-Esteban, "Survival Strategies in Freelance Journalism," 1–24.

49 Himma-Kadakas, and Mõttus, "Ready to Hire a Freelance Journalist," 27–43.

50 Judith Mcintosh White, "The Communicative Action of Journalists and Public Information Officers," *Journalism Practice* 6, no.4 (2012): 563–580; Lee Salter, "The Communicative Structures of Journalism and Public Relations," *Journalism* 6, no.1 (2005): 90–106.

51 Bittner, *Managing Change: Innovation and Trade Unionism in the News Industry*, 1–32; Martina Ladendorf, "Ethical Boundary Settings of Freelance Journalists Concerning Information Work", *Nordicom Review* 33, no.1 (2012): 83–98; Thomas Koch and Magdalena Obermaier,"Blurred Lines: German Freelance Journalists with Secondary Employment in Public Relations," *Public Relations Review* 40, no. 3 (2014): 473–482.

52 Van Leuven, Vanhaelewyn, and Raeymaeckers, "From One Division of Labor to the Other: The Relation Between Beat Reporting, Freelancing, and Journalistic Autonomy,"1203–1221.

53 Mark Coddington, "The Wall Becomes a Curtain: Revisiting Journalism's News-business Boundary," in *Boundaries of Journalism* eds. Carlson, Matt and Seth C. Lewis, (New York, NY: Routledge, 2015), 67–82; Josephi, and O'Donnell, "The Blurring Line between Freelance Journalists and Self-employed Media Workers," 139–156.

54 Coddington, "The Wall Becomes a Curtain," 67–82.

55 Deuze and Witschge, *Beyond Journalism*.

56 Marín-Sanchiz, Carvajal, and Luis González-Esteban, "Survival Strategies in Freelance Journalism," 1–24; Vandenberghe, and d'Haenens, "The Netherlands. On Media Concentration and Resilient Freelance Journalists," 257–296.

57 Norbäck, "Glimpses of Resistance: Entrepreneurial subjectivity and Freelance Journalist Work," 426–448.

58 Himma-Kadakas, and Mõttus, "Ready to Hire a Freelance Journalist," 27–43.

59 Christof Vanschoubroek, "De Politieke Strijd over uw Papieren Krant," *De Standaard*, October 27, 2022, https://www.standaard.be/cnt/dmf20221026_97563290.

18

WORKPLACE HAPPINESS, JOURNALISM AND COVID-19 IN SOUTH ASIA

Achala Abeykoon, Archana Kumari, Mohammad Sahid Ullah, Pallavi Majumdar, Sajjad Ali, Mou Mukherjee Das, Santosh Kumar Biswal, M. C. Rasmin, Shilpa Kalyan, Mohd Shahid, and Mamunor Rashid

The study is based on the theoretical underpinning of Frederick Herzberg's motivation-hygiene theory,[1] which suggests that job satisfaction and dissatisfaction are independent of each other and that each has its own set of mutually exclusive factors that cause job satisfaction or dissatisfaction.[2] The authors rely on qualitative research methods, using a case studies research strategy to gain a deeper understanding of how and why these positive practices contribute to workplace happiness. Thus, ten senior media professionals from Bangladesh, Bhutan, India, Pakistan, and Sri Lanka were interviewed to explore how they were treated by their media institutions during the pandemic.

The authors found that journalists were not heavily dissatisfied with their employment during the pandemic. They attribute this to the financial support that they received, relaxation of company policies such as leave-taking and the opportunity to work from home, and the safety, fringe benefits and emotional support extended by their organizations. It would thus seem that the satisfactory status of extrinsic facets has become a central hygiene element that positively impacted employee satisfaction during the pandemic. However, interview participants stated that media organizations could have played a significant role in extending emotional and psychological support to their employees during this period. These practices can become exemplary, allowing journalists to better cope with future traumatic events and enhance well-being in the journalism profession.

Happiness, COVID-19 and Media Institutions

The term "happiness" is mostly perceived in terms of subjective or emotional well-being such as the presence of positive emotions and pleasantness in life. Happiness is crucial for media institutions given that journalism is one of the

DOI: 10.4324/9781003364597-21

most stressful professions.[3] This is due to elements such as the physical and mental demands of the work, low salary, job insecurity, long and irregular hours, exposure to disasters and poor treatment by editors.[4] Compared to employees in other professions, the role of journalists during the pandemic became complex and difficult as they had to make the public aware of the danger of a little-known disease risking their own safety and well-being.

A 2020 survey of 1,406 journalists in 125 countries during the first wave of the pandemic, for instance, found that 70 percent of them experienced psychological and emotional impacts due to the COVID-19 crisis as the most difficult aspect of their work. Eighty-nine percent reported that their news organization had taken at least one negative measure due to the financial impacts of COVID-19, such as job and salary cuts and media outlet closures. Thirty percent stated that their news organizations had not provided protective equipment for field reporting. Respondents also stated that they urgently needed mental health support and interventions due to burnout. Sixty-one percent of them reported that their commitment to journalism has increased due to the pandemic.[5]

These findings speak to the importance of maintaining media workplace happiness, particularly during a crisis such as the pandemic. In this chapter, we discuss a few of the positive strategies employed by the journalists and their media institutions and the factors that motivated them to continue working in this crucial profession in several South Asian countries, namely Bangladesh, Bhutan, India, Pakistan, and Sri Lanka.[6]

Frederick Herzberg's motivation-hygiene theory

According to this theory—also known as the two-factor theory—job satisfaction and dissatisfaction are independent of each other, and each has its own set of mutually exclusive factors that cause job satisfaction or dissatisfaction.[7] Intrinsic factors related to a job such as achievement, recognition, responsibility, and advancement are identified as motivators. Extrinsic factors such as interpersonal relationships, salary, supervision, and company policy are identified as hygiene factors. In 1959, Herzberg found that motivators contribute to good feelings about the job and hygiene factors are associated with bad feelings about the job. Further, unlike other theoretical approaches to job satisfaction and dissatisfaction, this theory suggests that even though hygiene factors prevent dissatisfaction, they do not necessarily lead to satisfaction. Herzberg also argued that personal motivators or intrinsic factors are the real motivational factors for an employee.[8] Hence, the opposite of satisfaction is no satisfaction, but not dissatisfaction, and the opposite of dissatisfaction is no dissatisfaction.[9]

Several researchers have found that a number of factors that bring satisfaction to journalists are intrinsic to the job.[10] These include the quality of the journalism produced, goals that align with the goals of the employer, autonomy and working in a fast-paced and stressful environment. Several studies found that extrinsic factors such as salary, hours, competent management, and equipment are also important for determining journalist dissatisfaction.[11]

The focus of most of the studies on employee satisfaction in media and journalism conducted during and after the most critical period of the COVID-19 outbreak and lockdown periods (early 2020 to early 2022) is negative experiences such as physical and mental stress, burnout, and psychological impacts. However, little attention has been paid to how media institutions and their employees (particularly those living and working in South Asia) coped with these negative impacts and how they continued to play their role of informing, persuading, and entertaining audiences.

To gain an in-depth understanding of how and why these positive practices contributed to journalists' workplace happiness during the COVID-19 pandemic, this study relies on a qualitative research method using case study research strategy and interview method for data collection. Ten journalists from Bangladesh, Bhutan, India, Pakistan, and Sri Lanka were interviewed. Their experiences are thematically presented to explore the factors that motivated them to stay in their profession despite the immense hardships they had to endure during the COVID-19 pandemic.

South Asian Journalists, Media Organizations and COVID-19

Almost all the South Asian journalists who shared their experiences during the COVID-19 outbreak admitted that they were stressed and depressed during this period. They report that this was mainly due to the paradoxical situation they had to confront. However, across all countries, it became apparent that the organizations they work for played a significant role in determining their levels of happiness at work and in life.

Financial security provided by the media organizations

Most interviewed journalists were happy that their monthly salaries had not been cut despite the financial difficulties faced by their organizations.

> We are lucky that we were paid a salary every month and had the opportunity to work from home. There has been no major job cut during the pandemic.
>
> *(AKM Moinuddin, Bangladesh)*

A senior journalist in Bangladesh identified this as the "only comforting thing" that happened during the pandemic. In Odisha, a state in the eastern part of India, Odia language journalists were also glad that they were paid their full salaries and received other perks as usual even though media organizations were reeling from the dearth of advertising revenues. However, performance reviews were not conducted, which meant that the pay structure was not adjusted. The journalists interviewed in Sri Lanka and Pakistan did not offer any negative comments on their monthly salaries.

Owusu[12] asserted that financial knowledge and attitude have "a positive association with both financial management and financial satisfaction." Thus, the financial security guaranteed by organizations was one of the main sources of relief for journalists during the pandemic, and it brought happiness and relief to them and their families. These experiences contrast with the recent study conducted by Posetti et al.[13] in which 89 percent of interviewed journalists admitted that their news organizations had implemented at least one measure such as salary cuts, job cuts and outlet closures due to the gravity of the pandemic.

In the area addressed here, the print media industry in Bhutan, a country with one of the smallest economies in the world, has been most impacted by the financial insecurity caused by the pandemic. Over 90 percent of Bhutanese citizens are active members of at least one social media platform.[14] Legacy media that are heavily dependent on government advertising and hand-outs struggle for their survival. According to a senior journalist from Bhutan this situation worsened when the Bhutanese government took to publishing information on its official Facebook pages instead of holding regular press briefings to the mainstream media to disseminate information. The number of private newspapers dropped from 11 in 2013 to five in 2019. "We saw losing our jobs as the main threat instead of infection," a senior journalist shared (personal communication).

A journalist interviewed in West Bengal, India was critical of the salaries journalists receive. He said that employees are exploited, especially younger ones, and that salaries are not paid according to the standard norms. Journalism professionals are forced to work extended hours for no extra payment, significantly impacting the mental well-being of the journalists in the organization.

The opportunity to work from home and flexible time off

Under normal circumstances, journalists are generally unable to work from home because they must meet strict deadlines and travel to the field to gather news. Long and irregular hours of work are one of the main sources of stress for journalists.[15] However, during the COVID-19 pandemic, respondents from Pakistan, Bangladesh, Odisha and West Bengal of India and Sri Lanka were glad that they were given the rare opportunity to work from home.

> Introducing the home office was the best thing for the employees, as many colleagues tested positive for COVID-19. This decision brought the employees a great deal of comfort.
>
> *(AKM Moinuddin, Bangladesh)*

A journalist from Bengal, India who was assigned to New Delhi during the pandemic was allowed to report to work from the Kolkata office until the situation improved.

Further, female employees in a small-scale digital media station called Pahalavan, in northern Sri Lanka have very much benefitted from the work-from-home option, as they felt that traveling was not safe or that it was stressful, or that they needed to be home to take care of their family. Irregular and long working hours including weekends was an important concern in the journalism profession, particularly for women we interviewed.[16] For the safety and convenience of the staff members, Pahalavan also decided to conduct all live discussions using virtual platforms, meaning that staff members could conduct them from home. Staff members who were unable to set up a mini production facility in their homes were still given an opportunity to record their content in the form of audio file using simple equipment such as smartphones, laptops, and mini recorders instead of video. The audio clips were then re-edited by people in the office who added visual footage taken from archival footage when it was available.

A senior journalist in Bangladesh reported that he had to go to the office from time to time because he was the leader of a section. He felt that management pressured employees to resume certain duties, which caused stress and even death for some. The pandemic highlighted the peculiarity of journalism in Bhutan. The lack of competition in the industry meant that Bhutanese journalists could stay at home during the pandemic. "In 2020, there was an outbreak of COVID-19 in a remote village, but none of the journalists wanted to risk their lives to go there," explained a senior journalist. The fact that there was no pressure to go into the field can be interpreted in several ways. It could be a clear indication of a lack of drive to bring relevance and urgency to news reports. On the other hand, it could be a work culture that genuinely values journalists' lives.

This ease of working from home has positively impacted journalists' lives as they have been able to spend meaningful time with their family members and enhance their social communications during a difficult period. For most of them it was a rare opportunity to enjoy a break from their irregular and long work hours. Similarly, research found that journalists valued their friends and family more than before and experienced a deeper appreciation for life during the pandemic.[17]

Another benefit of working from home is finding time to enhance their professional and life skills. Shafi Ullah and Sabir Aman of Pakistan read books, enrolled in online courses and contacted international journalist organizations and unions. They attended numerous virtual meetings, workshops, and conferences.

When we started working from home, I had so much free time that I completed an online course called "English-language communication skills" and another online course titled "Become a Journalist: Report the News" on Coursera.

(Muhammad Shahid, Pakistan)

Further, most of the journalists interviewed were glad that they were allowed to take time off without losing pay during the pandemic. According to a journalist from Sri Lanka, reporters in his organization received 14 paid days off if they tested positive for COVID-19. In Odisha, India, media organizations were flexible when it came to giving their employees time off when needed. Journalists who were infected with the virus were given special leave so that they could quarantine, which meant that the time off did not impact casual and emergency leaves. It can be argued that the relaxation of policy and procedures practiced by some of these organizations on leave-taking and working from home during critical times might have enhanced the satisfaction of their employees.

Safety and emotional care provided by the organizations

The journalists were also happy that their management took measures to ensure their safety and physical well-being. According to several journalists in Sri Lanka, for example, roster systems were introduced during strict lockdown periods to minimize crowds. Employees were given private transportation because public transportation was not available during the lockdown periods. This was another way that management entities took steps to ensure their safety. Suitable nearby lodging was arranged for some employees who had to report to work from far away. It also became difficult for employees to find places to eat during the strict lockdown period in the country, so their organizations gave them three meals per day. Some media organizations even provided employees who contracted COVID-19 at work with hotel accommodations, food allowances, and dry rations to quarantined employees and their families. Some organizations allowed their journalists to participate in online press conferences, conduct online interviews, limit access to their premises, etc. to keep them safe. Media organizations in Sri Lanka, particularly those located in Colombo, the capital, took measures to reassure their employees and keep them safe.

Respondents who work in other countries were grateful of the support provided by senior management at their organizations. "Even when I tested positive for COVID-19, the top management was always in touch with me and inquired about my health" (AKM Moinuddin, Bangladesh). In Odisha, India, journalists contracted the virus during various waves of COVID because they were working on the front lines. They reported that they were provided insurance and given adequate mental health support by senior journalists and others in their news organizations. However, a senior journalist from Bangladesh described the treatment of employees by senior management as "not excellent."

Journalists reported receiving free masks and hand sanitizers and said that employees were given the opportunity to get vaccinated at work or in another suitable location. Organizations that were created to protect journalists' welfare such as the Press Club of Bengal held vaccination programs. The Journalists' Association of Bhutan (JAB) also recognized that journalists face stressful situations and need mental health support.[18]

A sense of professional obligation

Respondents also mentioned feeling that it was their professional responsibility to serve the public during the COVID-19 pandemic.

> Jammu and Kashmir, especially in Jammu province, faced lots of problems in terms of medical emergencies. So, I used the power of the mic and camera to highlight all the problems faced by the public for the Jammu and Kashmir administration. I found it very inspiring when a patient received the care he needed because of my reporting.
>
> *(Ashish Kohil, India)*

According to Rajat Vohra, a journalist from Jammu and Kashmir in India, the support and appreciation of the public was one of the main reasons journalists continued to do their work during the pandemic. Forty-three percent of respondents felt there was increased audience trust in their journalism during the first wave of COVID-19. Meanwhile, 61 percent said they were more committed to journalism than they were before the pandemic.

Were South Asian Journalists Happy in the Workplace?

Based on Frederick Herzberg's motivation-hygiene theory, the extrinsic factors discussed above, such as salary, company policies, interpersonal relationships between employer and employee, and fringe benefits can be identified as hygiene factors that are associated with bad feelings about the job. Although one could not argue that journalists were satisfied with their work during the COVID-19 outbreak, according to the findings of this particular study, they may not have been totally dissatisfied either due to considerable positive support provided by their news organizations.[19] It is also possible to argue that the support contributed to pleasant feelings towards their profession and positive experiences to a certain extent at work due to certain changes of rigid rules such as difficulties in taking leave, irregular working hours.[20]

The feeling that they felt a responsibility to carry out their duties during this critical period (an intrinsic factor) can be identified as a motivational factor that persuaded some of these journalists to remain in the profession despite the difficulties that they faced. Some of them were also satisfied and happy with their profession during this period that they could report rural news in-depth unlike prior to the pandemic due to there being more time available to spend on producing investigative news.

Furthermore, the findings of our study also suggest that when psychological resources such as hope, optimism, resilience, and self-efficacy that influence work stress are dealt with in a positive way, employee happiness at work increases.[21] As such, the measures taken by the South Asian media organizations in this study helped ease employees' stress, thus positively contributing to their happiness at work even though this could not be generalized. As discussed by our interviewees, their employers must pay more attention to the intrinsic factors such as mental health of their employees during a crisis such as COVID-19 while attending to the hygienic factors. The stress and trauma that they had to undergo during the pandemic, for instance, have not been adequately addressed nor given enough attention by their organizations. According to an Indian senior journalist of a reputed media house, female journalists were forced to leave their jobs due to non-supportive management. While this would be an area that requires further investigation, in conclusion, equal attention should be given to the intrinsic motivations of journalists as well as to extrinsic factors such as conducting regular non-formal meetings with employees or enabling workers to talk to an in-house or hired counselor in order to make them happier in the workplace.

Notes

1   Frederick I. Herzberg, "Motivation-Hygiene Theory," in *Organizational Behavior I* by John B. Miner. (New York: M E Sharp, 2005), 61–74.
2   Frederick I. Herzberg, "Work and the Nature of Man," (1966); Frederic I. Herzberg, B. Mausner, and B. B. Snyderman, *The Motivation to Work*, 2nd edn. (New York, NY: John Wiley & Sons, 1959).
3   DeFillippi, "Dilemmas of Project-based Media Work," 5–30; Fedler, "Insiders' Stories," 77–106; Reinardy, "Newspaper Journalism in Crisis," 33–50
4   Fedler, "Insiders' Stories," 77–106.
5   Posetti, Bell, and Brown, "Journalism and the Pandemic."
6   Herzberg, "Motivation-Hygiene Theory," 61–62.
7   Herzberg, "Work and the Nature of Man," 56.
8   Herzberg, "Work and the Nature of Man," 56.
9   Herzberg, "Motivation-Hygiene Theory," 61–74.
10 Grace H. Barrett, "Job Satisfaction among Newspaperwomen," *Journalism Quarterly* 61, no. 3 (1984): 593–599; Randal A Beam, "Organizational Goals and Priorities and the Job Satisfaction of US. Journalists," *Journalism & Mass Communication Quarterly* 83, no. 1 (2006): 169–185.
11 Barrett, "Job Satisfaction among Newspaperwomen," 593–599.
12 Godfred Matthew Yaw Owusu, "Predictors of Financial Satisfaction and its Impact on Psychological Well-Being of Individuals," *Journal of Humanities and Applied Social Sciences* (2021). https://doi.org/10.1108/JHASS-05-2021-0101.
13 Posetti, Bell, and Brown, "Journalism and the Pandemic."
14 *Bhutan Media Landscape*. (n.d.). Retrieved August 23, 2022, from https://rsf.org/en/country/bhutan.
15 Fedler, "Insiders' Stories," 77–106.

16 Schallom, *Satisfaction and Journalism*.
17 Posetti, Bell, and Brown, "Journalism and the Pandemic."
18 Chencho Dema, *The Stress of Being a Journalist*, March 23, (2022), Retrieved August 23, 2022, from https://businessbhutan.bt/the-stress-of-being-a-journalist/.
19 Herzberg, "Work and the Nature of Man,"; Herzberg, "Motivation-Hygiene Theory," 61–74.
20 Fisher, "Happiness at Work," 384–412.
21 Kim-Lim Tan, Tek-Yew Lew, and Adriel K.S. Sim, "Is Meaningful Work the Silver Bullet? Perspectives of the Social Workers," *Journal of Asia Business Studies* 13, no. 4 (2019): 612–632.

19

ENGAGED JOURNALISM AND PROFESSIONAL HAPPINESS

Lambrini Papadopoulou and Eugenia Siapera

What is happiness? How do people define and understand happiness in their professional lives and how does it affect their personal lives? And when it comes to a profession such as journalism, perceived less as a job and more as a vocation, what does it mean to be happy? In this chapter, we approach these questions through an in-depth discussion/interview with an engaged journalist. We also seek to understand the motivations and sources of deep satisfaction for an engaged journalist. What form does professional happiness take for an engaged journalist? What kind of obstacles are in the way of professional happiness? How does an engaged journalist balance the various tensions and conflicting demands? We begin exploring these questions by first outlining Maslow's hierarchy of needs and its embeddedness in studies of motivation and organizational practice.[1] We then discuss the focus on engaged journalism, referring to the kind of journalism that develops an ongoing relationship with its public, considering them as active participants in the news-making process and the use of a life history and narrative approach.[2]

Maslow's Needs, Motivational Theory and Engaged Journalism

Professional happiness, job satisfaction and motivation have been studied by organizational psychologists to identify what motivates people to work and under what circumstances they are enabled to not invest their energies into their work and also to develop and grow.[3] In this chapter, we focus on Maslow's hierarchy of needs, which is one of the first and most influential theories of motivation. Motivation, defined as the forces that push or propel a person to satisfy basic needs or wants, is a determinant of job satisfaction, and a component of professional and personal happiness.[4] Because of this relationship, we argue

DOI: 10.4324/9781003364597-22

that to understand happiness in journalism we need to understand how motivation works for journalists.

Maslow used his experiences as a psychologist to formulate a theory of needs, in which they are ordered in a hierarchy: needs at the bottom must be satisfied before an individual can move to the next level. The fulfilment of these needs is therefore what motivates a person. As soon as a need is satisfied, the person becomes focused on the next level of need. Needs exist in a hierarchy of repetency, which means that they are not all equal, but rather one need at a time becomes prepotent until satisfied. Maslow's[5] main argument was that people move from the bottom to the top of the hierarchy one step at a time.

At the bottom of the hierarchy, Maslow put physiological needs such as food and shelter. The next step up includes safety needs such as protection from danger. Hamner and Organ[6] found that job uncertainty, precarity and discrimination are all powerful motivators of the need for safety. Social needs come after these needs: love, friendship, belongingness and so on are important motivators here. According to Maslow, a person will not start looking to fulfil their social needs until the first two needs are met. Ego needs emerge after social needs are satisfied; these include the need for recognition, status, and prestige. Finally, at the top of the hierarchy we encounter self-actualization needs, meaning the need to fulfil one's potential, to grow and develop into what one's fullest potential.

While research has sought to refine these factors, our task in this chapter is different: to use this theory as a guide for understanding professional happiness in journalism. However, given the wide variation in the kind of journalism practiced, we decided to focus on engaged journalism. We follow Bélair-Gagnon et al.[7] in viewing engaged journalism as a kind of journalism that develops an ongoing relationship with its public, considering them as active participants in the news-making process. Ferrucci et al.[8] consider engaged journalism to be the successor to twentieth-century public journalism that centered journalism around citizens and created public debates[9] with the emphasis being on building a relationship of trust between journalists and the communities they serve.[10] This research is in continuation of previous work on this topic, in which we foreground the social role of journalism and an orientation towards community and especially marginalized social groups rather than towards the elites.[11]

Research Approach

Typically, theories of motivation are validated through surveys. Several studies on engaged journalism have also used surveys alongside in-depth interviews with a representative sample of journalists, newsroom participant observation and content analyses of engaged journalism's outputs. In this chapter, we adopt a different approach, because we are looking to explore engaged journalism in more depth and in a holistic manner. We are looking to gain a deeper insight into the motivations and sources of deep satisfaction for an engaged journalist. We are influenced by anthropological accounts and thick descriptions, which consider not only social actions, but their meaning and reasoning from the perspective of actors themselves.[12] We have therefore pivoted towards a life history narrative interview, which, following Dhunpath,[13] we take to provide a "means of understanding how motives and practices reflect the intimate intersection of institutional and individual experience."

Rather than viewing the life narrative approach as a method of elicitation of knowledge, we considered it as a co-production of knowledge, emerging out of an in-depth discussion and reflection on journalism between three participants who are all invested in developing ways to advance journalism and to make it accountable to the communities it serves. The focal point of this discussion was the life experience and views of a practicing engaged journalist, Mariniki Alevizopoulou. After a long career as a reporter in Greece, Mariniki co-founded a monthly political review, *Unfollow* magazine, which experimented with a new format for political reporting, in between investigative and activist journalism. The magazine peaked during the period of the sovereign debt crisis in Greece but eventually folded around 2018. Since then, Mariniki has worked as a freelance journalist and is involved in an investigative journalism start-up, The Manifold Files, which has had considerable success in receiving high profile grants, for example from Google News.

We invited Alevizopoulou to take part in this experimental co-production of knowledge because both authors know and admire her work, which involves covering high profile trials during the Greek version of the #MeToo movement in 2020–2022. Mariniki's reputation is that of a fearless, tenacious and principled journalist. It is these attributes that we are particularly interested in: where do they come from, how are they justified, and crucially how are they linked to professional satisfaction and perhaps even happiness? The discussion that follows seeks to provide some initial answers to these questions.

Engaged Journalism: Trauma and Joy

Using motivation theory as our guide, we begin from the most basic level of hygiene or basic needs, since their presence is a necessary condition for professional happiness. We then loosely follow Maslow's pyramid, while also allowing the discussion to flow and cover areas that Mariniki considered important to discuss. Mariniki provided important context for her motivations, based on personal experiences, not only as a working journalist, but coming from her own life trajectory, her commitment to feminist politics and her experiences as a mother of a young daughter.

The basics: money and making a living

Physiological needs, namely basic biological requirements such as food, drink, shelter and clothing are placed at the lower end of the hierarchy of needs and according to Maslow they are considered the most important as they must be satisfied first before individuals can attend to needs higher up. "So according to Maslow, I should find another job," was Mariniki's laughing reaction as we discussed the structure of the hierarchy. Mariniki seems to move between the different levels of the hierarchy without having first explicitly satisfied her basic needs since, as she explained, her work is not well paid. Nevertheless, she keeps going despite the low wages and job precarity. How or why do you do it?, we asked.

To explain, she referred to her recent experiences covering a high-profile case of rape and sexual abuse of young boys. The trial, which took place in 2022, was covered by all media, as the accused, Dimitris Lignadis, was the director of the National Theatre of Greece. Mariniki went to the trial every day. She recounted that she wrote four articles for a news website that paid her €250 in total. Why then did she do it? Because, she said, of a very personal and pressing need to record what was going on during the trial. "For me it was unthinkable that this trial would take place incognito and that any information we might receive would come through Lignadis' defence counsel and from the clique of reporters who covered the trial and have a friendly or even very friendly relationship with his counsel," she explained. Trauma, sexual abuse, and abuse of power are stories that need to be covered for the victims/survivors and on their behalf. Mariniki expressed the feeling that she had to be present in the trial every single day for their sake. To help us understand further her motivation and thinking around being present for survivors of abuse, Mariniki reflected on her personal life trajectory and its various intersections.

Weaving the personal with the professional

In accounting for her specific focus and insistence on covering the Lignadis rape trial, Mariniki disclosed that she was a student in the private school where he used to teach:

> I know what he's done; I know incidents that are relevant to the current accusations. I was "in" this case right from the beginning. So I got in touch with some of the victims, I believed them and I wanted to be there for them because I just could not think that they would be left alone to be eaten by the wolves. And by wolves I also mean my colleagues who cover this kind of beat.

She said that most of her colleagues would just report the most sensational parts of the case and then move on to the next story, following the prevailing notion "if it bleeds, it leads." However, Mariniki invested herself in the trial, formed real connections with the survivors and stood by them to protect them not only from the accused's defence counsel but also from the *wolves*, as she called her fellow reporters. This, Mariniki explained, is due to their covering the court beat and therefore being close to lawyers, especially high-profile ones, who are celebrities in their own right and provide headlines to journalists. This mainstream, narrow and self-serving type of journalism does not sit well with Mariniki. Her own experiences, knowledge and principles take her to a different direction: one that looks to offer voice to those silenced or, as the case may be, support them in deciding to remain silent. This enables her, she said, to "remain true to herself" and to validate and honour her own experiences as a survivor of abuse and trauma.

Contrary to the culture of masculinity that is sometimes associated with daily newsroom activities[14] Mariniki practices a more emotionally aware kind of journalism. She does not hide or suppress her personal experiences, nor does she try to shield herself from the emotional impact of the stories she covers. She remains aware of her emotions and uses them as motivations, allowing them to take over and guide her professional decisions. As pointed out by Wahl-Jorgensen[15] much of the best of journalism draws extensively on emotion. These, sometimes traumatic, life experiences constitute the resources that Mariniki mobilizes to make a meaningful contribution to journalism. By trusting her inner voice and following all the stories that "are burning her inside" as she put it, she is being true to herself and to the kind of journalism she practices. Importantly, motherhood acted as a catalyst for this kind of thinking.

Becoming a mother was an awakening experience that brought back various personal memories and traumas, leading her to pursue an investigative report, the first ever, on the failures of the child protection system in Greece. As she recounts, "when you bring a child into the world, you inevitably revisit your childhood self with a different look, under different terms." Recounting a story from her childhood, Mariniki explained how motherhood led her to find the story behind the story: a crying baby that breaks the side bars of her crib is not a strong baby but a scared and desperate baby, whose needs are not met. This realization helped her not only understand herself better but also identify with those whose needs society is not meeting. Mariniki explicitly mobilizes her feelings and values in practicing journalism. Her experiences, traumas, values and aspirations inform every decision she takes. By investing her true self in this work, she also provides space for her multiple identities, including being a mother, journalist and feminist to express themselves and help her practice a kind of journalism far removed from the role of a detached observer that still permeates understandings of journalism.

This is clear in another incident that took place while she was covering Lignadis' trial. While in the courtroom, Mariniki left to join a group of feminists who wanted to protest over a child custody case that was taking place in a nearby courtroom. She said she did this because:

> [T]he father was abusive and the mother a foreigner, so he was trying to take the child's custody by paying off his former wife's lawyers. So I barged in with them [a group of feminists]. I barged in as a feminist, as a mother and as a journalist. I barged in with all my roles.

This incident is closely connected to her own life experiences since as a child she also experienced her parents' traumatic divorce and custody fight. As she explained:

> I wish that someone did the same for me when my own custody was discussed and when my father was calling my mother a whore threatening to sue her for perjury. So, it is very important to not feel alone in the courtroom. I know how it is, I remember it and I will never forget it. It is very important, [to stand by that child], it makes you feel better and it gives you a sense of balance.

We interpret Mariniki's disclosure of the guiding role of her traumatic personal experiences as revealing an ongoing process of working through. In particular, these experiences guide and help her navigate her journalistic practice in ways that reconcile tensions between professional and personal identities. This in turn enables Mariniki to validate and honour her emotional experiences and trauma through supporting and giving voice to others going through similar processes and also having to deal with the added trauma of doing so in public and becoming part of stories reported in the news. By validation here we mean the recognition and acceptance of past experiences and associated trauma.[16] In these terms, Mariniki's professional position is consciously guided by a recognition of her past experiences, especially when she sees them replayed again and again among survivors of abuse and trauma. In this manner, we observe that for a journalist like Mariniki self-actualization emerges out of practising a kind of journalism that is consistent with her own experiences and trauma, and the principled positions that emerged from these. But what does this mean for "lower order" factors such as safety?

Community, Belonging and Safety

Investing herself into every story she covers allows Mariniki to create strong social connections around her. Journalists have been stereotypically portrayed as lone wolves who work hard to unveil injustices or scandals maintaining for themselves the position of a distant hero.[17] In contrast, community lies at the heart of Mariniki's journalistic practice. The communities she has managed to build with her friends, colleagues, readers, social media followers and sources provide her with emotional stability, satisfying her needs for safety, love/belonging and esteem.

Belonging to a community and social relationships inform the way Mariniki works and the stories she decides to cover. This was the case for another Greek #MeToo trial she covered, the trial of the actor Petros Philippidis who is facing rape charges. Covering these trials gave Mariniki the opportunity to get to know some of the actor's victims during the breaks of both the trials. As she explained:

> I never covered cultural and lifestyle stories, and I don't watch a lot of TV series so I didn't really know these actresses but we would meet in the breaks and talk and eventually we formed relationships. When we started talking, they were all saying how alone they felt as no one helped them and that no information regarding what was going on in the trial went public. They asked for help and so I began covering that trial as well.

We see here another occasion of an engaged journalist like Mariniki being driven by the needs of the community and choosing the side of those who are isolated and silenced. But sometimes, as we will see below, silence may be preferable.

Personal relationships over exclusive stories

Mariniki's relationship with her sources is also another example of the way she invests herself in her work. Notwithstanding the prevailing notion that journalist-source relations are reciprocal by nature as both parties need to feel they have something to gain,[18] Mariniki formed deep and honest relationships with her sources and in various instances preferred to miss a good or even exclusive story. She explained:

> Journalism gives you the opportunity to meet various people and get to know them deeply or spend time with them in their most difficult times. In essence, this relationship very quickly jumps through all the stages that a relationship under normal circumstances would go through and suddenly you find yourself talking with a person about their most important, deepest thoughts and issues.

Franklin argues that journalist–source relations are "driven by a strategic complementarity of interests."[19] This was not at all the case when in 2007 Mariniki went to the West Peloponnese to cover one of the worst wildfires in Greece's history. Forty-nine people lost their lives and among the victims were a mother and her four children. During her stay there, she got to know the victims' families:

> We formed deep relationships. I have eaten with these people, they invited me to the christenings of their children. I never wrote about them. I

never asked, for instance, to interview this woman's husband with whom we went out and drunk together. I knew that he wouldn't want it. This is the way I understand this work and I cannot do it any other way.

A key part of our argument here is that a strong commitment to principles and social values is fundamental to deriving professional satisfaction and contentment in engaged journalism, even if this came at the cost of what the profession would understand as a good story. What then is self-actualization, or the goal of working as an engaged journalist?

Self-Actualization through Communal Actualization

Self-actualization is defined by Maslow as the desire to accomplish everything that one can, to become the most that one can be. It should be pointed out that Maslow's hierarchy was revisited by studies that tried to advance his ideas but that he also highlighted a new highest level, that of self-transcendence referring to intrinsic and extrinsic developmental processes.[20]

For Mariniki, self-actualization is directly connected with the strong social bonds and communities she builds. Being an integral part of a supportive community enables her to grow personally and professionally and create for herself the kind of journalism she wants to practice.

In this context, self-actualization comes through communal actualization. The communities she creates and participates in help her meet her needs of belonging, of feeling loved and esteemed. The emotional connections she shares are deep and sincere and allow her to grow through them both as a person and as a journalist. She in turn invests herself in every story, lends her voice to those in need and provides them with the support and respect they deserve. Her own job satisfaction and professional happiness hinge on her ability to practice journalism while remaining true to herself and consistent with her principles. Does this mean she is happy? How does she understand happiness?

Happiness and Contentment

Mariniki's narrative told a story of an engaged journalist consciously driven by her own experiences and past trauma which led her to adopt a principled position in support of victims and survivors of abuse and trauma. Staying true to herself, consistent with her principles and values, and serving a community are central to Mariniki and her journalism. Can we therefore think of her as a happy journalist?

McKenzie defines contentment as a fulfilling relationship between the self and society. In western modernity, pursuits of happiness are prioritized over contentment. The latter is long lasting and involves a form of self-understanding that becomes a source of satisfaction or fulfilment.[21] Contentment may not sound as powerful or joyful as happiness but nevertheless entails a deeper, more meaningful and more long-lasting sense of satisfaction. Most importantly, contentment cannot be achieved in isolation. On the contrary, as McKenzie points out, contentment is a collective and long-term life project. Indeed, Mariniki Alevizopoulou's personal experiences may guide her professional decisions, but it is the social bonds she creates that essentially keep her going. In this sense, contentment just like self-actualization, or even self-transcendence to use the revisited notion,[22] resembles more a continual process of becoming rather than a perfect state one reaches of a "happily ever after."[23] Being embedded in society, listening closely to those in need, lending them her voice or supporting their silence, helps her keep her focus centered on the common good and essentially determines a different approach to journalism, one that we understand here as engaged journalism.

This kind of journalism entails tensions, some of which have been discussed in this chapter. Engaged journalists allow themselves to be invested in traumatic stories and are exposed to real dangers. So how can they meet their need for safety? We found that tensions as such can be resolved if journalists embed themselves within a community that is supporting and protecting.

Personal and professional lives of engaged journalists are quite often intermingled and this coexistence may create possible tensions. Guided by Mariniki's practice we argue that the only way for this tension to be resolved is by honouring and validating personal experiences and allowing true emotions guide one's approach to a story. Finally, engaged journalists may feel restricted or censored by their bosses as their ethics and values are in most cases not aligned. The solution here cannot come from any kind of compromise. Rather, just like Mariniki, we argue that engaged journalists should try to break free and turn to new and radical initiatives such as cooperatives, or other ventures that are aligned with their own values and don't measure success in terms of the profit they produce.

Notes

1 Charles, N., Weaver, "Job Satisfaction as a Component of Happiness Among Males and Females," *Personnel Psychology* 31, no. 4 (1978): 831–840, https://doi.org/10.1111/j.1744-6570.1978.tb02126.x.

2 Reid and Okoko, "Life History Narrative." In *Varieties of Qualitative Research Methods, Selected Contextual Perspectives* eds Janet Mola Okoko, Scott Runison, and Keith D. Walker (Springer, 2023), 287–293. DOI:10.1007/978-3-031-04394-9_46.

3 See for instance Lonneke Dubbelt, Evangelia Demerouti, and Sonja Rispens, "The Value of Job Crafting for Work Engagement, Task Performance, and Career Satisfaction," *European Journal of Work and Organizational Psychology* 28, no. 3 (2019): 300–314, https://doi.org/10.1080/1359432X.2019.1576632.

4 Weaver, "Job satisfaction as a component of Happiness Among Males and Females," 831–840.

5 Maslow, A. H. "A Theory of Human Motivation," *Psychological Review* 50, no. 4 (1943): 370–396.

6 Clay, W. Hamner, and Dennis W. Organ, *Organizational Behavior.* (Dalls: Business Publications, 1978).

7 Valérie Bélair-Gagnon, Jacob L. Nelson, and Seth C. Lewis, "Audience Engagement, Reciprocity, and the Pursuit of Community Connectedness in Public Media Journalism," *Journalism Practice* 13, no. 5 (2019): 558–575.

8 Patrick Ferrucci, Jacob L. Nelson, and Miles P. Davis, "From 'Public Journalism' to 'Engaged Journalism,'" *International Journal of Communication* 14 (2020): 19.

9 Jay Rosen, "Questions and Answers about Public Journalism," *Journalism Studies*, 1 (2000): 679–683.

10 Lindsay Green-Barber, "Towards a Useful Typology of Engaged Journalism," *Medium*, October 18, 2018, https://medium.com/the-impact-architects/towards-a-useful-typology-of-engaged-journalism-790c96c4577e.

11 Eugenia Siapera and Ioanna Iliadi, "Twitter, Journalism and Affective Labour, " *Sur le journalisme, About journalism, Sobre jornalismo* 4, no. 1 (2015): 76–89; Eugenia Siapera, and Lambrini Papadopoulou, "Entrepreneurialism or Cooperativism? An Exploration of Cooperative Journalistic Enterprises," *Journalism Practice* 10, no. 2 (2016): 178–195, https://doi.org/10.1080/17512786.2015.1125760.

12 Clifford Geertz, "Thick Description: Toward an Interpretive Theory of Culture." In *The Cultural Geography Reader* ed. Timothy Oakes and Patricia L. Pricepp, (Routledge, 2008), 41–51.

13 Rubby Dhunpath, "Life history methodology: 'Narradigm' regained," *International Journal of Qualitative Studies in Education* 13, no. 5 (2000): 543–551, https://doi.org/10.1080/09518390050156459.

14 Johana Kotisova, "The Elephant in the Newsroom: Current Research on Journalism and Emotion," *Sociology Compass* 13, no. 5 (2019): e12677, https://doi.org/10.1111/soc4.12677.

15 Karin Wahl-Jorgensen, "Questioning the Ideal of the Public Sphere: The Emotional Turn," *Social Media+ Society* 5, no. 3 (2019a): 1–3, https://doi.org/10.1177/2056305119852175.

16 Robert L. Leahy, "A Social-Cognitive Model of Validation." In *Compassion, Conceptualisations, Research and Use in Psychotherapy* ed. Paul Gilbert, (Los Angeles: Routledge, 2005), 195–217.

17 Raymond McCaffrey, "Stoicism and Courage as Journalistic Values," *American Journalism* 36, no. 2 (2019): 220–241, https://doi.org/10.1080/08821127.2019.1602443.

18 Marcel Broersma, Den Herder, Bas, Schohaus, Birte, "A Question of Power: The Changing Dynamics Between Journalists and Sources", *Journalism Practice* 7, no. 4 (2013), 388–395.

19 Bob Franklin, "A Good Day to Bury Bad News?: Journalists, Sources and the Packaging of Politics," *News, Public Relations and Power* (2003): 47.

20 Mark E. Koltko-Rivera, "Rediscovering the Later Version of Maslow's Hierarchy of Needs," *Review of General Psychology* 10, no. 4 (2006): 302–317, https://doi.org/10.1037/1089-2680.10.4.3.

21 McKenzie, J., "Happiness vs Contentment? A Case for a Sociology of the Good Life," *Journal for the Theory of Social Behaviour* 46, no. 3 (2016): 252–267.

22 Koltko-Rivera, "Rediscovering the later version of Maslow's hierarchy of needs," 302–317.

23 Hoffman Edward, *The Right to be Human.* (Los Angeles: Jeremy P. Tarcher, Inc, 1988).

PART IV

ESSAYS

20

HAS JOURNALISM FORGOTTEN THE JOURNALISTS?

John Crowley

Journalism is a fast-paced, dynamic profession which credits itself with writing the "first draft of history." While it can delve into fields like opinion, features, and investigation, it is most associated in the public consciousness with delivering the news. Largely depicted in fiction and on screen through a positive lens, the opportunity to get close to the world's most powerful politicians, business leaders, influencers, and celebrities remains a draw for those wanting to enter the industry. Journalism still carries with it a glamourous allure, but its most precious resource—the journalists themselves—are under severe strain. I welcome that this book is determined to address this under-reported need.

In recent years journalists have been beset on all sides by a so-called perfect storm: exposed to stress from failing business models, increased workloads, online harassment, a lack of representation and inclusion, job insecurity, macho news environments, disinformation, the pressure to be constantly connected and much more.[1]

Against this backdrop is an increasingly demanding news agenda: COVID-19 brought a new layer of complexity to news reporting. Journalists who were on the frontline faithfully telling people's stories during the pandemic were also putting themselves in harm's way.

Who was checking in on us?

While there are, as of 2023, multiple, long-running conflicts going on around the world, the Ukraine war has led news bulletins and front pages, bringing issues around vicarious trauma into sharp focus. One of the most important skills required of a journalist is the ability to engage empathetically. Bearing witness to people's stories can sometimes take them into conflict zones or disasters. But as graphic imagery and video from the battlefield is increasingly viewed on laptops and smartphones, far greater numbers back in the newsroom are being affected by vicarious trauma. Many journalists now

DOI: 10.4324/9781003364597-24

view disturbing material daily at work or, post-pandemic, in their homes without the usual newsroom support networks in place. Vicarious trauma is not just experienced through viewing graphic material from hostile environments. It can happen by being an eyewitness to any form of suffering—whether that is in a courtroom, hospital or at a crime scene. In some cases, it is felt more keenly when the experience was more relatable or closer to home.[2]

It follows that a news story can have adverse impacts on a journalist if it covers subject matter close to their own lived experience or a topic that is attached to their history or identity. Journalists bottle up their feelings from the moment they start training. I recall being told in journalism school to "never to become the story." But how does a journalist subsume their emotions when they are covering subjects such as racial injustice? Covering structural inequality through the prism of Black Lives Matter or feeling powerless to move the dial on the climate emergency can leave some reporters lacking agency. Journalists working on social media must contend with disinformation and false narratives only to find themselves the subject of online threats and abuse because of their professional status.

Many of these issues are not talked about openly when the ability to soak up pressure is seen as an integral part of a journalist's DNA. Complaining about your lot is viewed by battle-hardened co-workers as an admission of journalistic failure. This narrative needs to be challenged but few feel able to talk about such problems when awareness and support structures within newsrooms are patchy, invisible, or non-existent.

Happiness is subjective and, with such a busy in-tray of industry problems to be addressed, is it a newsroom leader or a mid-ranking line manager's responsibility to make their team happy? I would argue yes. Firstly, it's the humane thing to do. Secondly, when we are ready to preach how people should live their lives, then we need to hold ourselves to a higher standard. To really impress on newsroom leaders what needs to be done, we now need to illustrate the financial toll stress is exacting on our colleagues and make it clear that a journalist's happiness is a bottom-line issue. To my knowledge, no qualitative research exists on the impact sick days and journalists leaving the profession have on the industry. When news organizations around the world have spent many resources attracting young and diverse talent, it's beyond negligent not to consider how to retain them. The shopfront may look superficially attractive but when young reporters cross the threshold, many newsrooms remain toxic and intense environments.

How do you go about enabling happiness? The laundry list of challenges grouped all together can seem too momentous to overcome. While changes in newsroom culture cannot be tackled overnight a new approach to empathising with journalists can move the dial. For a long time, the adage "if it bleeds, it leads" has driven the news agenda. The annual Digital News Report of 2022 from the Reuters Institute of Journalism in Oxford[3] pushed back on that assumption. One of the report's major takeaways, it noted, is the growing tendency for "selective news avoidance" of so-called depressing subjects. Describing their own findings as "particularly challenging for the industry," it found the proportion of respondents that say they avoid the news, sometimes or often, had doubled in Brazil (54 percent) and the U.K. (46 percent) since 2017—and had increased in all other markets. "Across markets, many respondents say they are put off by the repetitiveness of the news agenda," the report stated. "[This is] especially around politics and COVID-19 (43 percent), or that they often feel worn out by the news (29 percent)."

One sentence felt like a wake-up call. "Subjects that journalists consider most important, such as political crises, international conflicts, global pandemics, and climate catastrophes, seem to be precisely the ones that are turning some people away from news." If news consumers are being turned away by negativity, what then for those whose job is to deliver it 24/7? As a working journalist I would welcome further research into the impact of news avoidance on our colleagues. How does covering news day in, day out, affect their happiness or their mood and their desire to remain in the industry?

A new form of reporting has emerged to counteract this. Organizations like the Solutions Journalism Network are leading a "global shift in journalism" exploring new ways to tell stories in a positive fashion. This doesn't mean solutions journalism can "solve" or "fix" an issue, but a particular topic can be looked at or reassessed through a positive prism.[4]

Journalists are intellectually curious, share a sense of camaraderie, and want to hold people and institutions to account. We need to think about measuring journalists' happiness. We also urgently need to think about providing training to newsroom leaders to support the mental health of their colleagues and, just as importantly, themselves.

Notes

1 John Crowley. "Journalism in the Time of Covid." URL: https://www.johncrow ley.org.uk/work-1/entry-03-8c3ap.
2 Headlines. "Vicarious Trauma." URL: chrome-extension://bdfcnmeidppjeaggn-midamkiddifkdib/viewer.html?file=https://www.mind.org.uk/media/4tybnie0/headlines-guide-to-vicarious-trauma.pdf.
3 Nic Newman et al. "Reuters Institute Digital News Report 2022." URL: chrome-extension://bdfcnmeidppjeaggnmidamkiddifkdib/viewer.html?file=https://reutersin stitute.politics.ox.ac.uk/sites/default/files/2022-06/Digital_News-Report_2022.pdf
4 Solutions Journalism Network. "What is Solutions Journalism?" URL: https://www.solutionsjournalism.org

21

HAPPINESS IN JOURNALISM AS A PUBLIC GOOD

Implications for Teaching and Research

Herman Wasserman

There are many reasons why practicing journalism today can make you unhappy.

Conditions for journalistic work around the world are often unfavorable. It remains dangerous to be a journalist in many places around the world. According to Reporters Without Borders' most recent index,[1] serious violations of press freedom have been noted in a record number of countries in 2022. Globally, public debate is increasingly characterized by social and political polarizations and contestations between publics and counter-publics, which is also reflected in the media. Social media and opinion content have been noted to fuel the increase in these socio-political tensions, while independent media is suppressed in many illiberal democracies. Journalists must contend not only with outright violent attacks and threats, but also attacks by populist politicians that undermine their legitimacy. These political attacks feed into a toxic online environment, which has created new threats to the safety and well-being of journalists. These include trolling, doxing, and online misogyny. Related to this deteriorating social and political environment is the continued decline in trust in journalism, which can be seen around the world. The annual Reuters Institute's Digital News Reports note that trust in journalism has fallen in almost half the countries they surveyed, with consumption of legacy news media such as television and print also declining. A further concerning development has been the phenomenon of news avoidance. News consumers say they cut down on their news usage because it is bad for their own sense of well-being.[2]

Adding to these threats and dangers is the ongoing economic stress under which journalists operate. The structural shifts in the global media ecology towards digital, mobile, and online platforms and away from legacy media, have been impacting negatively on the business models and financial viability of journalism for some time, but have been exacerbated by the COVID-19

DOI: 10.4324/9781003364597-25

pandemic. Ironically, these deteriorating conditions occur at a time when the global concern for disinformation, online hate, and conspiracy theories is on the increase, highlighting the importance of trustworthy, relevant, and ethical journalism.

Working in these conditions of danger, precarity, political polarization and public disengagement is bound to have a negative effect on the happiness and well-being of journalists. But what is happiness in journalism? Is it just a feeling that arises from the confluence of the right factors, an individual sense of fulfilment and contentment in doing a job that is meaningful and enjoyable, or something more systemic and fundamental? The chapters in this book suggest the latter—that happiness in journalism is connected to a broader, deeper sense of wellness, rooted in structural and procedural conditions, and embedded in journalistic routines and techniques. Happiness is not limited to—or perhaps, in the first place, not located in—individuals, but in a healthy journalistic community, which includes the public. The contributions in this book outline a variety of strategies in which journalists, working as communities of practice, can work together to create networks of care and support which create the environment within which journalists can flourish.

When happiness in journalism is viewed in this way, happiness becomes less of a vaguely circumscribed concept, but an attainable normative ideal around which objectives can be formulated and strategies constructed. This has implications for research and teaching in journalism as well. Paying scholarly attention to happiness as a noteworthy area of study means that it is taken seriously enough to devote time and resources into developing ways in which the world of academia can contribute to the world of work. Such research should not only focus on finding ways to improve individual resilience and mental health but should include critical studies of the political economy of the media industry to find ways that media owners and managers could create supportive structural conditions for journalists.

This book contains several important contributions arising from such research, which point to better retention strategies, collective bargaining, peer support, and job satisfaction. Contributors highlight ways in which editors and newsroom leadership can develop training programs to mitigate the impact of trauma, provide resources for journalists to cope with stressors, and teach them skills to stay safe from harassment and harm. The research into social media policies contained in this book is also crucially important to encourage editors and news leaders to develop standards and processes that strengthen the relationships between journalists and their publics, which can contribute to an increase in trust. Editors and news leaders should also take heed of research presented here which can help them treat journalistic happiness and well-being more holistically, not only in the workplace but outside of it as well. The suggestions of better security resources, safer practices and improved office routines and procedures can create more welcoming spaces for journalists.

Including the topic of happiness in teaching curricula means that journalistic resilience, coping strategies, and defensive techniques can become embedded in the journalistic skill sets imparted to student journalists. Valuable suggestions are made in this regard, such as embedding resilience and emotional literacy in curricula, creating training opportunities for educators to equip themselves with knowledge to prepare students for trauma, and creating wider and more inclusive networks for collaboration and support.

In the end, being concerned about journalistic wellness is about more than ensuring that journalists are happy. As worthy an ideal that might be, research and teaching into journalistic happiness is informed by the understanding that journalism distinguishes itself from other media-making practices fundamentally through its commitment to the public interest. This means that resilient journalism is an important social good, and it follows that happiness and well-being among journalists is a necessary precondition for such social good to ensue from journalistic practice. When journalists work in conditions that are conducive to their work, in a stable, supportive, and protective environment, with a realistic hope of sustainability, the quality, relevance and impact of journalism is likely to improve. It will be the public at large who will benefit from such journalism.

Notes

1 Reporters Without Borders (RSF). World Press Freedom Index (Reporters Without Borders 2022). https://rsf.org/en/rsf-s-2022-world-press-freedom-index-new-era-polarisation?year=2022&data_type=general Accessed on 1 April 2023.
2 Newman, Nic. "Overview and Key Findings of the 2022 Digital News Report." (Reuters Institute 2022), https://reutersinstitute.politics.ox.ac.uk/digital-news-report/2022/dnr-executive-summary Accessed on 1 April 2023.

22

NEWS, NEGATIVITY, AND THE AUDIENCE'S ROLE IN FINDING HAPPINESS IN JOURNALISM

Seth C. Lewis

This book has focused on the state of happiness in journalism and the issue of well-being among journalists—and rightly so, for the situation is dire. Journalists face a rising tide of hate and hostility in many parts of the world, often without adequate support from their employers. Journalists are harassed online and bullied in-person. They are struggling with trauma, anxiety, and depression. They are *tired*—like so many are these days, it's true, but their burnout is born of a unique confluence of circumstances: with media business models struggling and reporting resources thinning all around them, journalists are expected to do more with less. The occupational hazards are many, the opportunities for happiness too few.

And yet: While all the above is true and merits the book before you, if happiness in journalism begins with a reckoning about the well-being of journalists, it should not end there. It should also include an appreciation for what it's like on the other side—that is, what it's like not only to be in the complicated position of producing news, but also to be in the bewildering position these days of *consuming* news. To care about the mental and emotional welfare of journalists, we might say, should include corresponding care for news audiences: What would it mean to consider their happiness in the context of journalism?

Let's rewind for a moment to March 2020, when the world was turned upside down by the COVID-19 pandemic. Governments locked down countries and borders, companies furloughed millions of workers, and seemingly *everything*—office work, schools, wedding plans, vacations, all of it—went into a state of suspended disruption. Most people had more time at home, more time on their hands—and more time, as it turned out, for consuming *lots and lots of news*, particularly in those first few weeks and months.[1] While news is well-known for being negative,[2] news in the early phase of the pandemic was

DOI: 10.4324/9781003364597-26

acutely so, to the point that public agencies began advising people to cut down on their news consumption for the sake of their mental health.[3] News about the pandemic was all-consuming; it was frightening and fraught with uncertainty. I can speak from experience: like so many others, I could hardly keep from constantly refreshing news sites, looking for the latest bits of information that might provide clarity or reassurance.

I was doomscrolling like everyone else, sucked into the vortex of consuming a ceaseless stream of negative news stories.[4] Perhaps prompted by my own experience, and also looking to throw myself into a research project as a distraction (ahem, workaholism runs in journalism *and* academia, to the detriment of both professions), I plunged into a study seeking to understand how people experienced news during this period. Working with collaborator Jacob L. Nelson, we wanted to explore: How did people *feel* about the news they were consuming? And, given the degree to which life routines had been upended by the pandemic, what might this unique moment reveal about the nature of people's *experiences* with news on a visceral level?

Our research team conducted 60 Zoom interviews with a diverse cross-section of U.S. adults in spring 2020, and one of the themes that emerged was a profound dissatisfaction with news. People felt so distrustful about the news that many spoke of fact-checking it for themselves, in ways that left them worse off informationally.[5] People often felt confused, frustrated, and overwhelmed. There was *too much news*, and it was taking a toll on their well-being.

It's not surprising, then, to learn that there are broad trends toward detachment from news. In 2020, heavy news consumption was often followed by news avoidance; in one case, "to cope with feelings of being scared or overwhelmed, even the most connected [Norwegian] citizens deliberately and intermittently avoided news."[6] More and more people around the world report actively avoiding the news, in part because of the "anticipated anxiety" attached to the experience.[7] As Joshua Benton of NiemanLab summed it up (*emphasis added*):

> While the news on any given day is only metaphorically a horror show, many people treat headlines less as information than as scary stimuli. They'd rather not be regularly reminded of all that's broken in the world, with all-new horrors added by the hour. They've got plenty of other stuff to do, so why spend time doing something that will make them anxious? *This phenomenon can seem foreign to some journalists*—who, after all, are people who've chosen to spend most of their waking hours swimming in the latest news. But news avoidance is a very real phenomenon and, frankly, a deeply rational one for many people who see news as high risk, low reward.[8]

If the "metaphorical horror show" of news may be a foreign phenomenon to some journalists, it could be for journalism researchers, too, unless we attend more carefully to *why*, from the perspective of consumers, news might feel like such a "high risk, low reward" proposition. Of course, human beings are naturally attuned to threats, like those outlined in negative news, so it would be impossible, even undesirable, to expect that journalism should only accentuate positivity. Accountability journalism, of the kind so lionized for its influence in sustaining democracy, requires an audience—even an audience willing to put up with the horrors that investigative reporting might uncover. But that does not absolve us from paying attention to the larger story of happiness in and through journalism. That story will not be complete until the audience is part of it.

Notes

1 Nelson, Jacob L., and Seth C. Lewis, "The Structures that Shape News Consumption: Evidence from the Early Period of the COVID-19 Pandemic," *Journalism* 23, no. 12 (2022): 2495–2512.
2 Soroka, Stuart N., *Negativity in Democratic Politics*. (Cambridge: Cambridge University Press, 2014).
3 Mannell, Kate, and James Meese, "From Doom-Scrolling to News Avoidance," *Journalism Studies* 23, no. 3 (2022): 302–319.
4 Ytre-Arne, Brita and Hallvard Moe. "Doomscrolling, Monitoring and Avoiding," *Journalism Studies* 22, no. 13 (2021): 1739–1755.
5 Nelson, Jacob L., and Seth C. Lewis, "Only 'Sheep' Trust Journalists?" *New Media & Society* (2021). 14614448211018160.
6 Ytre-Arne, Brita and Hallvard Moe, "Doomscrolling, Monitoring and Avoiding."
7 Toff, Benjamin, and Rasmus Kleis Nielsen, "How News Feels: Anticipated Anxiety as a Factor in News Avoidance and a Barrier to Political Engagement," *Political Communication* 39, no. 6 (2022): 697–714.
8 Benton, Joshua. 2022. "The Relief of Missing Out." *NiemanLab*, September 19, 2022. https://www.niemanlab.org/2022/09/the-relief-of-missing-out-anticipated-anxiety-is-a-big-reason-why-more-people-are-avoiding-the-news/.

SELECTED BIBLIOGRAPHY

Aitamurto, Tanja and Anita Varma. "The Constructive Role of Journalism." *Journalism Practice* 12 (2018): 695–713.

Anderson, Stephanie and Brian Bourke. "Teaching Collegiate Journalists How to Cover Traumatic Events Using Moral Development Theory." *Journalism & Mass Communication Educator* 75, no. 2 (2019): 233–246.

Barrett, G. H. Job Satisfaction among Newspaperwomen. *Journalism Quarterly*, 61(3), 593–599 (1984).

Beam, Randal A. and Meg Spratt. "Managing Vulnerability." *Journalism Practice* 3, no. 4(2009): 421–438.

Josephi, Beate and Penny O'Donnell. "The Blurring Line Between Freelance Journalists and Self-Employed Media Workers." *Journalism* (2022): 1–18. DOI: doi:14648849221086806.

Bélair-Gagnon, Valérie, Diana Bossio, Avery E. Holton, and Logan Molyneux. "Disconnection." *Social Media + Society* 8, no. 1 (2022): 1–5.

Bossio, Diana, Bélair-Gagnon, Valérie, Holton, Avery E., and Molyneux, Logan. *The Paradox of Connection*. Urbana-Champaign, IL: University of Illinois Press, 2024.

Buchanan, Marla, and Patrice Keats. "Coping with Traumatic Stress in Journalism." *International Journal of Psychology*, 46 (2011), 127–135.

Burke, Ronald J., and Stig Matthiesen. "Workaholism among Norwegian Journalists." *Stress and Health* 20, no. 5 (2004): 301–308.

Caminos, Evelyn Daniela. "El Mundo del Trabajo y la Precariedad Laboral de los Comunicadores y Periodistas." *Revista de Estudio de Derecho Laboral y Derecho Procesal Laboral* 2, no. 2 (2020): 27–38.

Chadha, Kalyani, and Linda Steiner. *Newswork and Precarity*. London: Routledge, 2021.

Chan, Joseph Man, Zhongdang Pan, and Francis L. F. Lee. "Professional Aspirations and Job Satisfaction." *Journalism & Mass Communication Quarterly* 81, no. 2 (2014): 254–273.

Chen, Charles P., and Madia Javid-Yazdi. "Career Counseling Strategies to Enhance the Vocational Wellness of Journalists." *Australian Journal of Career Development*, 28, no. 1 (2019): 31–38.

Chen, Chun-Hsi Vivian , Wei-Chieh Chang, Chia-Hui Cheng, and Sheau-Cheun Paul Ma, "Emotional Intelligence in the Workplace: Exploring Its Effects on Journalists' Perceived Work Stress, Job Satisfaction, and Organizational Commitment," *Furen Management Review* 18, no. 3 (2011): 1–18, HYPERLINK "https://protect-us. mimecast.com/s/ILitCzpBnGH8zBKQ4F4nC_Q?domain=doi.org"https://doi. org/10.29698/FJMR.201109.0001.

Chen, Gina Masullo, Paromita Pain, Victoria Y. Chen, Madlin Mekelburg, Nina Springer, and Franziska Troger. "'You Really Have to Have a Thick Skin.'" *Journalism* 21, no. 7 (2020): 877–895.

Claesson, Annina. "'I Really Wanted Them to Have My Back, but They Didn't'—Structural Barriers to Addressing Gendered Online Violence against Journalists." *Digital Journalism* (2022): 1–20. https://doi.org/10.1080/21670811.2022.2110509.

Cohen, Nicole S. "Entrepreneurial Journalism and the Precarious State of Media Work." *South Atlantic Quarterly* 114, no. 3 (2015): 513–533.

Cohen, Nicole, Andrea Hunter, and Penny O'Donnell. "Bearing the Burden of Corporate Restructuring." *Journalism Practice* 13, no. 7 (2019): 817–833.

Cohen, Nicole S., and Greig de Peuter. "Collectively Confronting Journalists' Precarity Through Unionization." In *Newswork and Precarity*, edited by Kalyani Chadha and Linda Steiner, 203–216. New York: Routledge, 2022.

Craig, David A., and John P. Ferré. "Agape as an Ethic of Care for Journalism." *Journal of Mass Media Ethics* 21, no. 2–3 (2006): 123–140.

Davidson, Roei, and Oren Meyers. "'Should I Stay or Should I Go?'" *Journalism Studies* 17, no. 5 (2014): 590–607.

Deavours, Danielle. "Nonverbal Neutrality Norm." *Journal of Broadcasting & Electronic Media* 67, no. 1 (2022): 112–134.

Deavours, Danielle. "*Vicarious Traumatization of Broadcast Journalists and its Effect on Nonverbal Neutrality.*" Symposium on Media and Crisis Communication Research, 2020BEAOn-Location Virtual, 2020.

De Cock, Rozane, and Hedwig de Smaele. "Freelancing in Flemish News Media and Entrepreneurial Skills as Pivotal Elements in Job Satisfaction." *Journalism Practice* 10, no. 2 (2016): 251–265.

Deibert, Ron. "Digital Threats against Journalists." In *Journalism After Snowden*, edited by Emily Bell and Taylor Owen, 240–257. New York: Columbia University Press, 2017.

Deprez, Annelore and Karin Raeymaeckers. "A Longitudinal Study of Job Satisfaction Among Flemish Professional Journalists." *Journalism and Mass Communication* 2, no. 1 (2012): 235–249.

Deuze, Mark and Tamara Witschge. *Beyond Journalism*. John Wiley & Sons, 2020.

De Vuyst, Sara, and Karin Raeymaeckers. "Gender as a Multi-Layered Issue in Journalism." *European Journal of Women's Studies* 26, no. 1 (2017): 23–38.

Drevo, Susan. *The War on Journalists*. Doctoral dissertation, University of Tulsa, Oklahoma, 2019.

Edstrom, Maria and Martina Ladendorf. "Freelance Journalists as a Flexible Workforce in Media Industries." *Journalism Practice* 6, no. 5–6 (2012): 711–721.

Endres, Fredric F. "Stress in the Newsroom at Ohio Dailies." *Newspaper Research Journal* 10, no. 1 (1988): 1–14.

Everbach, Tracy. "The Culture of a Women-Led Newspaper." *Journalism & Mass Communication Quarterly* 83, no. 3 (2006): 477–493.

Feinstein, Anthony, Saul Feinstein, Maziar Behari, and Bennis Pavisian. "The Psychological Wellbeing of Iranian Journalists." *JRSM Open* 7, no. 12 (2016).

Ferrier, Michelle and Nisha Garud-Patkar. "TrollBusters." In *Mediating Misogyny: Gender, Technology, and Harassment*, edited by Jacqueline Ryan Vickery and Tracy Everbach, 311–332. London: Springer International Publishing, 2018.

Flores Morales, Rogelio, Verónica Reyes Pérez, and Lucy María Reidl Martínez. "El Impacto Psicológico de La Guerra Contra El Narcotráfico En Periodistas Mexicanos." *Revista Colombiana de Psicología* 23, no. 1 (2014): 177–192.

Gerd, Nies and Roberto Pedersini. *Freelance Journalists in the European Media Industry*. Brussels: European Federation of Journalists, 2003.

Gollmitzer, Mirjam. *Employment Conditions in Journalism*. Oxford, UK: Oxford University Press, 2019.

Gunaratne, Shelton, Mark Pearson, and Sugath Senarath. *Mindful Journalism and News Ethics in the Digital Era*. New York: Routledge, 2017.

Heckman, Meg, Myojung Chung, and Jody Santos. "'This isn't What the Industry Should Look Like Anymore': U.S. Student Journalists, Harassment and Professional Socialization." *Journalism & Mass Communication* 12, no. 2 (2022): 14–24.

Henrichsen, Jennifer R. "Understanding Nascent Newsroom Security and Safety Cultures.'" *Journalism Practice* 16, no. 9 (2021): 1829–1848.

Higgins-Dobney, Carey L. "Not on Air, but Online: The Labor Conditions of the Digital Journalist in U.S. Local Television Newsrooms." *Electronic News* 15, no. 3–4 (2021): 95–108. https://doi.org/10.1177/19312431211045741.

Hill, Desiree, Catherine A. Luther, and Phyllis Slocum. "Preparing Future Journalists for Trauma on the Job." *Journalism & Mass Communication Educator* 75, no. 1 (2020): 64–68.

Himma-Kadakas, Marju, and Mirjam Mõttus. "Ready to Hire a Freelance Journalist: The Change in Estonian Newsrooms' Willingness to Outsource Journalistic Content Production." *Central European Journal of Communication* 14, no. 1 (2021): 27–43.

Hoak, Gretchen. "Covering COVID: Journalists' Stress and Perceived Organizational Support While Reporting on the Pandemic." *Journalism & Mass Communication Quarterly* 98, no. 3 (2021): 854–874.

Holton, Avery E., Valérie Bélair-Gagnon, Diana Bossio, and Logan Molyneux. "'Not Their Fault, but Their Problem': Organizational Responses to the Online Harassment of Journalists." *Journalism Practice* 17, no. 4 (2023): 859–874.

Hopper, Megan K. and John Huxford. "Emotion Instruction in Journalism Courses." *Communication Education* 66, no. 1 (2017): 90–108.

Hughes, Sallie et al. "Coping with Occupational Stress in Journalism: Professional Identities and Advocacy as Resources." *Journalism Studies* 22, no. 8 (2021): 971–991.

Hummel, Roman, Susanne Kirchhoff, and Dimitri Prandner. "We Used to be Queens and Now we are Slaves: Working Conditions and Career Strategies in the Journalistic Field." *Journalism Practice* 6, no. 5–6 (2012): 722–731.

Huxford, John E., and K. Megan Hopper. "Reporting with Emotion." *Journal of Applied Journalism & Media Studies* 9, no. 1 (2020): 39–60.

Idås, Trond, K. Backholm, and J. Korhonen. "Trauma in the Newsroom: Social Support, Post-Traumatic Stress and Post-Traumatic Growth among Journalists Working with Terror." *European Journal of Psychotraumatology* 10, no. 1 (2019): 1–20.

Ireri, Kioko. "High Job Satisfaction Despite Low Income." *Journalism and Mass Communication Quarterly* 93, no. 1 (2016): 164–186.

Ivask, Signe. "Stressed out Print, Digital and Converged Newsroom Journalists Consider Leaving the Field." *Media and Communication* 8, no. 1 (2019): 83–99.

Jamil, Sadia. "Suffering in Silence: The Resilience of Pakistan's Female Journalists to Combat Sexual Harassment, Threats and Discrimination." *Journalism Practice* 14, no. 2 (2020): 150–170.

Jane, Emma A. "Gendered Cyberhate as Workplace Harassment and Economic Vandalism." *Feminist Media Studies* 18, no. 4 (2018): 575–591.

Jung, Jaemin and Youngju Kim. "Causes of Newspaper Firm Employee Burnout in Korea and its Impact on Organizational Commitment and Turnover Intention." *The International Journal of Human Resource Management* 23, no. 17 (2012): 3636–3651.

Koirala, Samiksha. "Female Journalists' Experience of Online Harassment." *Media and Communication* 8, no. 1 (2020): 47–56.

Kotisova, Johana. "The Elephant in the Newsroom: Current Research on Journalism and Emotion." *Sociology Compass* 13, no. 5 (2019).

Ladendorf, Martina. "Ethical Boundary Settings of Freelance Journalists Concerning Information Work." *Nordicom Review* 33, no. 1 (2012): 83–98.

Lee, Mina, Eun Hye Ha, and Jung Kun Pae. "The Exposure to Traumatic Events and Symptoms of Posttraumatic Stress Disorder among Korean Journalists." *Journalism* 19, no. 9–10 (2017): 1308–1325.

Lewis, Seth C., Rodrigo Zamith, and Mark Coddington. "Online Harassment and its Implications for the Journalist–Audience Relationship." *Digital Journalism*, 8, no. 8 (2020): 1047–1067.

Lim, Jeongsub. "The Relationships of Online Journalists' Emotional Responses to Competitors with Job Satisfaction, Workload, and Perception of the Quality of the News." *Asian Journal of Communication* 23, no. 2 (2013): 209–224.

Lindén, Carl-Gustav, Katja Lehtisaari, Mikko Grönlund, and Mikko Villi. "Journalistic Passion as Commodity." *Journalism Studies* 22, no. 12 (2021): 1701–1719.

Lu, Luo, and Robin Gilmour. "Culture and Conceptions of Happiness." *Journal of Happiness Studies* 5, no. 3 (2004): 269–291.

Liu, Huei-Ling, and Ven-Hwei Lo. "An Integrated Model of Workload, Autonomy, Burnout, Job Satisfaction, and Turnover Intention among Taiwanese Reporters." *Asian Journal of Communication* 28, no. 2 (2017): 153–169.

Löfgren Nilsson, Monica, and Henrik Örnebring. "Journalism Under Threat." *Journalism Practice* 10, no. 7 (2016): 880–890.

Lucht, Tracy. "Job Satisfaction and Gender," *Journalism Practice,* 10:3 (2015): 405–423, DOI: 10.1080/17512786.2015.1025416

Mabweazara, Hayes M. "Normative Dilemmas and Issues for Zimbabwean Print Journalism in the 'Information Society' Era." *Digital Journalism* 1, no. 1 (2013): 135–151.

MacDonald, Jasmine B., Anthony J. Saliba, Gene Hodgins, and Linda A. Ovington. "Burnout in Journalists." *Burnout Research* 3, no. 2 (2016): 34–44.

Marjoribanks, Timothy, Lawrie Zion, Penny O'Donnell, and Merryn Sherwood. *Journalists and Job Loss.* London: Routledge, 2021.

Marais, A., and A. D. Stuart. "The Role of Temperament in the Development of Post-Traumatic Stress Disorder amongst Journalists." *South African Journal of Psychology* 35, no. 1 (2005): 89–105.

Marín-Sanchiz, Cristian-Ramón, Miguel Carvajal, and José-Luis González-Esteban. "Survival Strategies in Freelance Journalism." *Journalism Practice* 17, no. 3 (2021): 450–473.

Martin, Fiona. "Tackling Gendered Violence Online." *Australian Journalism Review* 40, no. 2 (2018): 73–89.

Martin, Justin D. "Professional Efficacy among Arab American Journalists" *Journal of Middle East Media* 7, no. 1 (2011): 92–118.

Massé, Mark H. *Trauma Journalism*. London: Bloomsbury Publishing, 2011.

Massey, Brian L. and Cindy J. Elmore. "Happier Working ofr Themselves?," *Journalism Practice*, 5:6 (2011): 672-686, DOI: 10.1080/17512786.2011.579780

Massey, Brian L. and Jacqui Ewart. "Sustainability of Organizational Change in the Newsroom." *International Journal on Media Management* 14, no. 3 (2012): 207–225.

Matthews, Julian and Kelechi Onyemaobi. "Precarious Professionalism." *Journalism Studies* 21, 13 (2020): 1836–1851.

Mathews, Nick, Valérie Bélair-Gagnon, and Matt Carlson. "'Why I Quit Journalism'." *Journalism*, 24, no. 1 (2023): 62–77.

Mathisen, Birgit Røe. "Entrepreneurs and Idealists." *Journalism Practice* 13, no. 8 (2019): 1003–1007.

McCaffrey, Raymond. "Stoicism and Courage as Journalistic Values." *American Journalism* 36, no. 2 (2019): 220–241.

McGregor, Susan E. *Information Security Essentials a Guide for Reporters, Editors, and Newsroom Leaders*. New York: Columbia University Press, 2021.

McMahon, Cait. "Building Resilience in the War Zone against Hidden Injury." *Pacific Journalism Review* 16 (2010): 39–48.

Meier, Klaus. "How Does the Audience Respond to Constructive Journalism?" *Journalism Practice* 12, no. 6 (2018): 764–780.

Mellado, Claudia, ed. *Beyond Journalistic Norms*. London: Routledge, 2021.

Mesmer, Kelsey. "An Intersectional Analysis of U.S. Journalists' Experiences with Hostile Sources." *Journalism and Communication Monographs* 24, no. 3 (2022): 156–216.

Mesmer, Kelsey and M. Rosie Jahng. "Using Facebook to Discuss Aspects of Industry Safety." *Journalism Studies* 22, no. 8 (2021): https://doi.org/10.1080/1461670x.2021.1920452.

Miller, Kaitlin C. "Hostility Toward the Press." *Digital Journalism* (2021). https://doi.org/10.1080/21670811.2021.1991824.

Murphy, Colm, Pat Deeny, and Nigel Taylor. "A New Pedagogy to Enhance the Safety and Resilience of Journalists in Dangerous Environments Globally." *Education Sciences* 10, no. 11 (2020): 310.

Naldi, Lucia and Robert G. Picard. "Let's Start an Online News Site." *Journal of Media Business Studies* 9, no. 4 (2012): 69–97.

Ndlovu, Musawenkosi W. "What is the State of South African Journalism?" *African Journalism Studies* 36, no. 3 (2015): 114–138.

Nelson, Jacob L. "'Worse than the Harassment Itself.' Journalists' Reactions to Newsroom Social Media Policies." *Digital Journalism* (2023). https://doi.org/10.1080/21670811.2022.2153072.

Newman, Elana, Roger Simpson, and David Handschuh. "Trauma Exposure and Post-Traumatic Stress Disorder Among Photojournalists." *Visual Communication Quarterly* 10, no. 1 (2003): 4–13.

Norbäck, Maria. "Glimpses of Resistance: Entrepreneurial Subjectivity and Freelance Journalist Work." *Organization* 28, no. 3 (2019): 426–448.

North, Louise. "The Gender 'Problem' in Australia Journalism Education." *SSRN Electronic Journal* (2010).

Novak, Rosemary J., and Sarah Davidson. "Journalists Reporting on Hazardous Events." *Traumatology* 19, no. 4 (2013): 313–322.

O'Donnell, Penny, Lawrie Zion, and Merryn Sherwood. "Where Do Journalists Go after Newsroom Job Cuts?" *Journalism Practice* 10, no. 1 (2015): 35–51.

Ogunyemi, Ola and Joseph Akanuwe. "Should Journalism Curriculum Include Trauma Resilience Training?" *Journalism Education and Trauma Research Group* 10 (n.d.): 34–43.

Ogunyemi, Olatunji and Lada Trifonova Price. "Exploring the Attitudes of Journalism Educators to Teach Trauma-Informed Literacy." *Journalism & Mass Communication Educator* (2023). https://doi.org/10.1177/10776958221143466.

Opgenhaffen, Michaël, and Harald Scheerlinck. "Social Media Guidelines for Journalists." *Journalism Practice* 8, no. 6 (2014): 726–741.

Örnebring, Henrik. "A Social History of Precarity in Journalism." *Australian Journalism Review* 42, no. 2 (2020): 191–206.

Osmann, Jonas et al. "The Emotional Well-Being of Journalists Exposed to Traumatic Events." *Media, War & Conflict*, January, 14, no. 4 (2020): 476–502.

Parks, Perry. "Joy is a News Value." *Journalism Studies* 22, no. 6 (2021): 820–838.

Pearson, Mark et al. "Building Journalists' Resilience through Mindfulness Strategies." *Journalism* 22, no. 7 (2019): 1647–1664.

Posetti, Julie, Nabeelah Shabbir, Diana Maynard, Kalina Bontcheva, and Nermine Aboulez. *The Chilling*. UNESCO, 2021. Accessed April 1, 2023. https://en.unesco.org/publications/thechilling.

Powers, Angela, "An exploratory study of the impact of leadership behavior on levels of news convergence and job satisfaction." In *Leadership in the Media Industry: Changing Contexts, Emerging Challenges*, ed. Lucy Küng (2015): 11-28 (Jönköping: JIBS Research Report Series).

Reinardy, Scott. "Female Journalists More Likely to Leave Newspapers." *Newspaper Research Journal* 30, no. 3 (2009): 42–57.

Reinardy, Scott. "Newspaper Journalism in Crisis: Burnout on the Rise, Eroding Young Journalists' Career Commitment." *Journalism* 12, no. 1 (2011): 33–50.

Reinardy, Scott. "Job Security, Satisfaction Influence Work Commitment," *Newspaper Research Journal*, 33(1) (2012): 54–70. https://doi.org/10.1177/073953291203300105

Relly, Jeannine E. and Silvio Waisbord. "Why Collective Resilience in Journalism Matters." *Journal of Applied Journalism & Media Studies* 11, no. 2 (2022): 163–188.

Reyna, Victor Hugo. "'This is My Exit Sign': Job Control, Deficit, Role Strain and Turnover in Mexican Journalism," *Journalism Practice* 15, no. 8 (2021): 1129–1145.

Ricketson, Matthew, Andrew Dodd, Lawrie Zion, and Monika Winarnita. "'Like Being Shot in the Face' or 'I'm Glad I'm Out.'" *Journalism Studies* 21, no. 1 (2020): 54–71.

Rimscha, M. Bjørn von. "The Impact of Working Conditions and Personality Traits on the Job Satisfaction of Media Professionals." *Media Industries Journal* 2, no. 2 (2015).

Ryan, Kathleen M. "The Performative Journalist." *Journalism* 10, no. 5 (2009): 647–664.

Salamon, Errol. "Media Unions' Online Resistance Rhetoric." *Management Communication Quarterly* 37, no. 2 (2023): 368–395.

Seely, Natalee. "Journalists and Mental Health." *Newspaper Research Journal* 40, no. 2 (2019): 239–259.

Seely, Natalee. "Fostering Trauma Literacy." *Journalism & Mass Communication Educator* 75, no. 1 (2020): 116–130.

Siapera, Eugenia and Ioanna Iliadi. "Twitter, Journalism and Affective Labour." *About Journalism* 4, no. 1 (2015): 76–89.

Šimunjak, Maja and Manuel Menke. "Workplace Well-Being and Support Systems in Journalism." *Journalism* (2022). https://doi.org/10.1177/14648849221115205.

Smith, River J., Susan Drevo, and Elana Newman. "Covering Traumatic News Stories." *Stress and Health* 34, no. 2 (2017): 218–226.

Song, Haeyeop and Jaemin Jung, "Factors Affecting Turnover and Turnaway Intention of Journalists in South Korea," *Journalism & Mass Communication Quarterly* 99, no. 4 (2021): 1072–1098. https://doi.org/10.1177/10776990211042593.

Specht, Doug and Julia Tsilman. "Teaching Vicarious Trauma in the Journalism Classroom." *Journal of Applied Journalism & Media Studies* 7, no. 2 (2018): 407–427.

Steiner, Linda and Chad M. Okrusch. "Care as a Virtue for Journalists." *Journal of Mass Media Ethics* 21, no. 2–3 (2006): 102–122.

Stupart, Richard. "Emotion and Practical Ethics in Conflict Journalism." *Media, War & Conflict* 14, no. 13 (2021): 268–281.

Sybert, Jeanna. "Navigating Precarity." *Journalism Practice* 17, no. 4 (2021): 737–754.

Tyson, Gabriella and Jennifer Wild. "Post-Traumatic Stress Disorder Symptoms among Journalists Repeatedly Covering COVID-19 News." *International Journal of Environmental Research and Public Health* 18, no. 16 (2021): 8536.

Ugwuanyi, Lawrence O. "The Question of Happiness in African Philosophy." *South African Journal of Philosophy (Suid-Afrikaanse Tydskrif vir Wysbegeerte)* 33, no. 4 (2014): 513–522.

Van Leuven, Sarah, Bart Vanhaelewyn, and Karin Raeymaeckers. "From One Division of Labor to the Other." *Journalism Practice* 15, no. 9 (2021): 1203–1221.

Wahl-Jorgensen, Karin. "An Emotional Turn in Journalism Studies?" *Digital Journalism*, 8, no. 2 (2020): 175–194.

Waisbord, Silvio. "Mob Censorship." *Digital Journalism* 8, no. 8 (2020): 1030–1046.

Waisbord, Silvio. "Trolling Journalists and the Risks of Digital Publicity." *Journalism Practice* 16, no. 5 (2022): 1–17.

Wake, Alexandra and Matthew Ricketson. "Trauma in the Newsroom." *Ethical Space: The International Journal of Communication Ethics* 19, no. 1 (2022): 39–49.

Westlund, Oscar, Roy Krøvel, and Kristin Skare Orgeret. "Newsafety." *Journalism Practice* 16, no. 9 (2022): 1811–1828.

INDEX

affective labor 2, 98
anxiety: and audiences 194; and job security 14, 90; and journalistic norms 21, 48, 78; management 73; and reporting 141, 147; and well-being 75
audiences 1, 4–5, 20, 26, 168; and abuse 70, 101; care for 149, 193; engagement 97, 160; flattening 108; and social media 78, 80, 82, 84–5, 129, 149
authenticity 97
autonomy 2–4, 116; and CBAs, 89; and disconnection 98, 103; and entrepreneurial journalists 160–1; and technology platforms 111; threats to 106; and well-being 34, 116–20, 168

blocking 2, 98, 141
blurring 2, 63
bullying 1
burnout 1, 115; causes of 69, 115, 128, 131, 133–4, 158, 193; and leaving journalism 11; mitigating 71–3, 75, 151, 161; risk factors 97–8; and well-being 2, 3–8, 168

cognitive dissonance 6, 127–33
contentment: in engaged journalism, 7, 182; and happiness, 138, 148, 182–3, 191; and job satisfaction 116, 119
contract 61, 87–9, 91, 94, 117, 119, 158
Committee to Protect Journalists (CPJ) 19, 143

COVID-19 2, 7, 12, 193; and collective bargaining agreements 9; impact on journalism 12, 15, 97, 159, 167–71, 187, 190; institutional response to 171–2; and news avoidance 189; and well-being of journalists 2, 7, 150, 168

Dart Center 2, 103, 133–4, 143
digital attackers 105
digital-era newsworkers 88, 93
digital newsworker 87–90, 92–4
digital threats 105
disconnection 2–3, 6, 38, 96–103, 108, 150
disinformation 187–8, 191
door knocking 7, 138–41, 143–145

education 7, 101, 143; education strategies 40, 102, 152; and psychological capital 73; psychosocial education 154–5; trauma education 40, 47–9, 52–4, 154; and workplace benefits 89
emotional labor 69, 72, 152
emotional well-being 5, 20, 22, 36, 166
engagement 1–2; audience 78, 82, 160, 97–9; on social media 63, 99–100, 108; and well-being 35–8, 41, 47, 75, 109, 143
eudaimonia 19, 23–4
exit 11–13, 16, 65, 67, 140–1

Facebook 17, 87, 99, 108, 142, 169